A
Greater
Tradition

Seven Studies of Triadically Extended Symmetrical Narratives from *Beowulf* to *Ulysses*

Fred V. Bernard

Copyright © 2015 by Fred V. Bernard
All rights reserved. This book or any portion thereof may not be
reproduced or used in any manner whatsoever without the express
written permission of the publisher except for the use of brief
quotations used in a book review or for academic purposes.

Printed in the United States of America

First Printing, 2015
Revised 2019

ISBN 978-1-945637-58-2

Published courtesy of Diversity Ink Press.
(Author maintains full rights.)

Diversity Ink Press
173 Willow Way E.
Monmouth, OR 97361

Composition by BookComp, Inc.
Belmont, MI 49306

Contents

Preface   *v*

A Word From the Author   *ix*

1   A Few Subtleties in *Beowulf*   *1*

2   Shylock's Neighbors   *25*

3   Horatio, the "Ghost", and the Danish Succession   *55*

4   The Poisonings in *Hamlet* Reconsidered   *77*

5   The Heart of Hamlet's Mystery   *93*

6   "He Takes Her by the Palm": Heresy and Inquisition in *Othello*   *111*

7   The Paternities of Ishmael and Ahab   *131*

8   Queequeg   *155*

9   The Black Ambassadors   *173*

10   An Early Irish "Murphy Report"   *195*

Afterword   *213*

Notes   *217*

Bibliography   *239*

Index   *245*

Preface

The study about to be read is different from anything else the reader has ever read in that it addresses so much of the detail of the work addressed and thereby brings about the parity of labor between the writers' efforts and my criticism, as Henry James thought there should be. James states in a letter to Charles Eliot Norton:

> "I *do*, for instance believe in criticism more than that hyperbolic speech of mine would suggest. What I meant to suggest was my sense of its being, latterly, vastly overdone. There is such a flood of precepts & so few examples—so much preaching, advising, rebuking & reviling and so little *doing*: so many gentlemen sitting down to dispose in half an hour of what a few have spent months & years in producing. A single positive attempt, even with great faults, is worth, generally, most of the comments and amendments on it."

The critical work that does not address the detail of the work addressed is virtually worthless. This *does not* make my criticism correct. However, it does make the others more suspect and of very limited value.

Twenty years ago, when my efforts in using triadic analysis were regularly rejected, Peter Straubel suggested I needed multiple instances of such analysis, from a belief that many of them could not be explained away and dismissed. Setting about adding to my modest collection from Shakespeare and James, I decided to present a baker's half dozen of literature's toughest works. The following offering is the result of my efforts. For about a thousand years critics have been without the one tool equipped to

---

Henry James, *A Life in Letters*, ed. Philip Horne (London and New York: Penguin Books, 2000"), 53.

assess some of the greatest literary works we possess, and have been badly equipped to address their greatest mysteries for that length of time, though all the while acting as if we were equipped to handle everything except various nagging cruces—the Christian question in *Beowulf*, the ancient grudge in *The Merchant*, the heart of Hamlet's mystery, the motivation of Iago, and so on. These cruces are easily resolved by a structural method inherent in a few observations made but not developed by Marvin Feldhein sixty years ago. Structural studies are usually regarded as addressing frameworks that impart strength and unity to the works they serve. The structure inherent in Feldheim's study possesses enormous strength along with extraordinary surprises—neither of which he sees—that grow from a design which leads us to sections of their building that we had no idea even existed—floors and areas, rooms and inhabitants that we barely know. The following pages provide fresh readings of *Beowulf, The Merchant of Venice, Hamlet, Othello, Moby-Dick, The Ambassadors* and *Ulysses* by extending their inherent structured narratives (as far as I am able) according to the symmetrical necessities arising from their mathematical structures. The readers who have the training and familiarity with my method are physicists, mathematicians, and any one else smitten with a love of symmetry, though I believe that my writing is accessible to anyone with an interest in its subjects: I write to be understood. Ever since I first saw that academic writers were often citing somewhere close to a hundred books and articles as the foundations of their own articles of fifteen or so pages, and began asking friends what those scholars were trying to prove—and got smiles for answers—I steadily cut back on the number I used, but increased my citations from physicists, mathematicians, literary writers, and students who raised great questions for which at the time I had no answers. I now use as few footnotes as I can, and I believe that writers, not academic critics, are the persons who have said the truly productive and important things about the writing of literature. The theory I have found absolutely essential has come from Professor Feldheim's work, leading me to a fresh understanding of the theory advanced in the Prefaces of Henry James and a few essays of Arthur Miller. James wrote for a select few, and it is possible I am not among them, since he speaks of a number of matters that I so far do not understand. His Prefaces, I believe, offer the best theory I know of to explain novels, short fiction, and drama. I also believe he understood drama and wrote fine plays, which Jamesians have foolishly ignored. My view has long been that literary critics fail of their goal to understand our greatest texts because of not spending the necessary time to understand their requirements. The necessary time required is usually the length of time the author spent writing it. R. P. Blackmur once wrote of having read The *Ambassadors* I think it was four times, which he appeared to have thought was an unusual effort. I believe that perhaps two years of little more than reading it could be called a considerable effort. I should add that after two years of daily reading a great text, I have never found myself in possession of a full understanding of it, nor after a lifetime. Nor do I claim to have mastered any of the works I try to analyze. Least of all do I claim to be right about my interpretations. I am only certain they can be wrong. So too, in Jan Vermeer's "Girl with a Pearl Earring," the pearl may represent an analogy between it and the girl. Since within the pearl we would find a seed of sand, within the girl there may also be a seed of growth, producing a pearl for her. This kind of insight I have tried to present several times on each of the following pages. Each one can certainly be wrong, but each one may also be right.

A Word From the Author

I have dedicated my life to the study of literature and specifically Elizabethan Literature, which led me to the writing of this book. I taught literature for 34 years at the Wayne State, University of Michigan, and Aquinas College. All the people that gave so much to me are now gone, but I still want to say thank you to them as my great teachers. Leo Kirschbaum of Wayne State University, Warner Rice, and G. B. Harrison of the University of Michigan among others, and finally to my many good students who made me think as deeply as I hope my teaching made them think.

In this book I apply a mathematical pattern to the reading of poetry, novels, and plays, from Beowulf poet, Shakespeare, Melville, James, to Joyce. I will show that many of the difficult, dangerous, deeply offensive, and political subjects involved in these writings were handled as if their authors had never in the world heard of them. They are not seen on the surface of the works but are gotten to only by our working out the symmetries of the works that I deal with, so that we encounter what damns the human soul in *Beowulf*, what opens closed hearts in *The Merchant*, what exposes Horatio as the falsest of false friends, what shows Ishmael's voyage as one of unbelievable love, what shows James's virtually tunneling his way deep into American atrocities against American blacks, and what shows us atrocities of Irish Priests and Fathers against Irish sons and daughters. I may have succeeded in producing a work with something astonishing upon every page. I certainly hope so. That was my intention.

1

A Few Subtleties in *Beowulf*

Sixty years of disuse have erased most of my knowledge of Old English. Thus when I examined the structure of Beowulf for possible inclusion in this work, I had to read the poem in translation. Fortunately, structural elements are larger than poetic nuances so that I can offer my study of them to scholars for use in their own deeper work into the poem, though I am quite aware of how tentative my novitiate efforts are. Indeed, for all but structural matters, everything I elicit from the text must be regarded as provisional.

In any attempt to explain how literature came to possess the array of masking devices it presently uses, we must seriously address the earliest conditions that poets found themselves in. In the earliest times, their need was for audiences and sustenance. The one place they could have gotten each was a court. But at court, poets found themselves under powerful constraints upon what they could openly say. This fact brought into being figure, irony, and the other minor but important devices that we leave unexplained as to why they exist. The Beowulf poet needed as much figure as he could employ for telling the difficult story of the Flood-purged world his audience inhabited. In their world, violence, plunder, and human spoils involved them in a spiritual battle against infernal forces fighting, so they believed, for their very souls. The Beowulf poet sang his audience a story of a great hero who, simply as a Christian, had a fallen nature, which has slipped past the attention of the scholarly community that has also missed the great moral issues complicating the lives of those at Heorot who were being slain and lost to satanic enemies. Some bodies killed at Heorot were eaten, thus literally becoming part of their enemies in the service of the dark forces afoot following the fall from grace of our original parents. The attacks are physically rendered, but their ultimate meaning is moral. And that we have indeed not seen this speaks to the great skill of the Beowulf poet. Moreover, the terrorized community was aided by a hero who died in his third battle with Heorot's infernal enemies. Mingled here and there throughout the account are allusions that offer a study of blight and its pre-Flood origins It is all delicately handled and, like the biblical account of the Flood and its unspecified causes, allusive and disinclined to name the behaviors that brought it on.

Courts also were nervous about working poets because unflattering things occurred there that great lords even found threatening, especially when poets sang about them. Those lords would not much have liked Emily Dickinson's solution, which was to "Tell all the truth / but tell it slant." Great lords wanted the dreariness of court relieved by poets, who sang of other courts but not their own, except of course when they were useful for spinning after a great achievement, a failed policy, or campaign. The trouble was that poets absorbed much that was going on around them, saving it for audiences that wanted to hear it all. Even worse, poets knew how to make it all funny. So the problem for the poet became the problem of learning how to tell things "slant." Poets who were unsuccessful were dismissed from court, exiled, or killed. Those who succeeded probably studied subtlety, figure, number, and symmetry. What follows in this work are seven studies of symmetrical triadic literary structures that allow writers to tell certain things "slant," which otherwise could not have been told. Thus began a greater and secret tradition. Unlike those writers in F. R. Leavis's "tradition," every writer in this study likely knew he was a member of a highly exclusive group and was very proud of it.

It was inevitable that a great poet should find himself in the court of some weak prince with disastrous policies needed celebrating by skillful propaganda, that the poet should be "given" the job, and that necessity should require masking. What was necessary for telling the dangerous story so that the lord could not recognize it and absolutely not connectable to the author was the invention of a system that made the audience or reader complete an incomplete structure, much as we all do when we notice and replace a missing button on a shirtfront. You make your reader see a pattern of buttons, say, you make him then see a gap where a button should be, and you make him fill it—but you also show him how. Instead of dealing with seven or so buttons, as on a shirtfront, you use a smaller and more manageable pattern of, say, three elements allowing throughout your work the display of a very large number of tripled groups (as in *La Divinia Commedia* or *The Merchant of Venice*), from a fair number of which you withhold an element or two—buttons that will make some readers positively itch to replace them and thereby improve a slovenly appearance. A poet saw his way to do this the moment his shirt lost a button. The absolute safety in this arrangement comes from the poet's dealing in imaginary "buttons." They can never be traced to him. Indeed, they don't exist and can't even be seen. The gaps can be seen, except that gaps are also in the eye of the beholder and therefore provide deniability. And that this system works is clear because it relies on our need to right a wrong and make a deformity whole. Some of us cannot resist the aesthetic need to restore an ugly deformity to its original beauty.

In the eighth century, asymmetries involving buttons, or persons without fingers, arms, legs, or facial organs, would have stimulated imaginative replacement, along with any missing elements that made interested persons feel compelled to replace them. As soon as a poet saw that we can indeed be made to replace something missing from any ordinary scene, he had proof that he could be secure from anyone ever proving that an imaginary replacement was his. All that remained was for him to devise a structure in which we could see the symmetrical gaps and fill them ourselves. One structural tool that was devised was made of triadic elements (befitting a Christian time and an ethos filled with Trinitarian influences). Dante gave us such structure (having found it elsewhere), and among the hundreds of tripled elements that Dante arranged in groups were some with imperfections of a missing element or two, such as Dante poet's two named loves, God and Beatrice, which were left for us to complete with a third. So, too in *The Merchant of Venice*, where we find Gratiano living in a penthouse dwelling (with a lower apartment) next door to Shylock, we are left to identify the occupier of the lower floor. In *Hamlet*, we find two poisonings in need of a third. In *Moby-Dick* one person from the Pequod being saved leaves us to find two others. And finally in *Ulysses* where Simon pushes back Dilly's shoulders, we are left to name the two other things he also pushed back. In any case, the reader who first produced the missing elements for a story he was reading then knew the poet's secret and could replicate the matter in his own work. But though he could do so, he could not reveal the secret without peril to himself for spreading an idea noxious to the ruler. The solver could safely create only his structure. This apparent truth may explain, in part, why writers never disclosed what they had discovered in another writer's triadic structure.[1] Incomplete triads are made complete when the reader analyzes a complete triad and finds that the elements all involve the same subject but that each element has been assigned a distinct and different value or proportion, of most, less than most, and least, as we see in the monetary values of gold, silver, and lead caskets. Thus when the reader finds that Dante pilgrim has two loves, God and Beatrice, his third love must also be a person, but the least in the completed group, because no one else can come close to challenging his love of God and Beatrice. This produces the limitation that suggests Virgil as the third element. The reader sees the asymmetrical gap, sees the proportions involved, and mentally supplies the necessary element that symmetrically completes the structure. This is a highly sophisticated exercise on the part of writer and reader, each using one of the most powerful tools of human invention.[2]

Whenever first published, a triadic structure presented subsequent writers with conundrums but no hint that anything unusual was involved. All readers of that original work either figured out what was going on, or did not. The readers they attracted were the same type who continue to be attracted to them today—those who admire great genius devoted to great structure, comedy, narrative, character, and language. Those who not only saw but mastered the triadic tool for their own writings were certain to have hidden, astonishing revelations about their own societies, all of which await the labor that will reveal their hidden purposes. By implication, this includes all of Shakespeare, Melville, James, and Joyce, to mention only writers I analyze in these pages. Needless to say, one reason these writers still command a large number of readers is that a triadic structure ensures a new body of readers for the unfilled gaps, there being no other way to discover the real story apart from the extensions that triads supply. Without a continuing readership the authors face oblivion. Unsolved triads sustain interest and promote yet more reading, even if that work is mere flailing about, wide of the mark. I should add that my interest is solely in the extended narrative produced by filling important gaps, and not in discovering every triad, the whole of which produces organic unity.[3]

Prior to the introduction of a triadic structure in a literary work, literature was generally homogenous, in that all texts told completed stories. Following its introduction, most texts told complete stories on their surfaces, but one did not. This meant that a reading of the completed stories satisfied the reader, who had no reason to continue reading the work. Only the incomplete story insisted on more readings. It did so because writers write to be understood, and those who presented incomplete stories presented them with conundrums and cruces which could not be solved without more readings. The incomplete structure assured its creator of an unsatisfactory experience, which would remain unsatisfactory until the reader had answered the last question raised by the structure of the text. The writer of the incomplete story thus had a great advantage over the writer of the complete story; he was assured of the sustained attention of the unsatisfied reader, and his work had a future. And not only a future, but imitation in the form of other veiled masterpieces. The first person I know of to devise the triadic tool, is the Beowulf poet, followed by Dante, Shakespeare, Melville, James, and Joyce (I leave out a few others). But how it passed from the Beowulf poet ultimately to Dante defies my explanatory powers. Passage from Dante to Shakespeare seems more obvious since the English poet wrote so many plays set in Italy and for them carried out many researches into matters Italian. How it got to Melville is also easier to say because he loved and was strongly influenced by both Dante and Shakespeare. Similarly, Shakespeare was James's great master, who was deeply read in play and novel, making it likely that Shakespeare and Melville taught him much about structures. And Joyce knew Dante and Shakespeare and likely read Melville's work,[4] but possibly not the Beowulf poet. More important still, each writer had the necessary genius to absorb the structural peculiarities in the work of his predecessors, and to master the structural tool and use it. And equally important, each was a great genius who naturally attracted readers with great skills, so that the literatures of Italy, England, America, Ireland (for starters), are likely to offer some interesting and exciting surprises for the critic who, studying their universes for signs of planetary life elsewhere, looks into these galaxies.

II

Many readers of Beowulf pass over the seemingly innocent reference to Scyld Scefing in the beginning of the poem and thus miss catching a moral overtone that follows our realizing that Rolf Kraki was the most famous Scylding chief. Talbot Donaldson calls the passage "mysterious," which it is. But it is even more like a riddle, placing before us the question, what offense could a mere babe commit to bring down upon it the curse of death so clear in the baby's being set adrift and directed by wind, current, and fate? The most persuasive answer I can see is that the baby represents a great danger to its people who, even so, were loath to kill it, and who thus left the outcome up to fate. Furthermore, the great danger would involve some fear of the people, such as their becoming cursed if led by a child who was the product of incest. Line one of the poem gives us a sexual context in which to place Scyld because the line connects him with the Spear Danes, and Spear Danes gives a phallic identification to this incestuously-born child. Of the two sexual possibilities, that he is illegitimate and that he was produced incestuously, the first is lacking in anything threatening to his people, whereas the second violates a powerful taboo, which they would grossly flout by accepting his ultimate leadership. Such leadership from such a child was useful to the Beowulf poet, and R. H. Hodgkin presents us with two versions of events that the Beowulf poet apparently blended into his tale.

The English, in the epic of *Beowulf*, remembered the Scyldings for the magnificence of their hall Heorot, for the stateliness of their court and their lavish generosity; but in the Danish tradition they were handed down as a family doomed by its passions. Brother murders brother, father commits incest with daughter; and Rolf Kraki, the offspring of the incest, though raising Denmark to a short spell of empire over its neighbours, in the end by threefold treason—that of a sworn vassal to his lord, that of kin to kin, and that of the guest to his host—is brought to destruction; for the last scene in the hall of Leire, the hall in which Beowulf had fought with the monster.

Grendel is the slaughterer of Rolf Kraki and all his men save one in the dead of night by the hands of their guests.[5] Apparently, the Beowulf poet mingles aspects of the English and Danish versions for his story (producing a third version), a sleight of hand that some in his English audience could have grasped more readily than we can. Why he would give such prominence, as we shall see, to the Danish version is clear, simply by the dramatic power of its account. But, without saying a word on a taboo subject, the poet likely became the earliest English writer to connect incest with royalty and dared to show it infected with the deepest stains in a society. In any event, we are still in the opening lines of the poem, and right at the start, the poet is presenting his audience with large difficulties and dangerous subjects. Not only can we suppose that other difficulties lie ahead, but we have evidence of his belief in the skills of some in his audience—skills that deserve comparison with those possessed by the finest audience anywhere. Some of his listeners were very sophisticated.

Some readers of *Beowulf* have long had trouble accepting the poem because of its supposedly infantile giants. If those readers had been able to see that Shakespeare adopted this incestuous spine of the poem for *Hamlet*, the standings of poem and poet might have been greater than they are. When we sift through the two works, we find that each is set in Denmark, each with a drinking hall, one Denmark attracting giants, the other Denmark a "ghost." Each country attracts a warrior lord at the head of a band of irregulars, one being Norwegian, the other Geatish. Each Denmark is ruled by a weakened king and his strong, matronly queen. The one king uses "horses and weapons"[6] (XV, 1042) to reward Beowulf for fighting Heorot's three opponents; the other king uses a bet of Barbary horses and foils to induce Hamlet to expose himself to Laertes' lethal rapier, dagger, and poison. The doublings in these matters make an inescapable pattern in each work, a pattern that in each rests side by side with another pattern of threes, also inescapable. Shakespeare seems familiar with the poetic account of Hrothgar making Beowulf his son, and to have used it for Claudius's making Hamlet his son. Indeed, his keeping wassail reflects the influence of Heorot, as does Fortinbras's name (=strong of arm=Beowulf).

Moreover, John Grigsby points out that Heorogar was king before Hrothgar, but had died, and his son was not old enough to reign effectively, though he says nothing about the parallel of young Hamlet's being withheld the Danish throne, and also remains silent before the obvious parallel to Hrothgar's seizing the throne in place of his nephew Heoroweard,[7] which so neatly parallels Claudius's usurping the Danish throne from young Hamlet. For now, these similarities are enough to show a parallelism between the two literary actions. I will return to other very important parallel matters between the two works later in this chapter.

Some readers who failed to see and understand this structure may have regarded *Beowulf* as immature art because of the presence and importance of its monsters, three in number, the first two of whom are no sooner dispatched than they are replaced by a third and greater one, an entirely non-human dragon. It may have proved too much for the credulity of some readers. But the fabulous need only be given the suspension of our disbelief in order for us to see that it exists to introduce highly important thematic matters, especially the giants, who come with biblical antecedents. From them, we can determine the proportions of the three elements in the triads we find in the work. Let us therefore now analyze them.

First, there are the humans. Next, and probably a full head or two taller than them, are Grendel and his dam. And third, and much larger than either, is the dragon. This arrangement gives the poet a perfect triad having relatively strict proportions of most, less than most, and least.[8] Triads so proportioned are the key to the entire structure of the poem.[9] Of course, the poet's alliterative line, with its tripartite structure of a whole displaying two halves plunges us even more quickly and efficiently into the triadic form than Dante's terza rima does into the Comedy, for the latter requires three lines to the Beowulf poet's one.

Whether or not he was the first creator of the literary triadic structure, the Beowulf poet was interested in the Flood and presumably in the unnamed sins that brought it on, sins that people returned to once the population thickened again and took up its former ways. For these sins, never named in the Old Testament, the poet saw the need not to specify them, but either to use or devise a system that made them unmistakably clear. Hence the triadic structure, so suited to mask very ugly moral matters (and often just to make us think), matters that we need to confront but that make uncomfortable reading. The monsters are powerful symbols of strength, and their strength is seen in the poem's references to the Flood because that event overcame the great moral depravity in the world, the moment when God was so repelled by human behavior that nothing would serve but drowning every person on the face of the earth in order to expunge their offensive habits and practices and start afresh. Monsters in this unique moral context sober the reader and assure him of a deeply serious study. Befitting their seriousness is their being so darkly rendered. Readers who are amused or disgusted by them may bear greater witness to their own critical inexperience about the nature of poetry than to the puerility of the poet's imagination.

That imagination was at pains to create a difficult but successful tri-partite time frame, from the Expulsion to the Flood, from the Flood to the time of Grendel's attack, and from Beowulf's appearance to his death. The first involves Cain, Grendel's dam, and Grendel, the second involves the early and successful attacks of the giants on Heorot, and the third Beowulf's feats at Heorot and death in battle with the dragon. These are presented as if succeeding each other, which is impossible except for their poet's great masking skills that seem so far to have escaped notice. It is also remarkable how lightly touched with Christian practices the surface of the poem is, lacking church, priest, cross, or baptism. Lacking such things is a strong inducement for us to dismiss Christianity as having significance in the poem. But there is enough Christianity to balance the poem's pagan atmosphere. That atmosphere is consistent with a small Danish community, close to the northern edge of eighth-century tribal life, visited by a Geatish warrior from even farther reaches of the north. Christians hearing *Beowulf* recited would have been familiar with the pagan and Christian characters, probably viewing the pagans as descended from Adam and Eve and therefore as fallen souls who had replaced fertility gods such as Nerthus and others first noticed in Tacitus's Germania. John Grigsby's recent study, *Beowulf and Grendel*, offers an examination of the early pagan tribal and archeological evidence for cultic customs throwing light upon Nerthus and other influential fertility practices. That body of evidence adds considerably to our knowledge of the second person in Grigsby's title, Grendel, but less to the first, Beowulf. To clarify crucial matters for Beowulf, we need a Christian background, and that is supplied by Genesis, chapter 6, and by some of the salvific ideas in the New Testament, Genesis 6:4 being of particular interest and offering us a fascinating glimpse into angelic matters. The much discussed absence of Christian emphasis in the poem tells us nothing about the importance of that religion to the meaning of the poem, but rather perfectly reflects the triadic values of matters infernal, pagan, and Christian in a poem much of which takes place in an early pagan country attacked by infernal creatures and saved by a Christian hero, who comes on a military mission lacking any evangelizing aspects. His gospel is a sword, not a bible.

Genesis is an extraordinary book, devoted to much more than the story of mere human beginnings. It states that angels preceded humans as creatures who walked upon the face of the earth, and that after the creation of Adam and Eve, but apparently before the Flood, some male angels sought union with human female descendants of the original human pair, as we learn from Genesis 6:4:

> Now giants were upon the earth in those days. For after [,] the sons of God went in to the Daughters of men, and they brought forth children, these are the mighty men of old, men of renown.[10]

The daughters so visited seem to have had no voice in the matter, nor however are they making any complaints, and some of the offspring enjoyed important status. The offspring possessed greater than average human stature (being probably at least six feet or taller and called giants here in Jerome's Vulgate); so that it seems fair to suppose that their physical size sometimes attracted or coerced control over certain human females. Such unions accord with Lucifer's intent to hold sway on earth, if not in heaven, and were an offence that brought on the purifying Flood, in which any unprotected angels would have been killed along with their offspring.

As various early writers have noted, the Beowulf poet did not offer his audience an eighth-century story. Instead, he chose to use the sixth-century actions of Hrothgar after the failure of his attempt at peace by marrying his daughter Freawaru to Ingeld, as Beowulf hints to Hygelac. Such distancing avoided agitating any still active feelings on the matter among members of the audience. Two thousand years separate the Greek and Renaissance dramatists who practiced such distancing, and squarely in their middle we find a single, nameless, unknown and unprepared-for poet[11] (who is his Marlowe, his master?), who appeared like the mythical Phoenix and then disappeared, but not before leaving us a work that has won its way to be seen as involving sophisticated devices[12] that, if I am correct, have not even been recognized for what they are, in a work that has elicited complaints about its inspiring childish responses.

Moreover, the Beowulf poet, by means of his references to Cain and the Flood seems to suggest that his distancing or placement of the event from his own era is doubled, going back to the Biblical time of Eden itself, especially since Genesis gives us an account of giants, and we certainly find giants playing a very large role in the poem. Flickering like fire throughout the poem are touches not of the early Eden of harmony and peace, where life was rapturously lived in the murmur of divine voices, but in the Eden of defiance, and corruption, and expulsion, the later time after Cain slew Abel and became a fugitive estranged from God as Lucifer was gaining sway over humankind in his infernal struggle for dominion in the world. The Beowulf poet told his audience a story touching the edges of Eden's former glory, but so vitiated that nothing short of a flood, drowning every living, unmarked soul, could achieve a second and restorative condition. This choice of time and events will account, as nothing else can, for the poem's brilliant, sustained, dark tone and for the spellbound interest the work cast upon its listeners, then and now. It was a masterstroke—and cunningly done when we consider that the poet silently collapses his time frame so as to make the Flood matter lead directly into Heorot's being attacked by a woman and son who belong to the former period, possibly two thousand years back! This is a prodigious leap over an enormous chasm of time, and the Beowulf poet is so skillful that he causes the matter to appear to be seamless and to go undetected by some who think he is unsophisticated.[13] But while the Flood killed all that Noah's ark did not spare, the account is silent on the highly interesting question of whether all earth-visiting angelic creatures were also wiped out. *Beowulf* offers one possible answer to this question.

When the poem speaks of Grendel and his mother as monsters living underwater in the lake of a fen, the Beowulf poet seems to have thought of a way to allow some creatures to have escaped drowning by their having adapted to underwater life before the Flood. But antecedent to this riddle, to which we shall return shortly, is the fact of an unnamed mother and son living together, indeed, being paired and apparently inseparable for all of their life, where we would expect father and son or brother and brother. Thickening the mystery they present is the further fact that Grendel attacks Heorot alone, when mother and son's combined strength could likely have overpowered Beowulf in the hall. Would the mother have sent Grendel alone, or is there a reason for Grendel to have ventured forth without inviting her? If the oddity of this pair sharing a life and a home suggests an unnatural union and we ask when the attraction started and by whom, then the answer would seem to be very early and by the mother because the son's leaving her alone suggests aversion to her company. So distraught is she over the loss of one of his limbs that she attacks the hall to retrieve it and make him "whole" again, rather than having him maimed even in death. All of this emphasizes her too great an interest in him, an interest he has not reciprocated. The emphasis allows us to see that she has had three male interests, one in Abel, one in Cain, and one in Grendel, two shared and one avoided. As for the triad of incestuous unions in the poem, that is still an incomplete, important group, but the remaining elements will appear in due course.

The striking aspect of this complex arrangement is how well the poet has thought the matter through and how skillfully he handled complication, capable of keeping devoted scholars from seeing even these most basic poetic matters. What is also striking is how little we are able to learn about the story this poem tells without a knowledge of its triadic structure. Language plays a lesser role than simple mathematical symmetry in working out the extended narrative structurally conveyed in this work. To see some of the poetic subtlety requires not mastery of nuances in Old English but seeing what is nearly impossible to miss, that the poem contains an underwater den in which inhabitants could survive the biblical Flood. In this context, God's strategy for expunging evil produced for the scop's audience a kind of carpenterial riddle, for the onlookers of the ark's construction could have seen the emerging shape of a massive, dry-docked vessel, which, during months of building, would have been visible to Lucifer's earthly brood, and which would have permitted Grendel's mother to solve the riddle (once she saw the huge size of the ark and the large roundup of animals to be saved) and realize that if it was time for the latter to get aboard, it was also time for mother and son to devise an underwater home.[14] The Beowulf poet gave his audience no easy job. The cunning involved in the matter would have shown the audience evil's potent opposition in its struggle with heaven for dominion over earth that finally ended with God's sacrifice of his son, and its gruesome, inverse poetic analog, the elevated "crucifixion" of Grendel's arm producing for his mother the loss of her only son in the same contest. This may be the second of the much looked-for but unfound uses of New Testament ideas in the poem. If so, the pattern governing their treatment may be analogical and dependent on our sharpness of knowledge, it being more likely the poet is testing our knowledge of the New Testament than that we are testing his. In such veiled work, the poet outdoes even Milton in allowing us to see, almost a thousand years before the epicist, the outline and duration of that contest. One sees one's way to saying such things thanks to the work of all our predecessors, including Fredrick Klaeber, who laid out an early case for the Christian thrust of the poem—in noting that the Old Testament matters of the giants and the deluge, and especially in becoming the first to identify a New Testament influence on *Beowulf* in suggesting that "It would indeed be hard to understand why the poet contented himself with a plot of mere fabulous adventures so much inferior to the splendid heroic setting, unless the narrative derived a superior dignity from suggesting the most exalted hero-life known to Christians," (Tuso, 104–105).

To early critics who asked why Cain figures so prominently in the poem I owe one set of expansions. Shakespeare himself adopts the Cain matter for *Hamlet* when Claudius speaks of his murder of his brother, old Hamlet, as having "the primal eldest curse upon it," that is, Cain's murder of Abel. Claudius then married that brother's wife, Gertrude, and introduced the theme of incest into the play, as Hamlet indicates in calling him an "incestuous" beast. For both writers, Cain represents the dregs of depravity, incest, especially because in *Beowulf*, Cain's murdering his brother suggests that it too was prompted by Cain becoming enamored of Abel's wife, but fleeing without sexual consummation. What stunningly happens here, then, is that the woman who flees is Abel's wife at the time of flight but who, thanks to being unnamed, can be morphed into Grendel's dam the next time she appears. Her addition to the poem adds massively to the thematic power of Beowulf, thematic power exactly of the kind that can be associated with the need for an ensuing Flood. Her being followed by Cain suggests her helping instigate the murder, thus making her, as it were, a second Eve (and the third original sinner). Since flight seeks to avoid punishment; the question what has she done that is punishable produces complicity as the most eligible explanation of her behavior. It is simply dazzling, daring courage that pulls off such an extraordinary transformation. Of course, we will never know the truth in this or any other matter I am discussing, since the only certainty concerning any interpretation of any poem is that it can be wrong. But the poet is a master who takes great risks that put him in a class by himself. We might finally notice that the fenland we find in *Beowulf* is to be found also at and around Lindisfarne, which has an ancient association with fens, religion, interlace symmetrical design, gold work, and poetry, making possible an association with the Beowulf poet, too.

If Cain does the important work of connecting the poem with his own sins, we see this continue in the poem's emphasis on Grendel's (phallic) limb, its dismembering, and its being hung "high on the roof" of the great hall (XIV 872) as a (sexual) trophy and cunning lure to attract the mother. Moreover, the incestuous involvement of Cain and his sister-in-law will explain her further intense but one-sided interest in Grendel, once she comes forth as Grendel's dam. This account provides us with one incestuous union, leaving us to find two more. They are sure to be surprises because as gaps that in a triadic structure require filling we have no idea what they will prove to be.

But answers are not far to seek. To fulfill the triad of the three incestuous unions, we need go no farther that the marauding life that forms the basis of the seafaring existence that the poet weaves into parts of his account. Such a life continually carried with it the obvious inherent dangers of battle, pillage, and rape. When these three are easy and rewarding, they invite return visits. Extraordinary things now occur. Since Beowulf is younger than Wealhtheow, we may surmise that Ecgtheow, Beowulf's father, had been an early voyager, followed, about twenty years later, by Beowulf. And since Wealhtheow is well disposed toward him now, we can assume she doesn't recognize him as the son of her mother's attacker many years earlier, in a darkened room, her shift thrown over her head, an ugly, brief act, and a parting after an encounter of a few minutes. Such rape happened to women who were taken for rewards for the privation that accompanies dangerous voyages of men with violent tempers. If pregnancy results, the mother would have only the shared child's features as an indication of the father's appearance to identify the latter. Since Beowulf's appearance produces no premonitory warning, we must assume that she and Beowulf do not significantly resemble each other. Similarly, Beowulf would have no way of recognizing the offspring of his father's victim upon encountering Wealhtheow far removed from her birthplace and married to Hrothgar. What else then is the poet telling us at the start of the poem when we learn that Scyld Scefing was a Spear-Dane, and at the "fated time" (l. 28) died and was placed in the hollow of the boat at the mast (l. 36) than that the image here is a kind of synecdoche? Why does the poet expend three phallic images on this king—spear, hollow, and mast— and appear to do nothing with them? We seem to be expected to understand the nature of the lives the poet puts before us. At death, such kings would be laid, face up, in the hollow of a boat, next to the mast, giving them a caricature-like appearance of huge potency even in death. Needless to say, Beowulf himself is included among those fated, potent kings. And because Wealhtheow is made a gift of to Beowulf, and her father is never named, it becomes possible that Beowulf's father Ecgtheow fathered her and that she or Beowulf had a twin who did not survive, thus completing the triad of his children, two fated to live and one to die. In the heyday of Viking attacks, the men in a *Beowulf* audience would know (as modern scholars forget) what Spear-Danes did once ashore and hot for their share of spoils. At some point in this repeated cycle, every sexual pairing would have been attended with the possibility of proscribed, fated relationships, all of which would trace back to Cain. And to help his audience see this possibility for Beowulf, the poet provides Wealhtheow and Ecgtheow, names in which to hear a possible fatal link that doomed Beowulf and his half-sister. The final point to make about this matter is that the third element of the triad comes with Beowulf's accepting Wealhtheow's offered cup, and the pair of acts produce no small Christian problem for Beowulf's ultimate salvation.

So why then Cain? The first reason is the need for a figure of malevolent evil, someone bearing association with the darker sins that brought on the need for the Flood. This darker side is better represented by Cain than by Adam and Eve.[15] Also, without

Cain there would be no Grendel's dam, no Grendel, no need for Beowulf, and no powerful story for Beowulf. But with Cain as incestuous companion of Grendel's dam comes a son. It seems obvious that the mother has an (unreturned) incestuous interest in Grendel because of her earlier incestuous union with Cain. And Cain, along with large numbers of others who ignored Mosaic law, made the Flood a necessity.

Heorot, a pagan temple of drunkenness, trophies, great gifts of thane gold, and death, further develops the theme of incest. Beowulf baits his trap for Grendel's mother in a fashion hinting at their incest. He rips out Grendel's arm and mounts it at the roof where her yearning look upward will see the priapic-appearing body part, thus advantaging Beowulf, who will have a momentary opportunity, behind and unseen, to approach the aggrieved mother adoring a part of her too-deeply loved son. In risking her own life to retrieve it, the mother treats it as an object of "love" that she cannot live without, which suggests that foulness has passed from Cain to her, but imperfectly from her to Grendel. By decapitating her Beowulf suggests how deadly he regards her taint (but not, it seems, his own). Her union with Cain has probably changed her greatly, especially physically, and his sway has been only slightly passed on to infect Grendel, who resists its force, for a properly formed triad.

Her having been deeply changed deserves a bit more scrutiny because the ordinary woman who was Abel's wife emerges as Grendel's dam, a woman of infernal allegiance who thinks she is strong enough physically to challenge Beowulf. When we ask what was her transforming agent, the answer the poem offers is her very blood. She is the third and final element in the nearly completed group made up of the transformed sword hilt (by reduction), the dragon transformed from a worm (by enlargement), and herself by infusion. The hellish power of her blood contrasts with a later and concluding instance of redemptive power, as we shall see.

Hrothgar's payment for Heorot's delivery is especially base because he seems willing to make up for his cheapness by a second means of payment that is even cheaper, though unusually ironic. It personally costs him nothing, and so far seems to have escaped detection. On their meeting, Wealhtheow frankly tells Beowulf she "thanked God that her wish was fulfilled, that she might trust in some man for help against deadly deeds" (IX, 627–29). The irony of her statement is stunning, given her possibly possessing an incestuous link with him at this very moment, a link that many years ago produced her son through "deadly deeds." She believes her son's vulnerability as heir-apparent would be better protected by Beowulf as his father than by Hrothgar as her cuckolded husband, though I am not clear how much the king knows of the matter. But whether he recognizes the possibility or not, he lacks the strength to protect the boy, and so is useless in the matter. Upon her offering herself to Beowulf through her phallic cup, apparently with Hrothgar's blessing, Beowulf instantly takes it (IX. 629), thereby showing that God has not answered her prayer. (The poetic fare we meet up with here is rich with multiple ironies.) Her compliment to Beowulf would appear to reunite the pair in another bit of legerdemain: she is younger, not older than he is, though she is presented as the matron and he as the younger hero, reminding us in turn of matron Gertrude's interest in young Hamlet. That Wealhtheow would offer Beowulf her "cup" without Hrothgar's approval, indeed order, is unlikely especially because the poet makes such a point of saying, "I have not heard of many who gave four precious gold-adorned things to another on the ale-bench in a more friendly way" (IX. 1032), after we have been told that the queen "came forth . . . gold adorned" (IX. 618–19), making her so brilliantly eligible to be another gold Hrothgarian gift[16] and also possibly explaining her curious name, apparently a compound joining "weal"=wealth or riches with "theow"=slave or servant, so appropriate in one who serves the wishes of a rich king. The matter further unfolds when she offers the cup to her husband, and we are not told he takes it (IX. 1176), as if she is now damaged goods. In what seems like a highly nuanced passage, she urges that he use "mild words" to the Geats "as a man ought to do." Her use of "man," instead of host or the second person pronoun, is withering. She even stresses that he be "mindful of gifts" (IX. 1178–80). Her subtle implication suggests that giving goes so against his grain (though he seems to have made a gift of her to his rival) that he is lacking in a basic, lordly trait, and loath to be generous. Her advice isn't lost on him; he apparently believes the timing is disadvantageous and therefore waits till Beowulf is about to sail for home to ensure a lasting impression with a third, triadic, and lavish set of gifts, together with tears, a kiss, and a plea that he "quickly come back" (XXVI. 1868), should a now unprotected Hrothgar be attacked again. The king seems to believe the insincerity of this farewell will not be seen through. Beowulf's contrasts still show up the king for the weaker person at this point in the poem, though Beowulf is not so strong morally as we have thought.

Wealhtheow's offers of the cup define them as sexual by the simple phallic nature of a cup, which is a veiled allusion to the female phallus. The poet explicitly tells us that Beowulf "took the cup" (IX. 629). And to be sure that we see this, the poet re-emphasizes the matter when Wealhtheow gives her guest not four "things," but five rich gifts ending with "the largest of necklaces of those that [the poet has ever] heard spoken of on earth" (IX. 1194–96), another phallic image. But Hrothgar seems to have given five gifts, too, one being his queen which, as I have shown, we must work a bit to see and which is a gift differing from the other four. Clearly, though, the queen also knows how to reward a guest. Clearly, too, the guest knows how not to offend: Donaldson's note on the necklace tells us that Beowulf later gave it away. It would seem this means that Beowulf publicly and diplomatically accepts what he privately declines. Moreover, Grigsby notes that the necklace is tied to evidence showing it to involve lovemaking (Grigsby, 132) though he draws out none of the implications of the act. Such careful control over the poet's story is another sign showing us that the poet is worthy of standing amongst our finest writers.

Two sexual offers of the cup leave us one gift short of a triad. That the third gift has been the fleshly cup of herself is confirmed, triadically of course, by an incomplete triad of Beowulf's sleeping places. The first is the hall bench where he awaits Grendel. The second is the place where he is supposed to sleep but doesn't because it is decided to move him elsewhere (XIX. 1302–3). This means he has slept on a bench and in a bed, and the third place would have been in the queen's bed, the triadic values being clear enough now to suggest that on this night Beowulf possesses her though later still he sets her aside. This argument darkens the moral stature of Beowulf, whose Christian strength deserts him here, so that he may enjoy the queen. He becomes not just human but a sinful human, which is important for the conclusion of the poem. The author, however, is shown to be skilled in working in two directions at once. This interpretation is rendered possible because readers of Genesis meet the same anomaly of a well-populated world of tribes, clans, and nations all having descended from three men and one woman, which makes incestuous sharing appear to have been inevitable. And sharing would have been a source of jealous tension that could have led to the unexplained murder of Abel. Adding strength to these important suggestions is the description of the mother's blood as so boiling hot that it melted a sword blade—making Beowulf the third possessor of the hilt that had possibly been Abel's death weapon and had belonged to Cain, and now is a phallic image united with and dissolved by hot destructive blood, pointing to great sexual excess. Joining such images is the peculiar, dark, almost unrelieved, tone of the first two sections of the poem, a tone that to my ear matches as nothing else can the sustained sexual foulness eliciting so mournful a response. The carrier of the tone is the extraordinary language itself, seldom ever straightforward, but constantly and variously challenging us to choose, in almost every line, between an interpretation that the words say more than they appear to say or not quite as much as they may seem to say.

Our task is further complicated because the poet is drawn to working beyond mere narrative lines: he almost turns the work into drama at certain points because some portions slip so effortlessly into indirect or direct quotations from characters of unclear, difficult relation, both physically and emotionally, to each other. Their language is often as nuanced and subtle as anything found in Shakespeare[17]—and we are supposedly prohibited from resorting to speculation even though the language always remains poetic and no other choice is available—language that is allusive, never choosing between possible meanings for us, but always confining us to closer and closer paraphrases that show ultimately no difference between our efforts and those of bright high school and college students. And this truth identifies the common curse of literary criticism, as we practice it, as an elaborate effort that simply restates the original work and is thought best executed when it produces a veritable twin—in short, when no differences are apparent, save, of course, for a bit of incremental interpretation.

The unnamed foulness so subtly hinted at when Grendel's mother seeks out her son's "arm" is powerfully heightened by the poem's triadic structure. The proportions displayed by these triads are similar to those found in Dante and antedate them by about five centuries. When, therefore, we read that Hrothgar intends to make Beowulf his son (XVII. 1180). Beowulf will become his third heir after Hrethric and Hrothmund. This intention dramatically increases the potential for political intrigue among the three heirs, in addition to possibly allowing Hrothgar a "cheap" way to postpone paying Beowulf for delivering him from his scourge. Beowulf thus is beset by a double set of opponents, those in court and out, in what amounts to another balance of the sort that Tolkein called to our attention (Tuso, 108). To underscore the court split, the poet has Beowulf sitting with Hrothgar's sons, Hrothgar sitting with his nephew Hrothulf, and Wealhtheow unattached and alone (XVII. 1157, 1190–91, XVIII. 1236), an arrangement that stresses the perils confronting them because of the new enemies they may face, and their safety, such as it is, residing in their wits and sometimes trustable sword blades.

One set of antagonists is quite old, however. When Wealhtheow offers the meadcup to Hrothgar and then to Beowulf and the text is silent on either one accepting it (XVII. 1176, 1192), triadic necessity requires that a third person have been offered her cup, and this opens the door to our considering Hrothulf, to whom Wealhtheow, the queen of hospitality, does not offer the cup, he and his host at the moment being "still unbroken" as of (I. 1158), though "still" seems to hint that a break is forthcoming. There is obviously a flat loss in poetic value should the poet allow the choice to go to a person without connection to Wealhtheow and Hrothgar. Hrothulf represents a powerful choice because he then can have been involved with Wealhtheow in an incestuous union, one that reinforces the successional problem at Heorot. Grigsby's genealogical tables affirm the problem by having Hrethric identified as Roricus in Scandinavian legend and not recognized as his father's son, as well-informed listeners in the early audiences would have known. If this is the case, then to Grigsby's question "To what does Hrothgar owe the presence of his uninvited guest [Grendel]?" (Grigsby, 123), one answer would seem to be Heorot's double attraction as a place of Satanic victory through incestuous union and as the place where Grendel may hope to vanquish his moral opposite Beowulf, as one who has partaken of Wealhtheow's offered cup, a grave sin.

The Beowulf poet misses none of the fine psychological tensions arising from such unions, as we see when Beowulf smoothly, even bitingly, asked Hrothgar if his night had been "pleasant according to his desires." This can be asked in perfect innocence, but the question displeases Hrothgar, who curtly replies, "Ask not about pleasure" (XIX. 1315–17), which can be read as the king's denial of having such desires for his queen, or as displeasure at his guest's possible mockery. Reading the passage both ways may bring us pretty close to the truth, I believe. Our license for so doing comes from the queen's bitterly sharp comment that Hrothgar should "Enjoy while you may many rewards and leave to your kinsmen folk and kingdom when you must go forth to look on the Ruler's decree" (XVII. 1181–83). This remark is triply inflammatory because it glances at Hrothgar's, large loss of people, shrunken territory, and forthcoming death. It also witnesses the queen's apparent Christianity—and suggests that she is a convert and perhaps one who advised Hrothgar to invite Beowulf to Heorot. Her statement acts as a black velvet ground displaying the fire of the various passages in the poem naming Hrothgar as protector, defender, and leader of his people, and other similar courtesies. The psychological lights that play upon this scene may well be among the earliest such illuminations found in a work of English literature.

But of greater importance to this scene is a matter concerning the royal children, "her sons" as Wealhtheow speaks of them (XVII. 1288). By using "her" instead of "our," she allows us to question Hrothgar's paternity of one or both of them. She reinforces this possibility by asking Beowulf to protect them and also "yourself counsel them," for which she will remember to reward him. Wealhtheow seems to have one child specifically in mind when she protectively implores Beowulf to "be kind of deeds to my son" (I. 1218). She clearly trusts Beowulf more than Hrothgar both as regards counsel and physical protection. She appears to want him to protect an especially vulnerable son, apparently the eldest, the "heir" to the kingdom, who would attract the notice of remoter heirs or other ambitious souls. The boy is about twelve years of age, and since Hrothgar is so weak that he needed Beowulf's help (which will soon depart with him), should anything happen to Hrothgar a twelve-year old is even more vulnerable to anyone with an eye on the crown.

Up to this point, that is, through the death of Grendel's dam, the power of the poem is unimpeded. But in the final section dealing with the dragon, the mere physical luster of the material sharply diminishes. It starts off brilliantly, however, because the poet balances the under-girding of murder and Flood from the first book of the Old Testament with the dragon's subjugation in the last book of the New Testament (chapter 12), the symmetry here being obvious and no accident. But the poet faced an enormous problem, one without apparent solution, a total structural collapse, the result of his completing the triad of son, mother, and dragon, that is, the triad of the three daemonic figures. All that remained for him was to establish the proportions between the dragon and his underling predecessors, Grendel and his dam. But the latter had already been assigned powerful values through their connection with the great theme of incest. So with Grendel allotted the most important emphasis and Grendel's dam occupying second place, the dragon has only one spot to fill, the third and lesser important element. This, of course, handed the poet the strangest of tasks, namely, assigning the Satanic figure a position lower than that of his clear subordinates by having him trail them in third place. But as an agent of evil, the dragon is the most important member of the triad because it is the "worm," or snake, and therefore Satan. You sustain the magic of this inversion by doing almost nothing at all, that is, by taking only the names of dragon and worm from chapter 12 and ignoring all else, while exchanging Mary's subjugation of Satan in Revelations with Beowulf and Wiglaf's fighting the dragon, and all the time you build weakness into Beowulf, stressing his advanced age, his weariness, his ebbing strength, his need of Wiglaf's help in overcoming the dragon, and the general, resigned mood of a man about to bodily die but spiritually live, thanks to God himself, the third power in the triad of the dragon's opponents. And you do this by subduing the entire forward momentum of the force that has impelled your poem forward, a force that respectably rivals Sophocles' massive line by line power in Oedipus, and turn the momentum from its bed and bearing to what looks like a weaker course, which turns out to be more powerful still. Satan of course does not literally die. He lives, but he loses his fight for Beowulf's soul, because Beowulf's final act is devoted to overcoming his great foe, which both lose. This loss for Satan (but victory for God) ends the poem on the weakest triadic element, which is what the triad requires.

With the clear change in momentum comes the stunning realization that all the time we have been dealing with another and vast triad, the triad of the poem's momentums, the dragon episode being the final and least element, and the post-Flood intensities at Heorot and pre-Flood background portions being the most and the less than most. The ease with which the poet pulls this triad off frankly left me dumbfounded, since I did not have an inkling that a triad could possess such great dimensions. Yet there it was, brought to light at the very end of the poem, a subtlety sophisticated and surprising, and affixed to an episode with a fifty foot dragon that raises disgust in one class of reader. And I emerged from that reverie, only to realize there is much more to the poem.

The death of Beowulf is the great spiritual note, the victory that his soul requires because the poet achieves a maximum of power that at once satisfies the needs of his Christian story, which must end with Beowulf's losing to Satan even as God triumphs over him in a huge paradoxical anticlimax. And the reason that the poet is forced to invert the values of the triad is because there is no possible way to attach the incest theme to the dragon. Take that theme away from the dragon and you are left with the weakest element, which none the less involves the figure who was strong enough to remain the defier of God himself. In short, the poet, completing his crucial triad of New Testament influences, returns to the oldest and greatest Christian belief we possess, namely the further paradox that Satan's victory over Beowulf is nothing but a defeat because, thanks to the power of Christ's transformative blood, death gives Beowulf the victory of eternal life, and a salvific ending is plainly the most powerful Christian event available to the poet.

Moreover, the message is unmistakable that Beowulf dies as a Christian fighting Satan (already having killed his two lesser agents), and therefore has spent his adult life fighting the enemies of God, which we are allowed to assume is enough to redeem him from one of the worst of sins, incest. The poem concerns three transformative bloods, two given and one implied: the blood of Cain that advanced the fall of man by corrupting, for a second time, the world; the blood of Grendel's dam, able to melt a phallic sword blade up to the hilt; and the never-mentioned blood of Christ, capable of saving every repentant, sin-stained soul, including those guilty of incest itself. Beowulf, a friend of God, not an enemy, is a Christian sinner, who has cuckolded and mocked his lord, coveted his neighbor's wife, his half-sister, and drunk from her "cup" so that the poet can show his audience that no sin whatever is beyond the redemption of the blood of Christ. Far, then, from writing a poem of uncertain Christian significance, the Beowulf poet has created a work that deserves ranking among the greatest such efforts that we possess. It should bow to *The Divine Comedy*, but it need not drop to its knees.

One of the poet's achievements is having written a study of great court intrigue a full eight centuries before Shakespeare displayed the corrosive court tensions that we find in Hamlet (some of which appear plucked straight from Beowulf) arising from character, intrigue, and succession. If it should turn out that the Beowulf poet introduced the greatest structural tool known to literature, he then deserves mention among our foremost writers. And if this proves true, then as an unknown poet, writing in an unknown place and at an unknown time, he will have had the distinction of writing not only a brilliant and astonishing work himself, but one that arguably helped make possible the structural work of Dante, Shakespeare, Melville, James, and Joyce, while thereby contributing a highly interesting story to literature.

We have seen a portion of that story, namely the poet's extraordinary gamble. That gamble reveals his mind and his supreme, unflinching confidence that he can leave unstated any mention of Christ while showing Beowulf's redemptive acts. With this stroke the Beowulf poet brings his one known work to a close with the most powerful reaffirmation of the biblical message we possess, while showing Anglo-Saxon poetry to be writing in which massive structural problems can be identified as overcome and really anything "modern" is possible, so that we become aware that the Beowulf poet is well qualified to head the group of writers that we can now move on to examine in his great structural tradition. Chaucer is the father of English literature, but the Beowulf poet is the alpha father of modern symmetrical structures. From his structural tradition, perhaps begun in the eighth century, would be excluded more than half the literature that awaited authors and writing, and in which would be included, safe from accidental discovery, any secret known to the writers discerning enough to recognize and master a superior structural form. At the time of its writing, Austen, Eliot, Dickens, Hardy, and others, to name a few, were structurally obsolete and doomed to the creation of works that a reading or two would appear to exhaust.

The Beowulf poet possessed a structural greatness that few other writers would command. My study leaves the poem far from being exhausted, though there is one final matter that deserves attention. Triadic structure can now and then validate editorial conjectural readings of a physically damaged text. For example, one of the passages damaged by the fire that affected various parts of the poem occurs at Beowulf's funeral. The damaged text ends when "the Geatish woman, wavy-haired, sang a sorrowful song about Beowulf, said" (XLII. 3132–33). Donaldson then offers his reading of a few damaged lines, one of which says "she sorely feared for herself" (loc. cit.). This can only mean that Beowulf's death leaves her without a protector. Another woman, Wealhtheow, sorely feared for the safety of her children, whom she implored Beowulf to protect. His acting in that capacity for them means that he also will serve as a protector for a third person, and Donaldson's reading of the damaged passage produces that person and completes this important triad. Who this woman may be is a mystery—but not for long because with two mothers in the poem, Grendel's dam and Wealtheow, we must have a third. This woman, the most prominent person at the funeral, bids fair to be Beowulf's mother. Donaldson's conjectural reading of the damaged text is as validated as a completed triad can make it. And why this woman should fear for herself is explained if, as Beowulf's mother, she has too great a love for him. It is so strong that she appears out of nowhere and thrusts herself forward during

Beowulf's final rite honoring his greatness. The woman with the wavy hair is tolerated but avoided by those around her. What has she done to be ostracized now that she has lost a protector?

This journey began with a fated infant being protected and its life spared because of its rank. It now comes full circle at the very end with two fated adults losing life, one physically and the other (for the moment) spiritually, in fulfillment of the mighty theme the poet places before us and over which he demonstrates such total control in this ominous moment of mother and child making an incomplete family triad, completed when we see that Beowulf needs a brother who is attracted to a woman who appears with wavy hair that will perpetuate the curse we first meet at the poem's beginning. The answer to the obvious question, the mystery of what the Geatish woman has done, is simple. She has broken a taboo, and now lost one protector while gaining another, his brother, who appears now to be king. Her intimate feeling for him is delicately hinted at by the touch that her hair is not rent, as we would expect, given the death of Beowulf and the obvious parallel she makes with Grendel's dam at the time of Grendel's death.

That Beowulf appears to have a brother is strikingly borne out by a vivid triadic necessity required by the pair we already possess, those of Cain and Abel and Wealtheow's sons, which is neatly finished if Beowulf has a brother all six being related to rulers. No other answer so neatly supplies solutions to such important questions so completely, so powerfully. No other answer lifts its author into the ranks of the western world's greatest poets—Homer, Virgil, Dante, and Shakespeare. The poem deserves the kind of respect Shakespeare gave it, the respect that comes with our seeing how great it really is and how much we are indebted to its poet.[18]

2

Shylock's Neighbors

In 1968, the late Professor Marvin Felheim opened an investigation into the triadic pattern of elements,[1] the most pervasive pattern found in *The Merchant of Venice* and the raw basis for the symmetrical structure that permeates the play.[2] Unmentioned by Felheim, this structure originated with the Beowulf poet, appeared later in Dante, and later still was adopted by Shakespeare, Melville, James, and Joyce, among other great writers. The triads of Grendel, Grendel's Dam, and the dragon, and Inferno, Purgatorio, and Paradiso are virtually the same as the triad of gold, silver, and lead caskets in the play, the triad of Pequod captains in Moby-Dick, the triad of ambassadors Strether, Sarah, and Jim, and the triad of Stephen, Bloom, and Molly in Ulysses, each triad being a group of three like proportioned elements, the first elements (Paradiso, gold, Ahab, Strether, and Bloom being the largest and most important, followed by the slightly less important or valuable elements made up of Purgatorio, silver, Bildad, Sarah, and Stephen, and the smallest and least important elements made up of Inferno, lead, Peleg, Jim, and Molly). The proportioned gradations among the elements act as a true fingerprint, objectively identifying the work as that of the author, not of us. The elements themselves are alike and therefore symmetrical. Felheim noticed, without comment, that the two larger were similar and paired, and the smallest one was separate and different. This is a crucial but limited observation, and it represents the foremost features of every triad in the play.

Symmetry is the most powerful tool available to mathematicians, physicists, writers, composers, and many others, and it comes into use and manifests its literary power when a writer addressing a moral or political matter that is dangerous to treat openly, then creates an open, or incomplete, triad. The omitted element often deals with such a subject but is left for us to complete, and it makes the triadic tool a producer of extraordinary power and surprises. Such subjects are usually the most powerful ones a writer can address and the state suppress. In the context of a system of hundreds of completed groups, the reader will recognize the need to complete incomplete ones and make them like the others, this being what symmetry demands. We can see this demand in medical cases of deformities so ugly that a surgeon will attempt to restore a severed limb or appendage, or rectify a disfigurement, such as a cleft palate. In slighter instances, we all do this when we replace a button on a shirtfront or a sleeve. Along with beauty, function is restored. The writer simply counts on our converting ugliness into beauty. We become surgeons of sorts, and we take this work seriously and make it scrupulously conform proportionally to the given elements: we have a model, and we match it. The completion safeguards everyone from prosecution—writer, printer, and us—the transfer occurring only between the writer's mind and ours: there is no prosecutable offense. The writer devises a way to express anything at all of a volatile, political or moral nature, and we are free to complete it—or miss it, if we are unaware of the structural necessities of his system.

The Merchant of Venice poses the great question of whether it is anti-Semitic and its author an anti-Semite, or, put another way, whether Shakespeare sees Jews as human beings (which the state seemed to fear as Jewish sympathizing and perhaps as disapproval of its 1594 execution of Roderigo Lopez for allegedly trying to poison Elizabeth), or as dangerous, reprehensible creatures (which Shakespeare seems to have thought the government preferred). Triads provide a solution to this matter in an especially elegant manner, through our determining who Shylock's next door neighbors are.

Shylock's relationships to his neighbors, and theirs to him, are defining aspects of his character and of theirs. And on this matter of character and relationships, the best analysis we possess comes from Arthur Miller. He drew an important distinction that has generally gone unheeded and ignored when he said that

> "'maybe more than any other art, the play lacks independence as an artifact. It is a set of relationships. There really are no characters in plays; there are *relationships*. Where there are only characters and no relationships, we have an unsatisfactory play. A work has to be supported by its time. It's an old story. A

work can appear and the audience might not quite know what to make of it. They don't get the clues the work is sending them."

Without relationships, tensions and conflicts are reduced and removed, and in the study that follows we shall see the positive truth of what they contribute to this play. Miller also strongly approved of an audience "constantly trying to supply what is missing."[3] Miller obviously believes that certain works are missing a great many things, since we are constantly to be trying to supply them. This flies straight in the face of what academics believe and are comfortable with, for they generally suppose that the author has delivered a completed work that is not to be tampered with. I believe Miller is right and therefore offers important support for my attempts to fill many gaps, Shakespearean gaps being usually only asymmetrical notices of symmetrical structuring. Whether I've filled them correctly or not is an entirely different matter, for which my support is simply the arguments I produce. Completed gaps extend narratives, and extended narratives matter greatly to a writer using them, both for symmetrical beauty and acquiring readers now and later. An extended narrative rewards patient readers with a very great story indeed, and it can extend the life and interest of the work far into the future. Shakespeare begins his very great story with Antonio's sadness and helps us begin seeing into it when Lorenzo and Jessica walk off with Shylock's ducats and jewels.

At 2.4.25–6 Lorenzo plans meeting Salerio and Solanio "At Gratiano's lodging some hour hence." This meeting occurs at 2.6.1–2. As they stand beneath Gratiano's penthouse, Lorenzo arrives 25 lines later, and Jessica calls down from Shylock's adjacent upper windows and shortly reappears in order to throw down ducats and jewels. The wine-loving, party animal Gratiano, in short, lives in the penthouse right next door to sober Shylock.[4] Few if any Venetian houses were unattached, so that Gratiano's building likely shares a wall with Shylock's. The most interesting matter here is not architectural but occupational. Who lives under Gratiano? The play's silence on this matter is total.

The play is also totally silent about where Antonio lives. This question is stressed anew when we consider that we spend significant time in the living quarters of two of the three most important characters in the play—Shylock and Portia—but not one second in the third—Antonio's. His house's location is never identified. Though Antonio

is the elegant answer to the question about who lives below Gratiano, and the answer
that gives Shakespeare greater drama than any other occupant he could choose, Antonio's residency there would obviously mean he is a Christian living in the ghetto. If we
assume that this could not be, we would be wrong, because Gratiano is also a Christian
and a great friend of Antonio. And his being a Christian living above makes it quite
possible that Christian Antonio may live below, where the two of them can berate Shylock. Of course, since we aren't told the lower unit is occupied, we are free to suppose it
is empty, and free also to suppose it is occupied by some minor character—except that
Shakespeare is a great dramatist who must know there is dramatic value only in a comically volatile choice. Like Gratiano, Antonio is then not only a Christian and a neighbor of Shylock's, but his enemy as well. And if we imagine the two structures sharing
a common wall and housing Shylock, Gratiano, and Antonio—one building having
double residency because of its penthouse and the other being a single dwelling—we
see two buildings containing three residences, which make a perfect and completed
triad of three elements, doubly distributed, an arrangement Felheim drew silent attention to. But what kind of Christians lived in the Venetian ghetto? Obviously not
born Christians. That leaves conversos, Jews who had converted to Christianity. Jews
living next door to conversos were quite historical. Such Jews were not welcomed into
Christian neighborhoods. And as Salo Wittmayer Baron says, they soon adopted the
habit of seeking out their old families, friends, and associates, with whom there would
have been frictions but long-standing relationships.[5] Moreover, those conversos trying
to buy houses among Christians would have found age-old animosities against them,
leaving them able to live only in their old residences in their old and familiar ghettoes.
Shakespeare's ghetto was occupied by Jew and converso alike, living next door to each
other. Such a makeup of the ghetto renders it certain that *The Merchant of Venice* reflects
the realities of Venetian life. But whether it does or doesn't, his arrangement of neighbors instantly makes questionable much of the last hundred years of scholarship that
holds the play to be anti-Semitic and its author an anti-Semite. We have good reason to
begin the serious work of addressing the carefully nuanced play that Shakespeare did
write and the subtle story he tells.

Since the characters wear no sandwich-boards saying they are Jew or converso, we
have to determine such matters for ourselves. Moreover, Elizabethan licensing authorities would be perplexed by a play dealing with such mixing and well could wonder

about its author's religious allegiance. Shakespeare may address this ambiguity by the most striking feature of the play: its employment of so many unexplained groups of three. This is the only play Shakespeare wrote that makes this feature not only visible but impossible to miss, though many of its predecessors—and followers—use the triadic form but keep it unseen (such as *Romeo and Juliet* and *Hamlet*). The only other great literary work with so insistent a show of threes is Dante's *La Divina Commedia*. Each writer's subject was sufficiently suspect to state political powers (Dante for putting popes in Hell and in one brilliant tactical move called "Inferno" instantly making literature of and putting into discussable play every vice known to humanity, and Shakespeare for making a Jew his main character) that each writer apparently thought it wise to drape his text with absolutely visible, oft-repeated trinitarian-like triadic groups to establish his bona fides. It is quite certain that the Stationer's Company knew what modern scholars do not (they had only to ask any Venetian traveler), that given the prejudices of the time, Shakespeare's Venetian characters were highly likely to include a number of Jews beyond the few explicitly identified as such. The state censors would have been suspicious of a dramatist so taken with Jewish themes and characters and needing a legalistic trap, sprung by a young woman, to keep a Jew from maiming a "Christian" merchant, that he employed hundreds of obvious tricks.

Positing Antonio as the neighbor of Gratiano above and Shylock next door not only is the best housing arrangement Shakespeare could possibly devise, but it answers a number of other questions that otherwise are hard. Why house Shylock squarely next to the two persons who dislike him more than does anyone else in the play, except as a fine source of comic amusement to us? Shylock's chief dislike of Gratiano involves the boisterous noise that characterizes the lifestyle of this hot-headed bachelor, who is the most vindictive and vocal of Shylock's enemies. Gratiano and Shylock are splendid opposites, Shylock being usually as sedate as Gratiano is loud-mouthed. Small wonder Shylock is seldom at home: he lives next to a party animal, and smaller wonder Jessica dryly says, "Our house is hell" (2.3.2). She can say this with a neighbor's certitude of the effect Shylock's next-door enemies have had on him on an almost daily basis. Gratiano's loudness clearly bothers Shylock, as we see in the court scene. There, Gratiano is bellowing insults at Shylock who, knife in hand, calmly whets away while acting the role of your ordinary, moderate, reasonable enemy, and urging, as he scrapes an edge onto his blade, that Gratiano should practice vocal restraint: "Till thou canst rail the seal from off my bond, Thou but offend'st thy lungs to speak so loud" (4.1.139–140). Obviously, Gratiano's bluster offends Shylock. Obviously too, over time, Shylock has often had to yell at the loud-mouthed fellow next door to be quiet. Gratiano knows such a muzzler too well, for he tries to cheer a downcast Antonio with a story of an unnamed gloomy silencer, "As who should say, 'I am Sir Oracle, And when I ope my lips let no dog bark!'" (1.1.93–94). This is a personification that points to their oracular neighbor Shylock. Along with Antonio, Gratiano asks that we catch his drift. At home, Shylock seals off his house from the rowdy youth by closing his windows and trying to deaden Gratiano's noise by entombing himself. He even orders Jessica to "stop my house's ears, I mean my casements," and not let "the sound of shallow fopp'ry enter My sober house" (2.5.33–36). For more than two thousand years the relationships of warring neighbors have been the stuff of comic drama. But to the personal differences in lifestyles, Shakespeare adds a social tang; it is not anti-Semitic, but rather classist, for it conveys the feeling of superiority that marks the owner of a religion which he is certain is superior to that of his neighbor. Genuine anti-Semitism does not seem to be expressed by a loudmouth converso youth living next door to a quiet, elderly Jew. The only cards that a poor, youthful Gratiano has to play against a rich, older, killjoy are the cards of youthful strength, social superiority, and obnoxiousness.

Antonio also plays the religious card—and more viciously—because he is far more defensive than Gratiano, and with very good reason as we shall see. Moreover, neighborly proximity, if such is the case, would allow him to play his card often. One reason he knows so much about Shylock is that he lives close enough to see the contraction in Shylock's life as various people leave—Leah, Old Gobbo, Jessica, and Launcelot. But there is another and more important reason as well, which Portia tips us off to when she famously asks, "Which is the merchant here? and which the Jew?" (4.1.172). One explanation of this odd question is that she sees a family resemblance. And since both are Jews, of the right ages, and apparently living next door to each other, it becomes possible that they are brothers. Sibling rivalry, which can become quite intense, may explain some of their mutual dislike. Their apparently ethnically-visible physical appearance is borne out by Shylock's own remark about Antonio, "He hates our sacred nation" (1.3.43), where the pronoun *our* should be understood to include Antonio. His presence in the ghetto (2.6.59; 3.3 s.d.) is not only consistent with residency, but his intense dislike of Shylock is not necessarily proof of anti-Semitism. This carefully worked-out arrangement of making Shylock's most vocal antagonists his neighbors, and one of them his possible brother, shows Shakespeare compounding the intensities of their lives so as to subject them to an absolute maximum of stress, already quite considerable because as dwellers in the ghetto, they have been segregated as inferior from Christian Venice. To their usual daily stress, they live under a doubled amount as each other's tormentor. Lives so pressured and studied yield a maximum of drama. And throughout his career, Shakespeare chose such intense arrangements for every conceivable stress and dramatized exposure. And for this one, he has Gratiano and Lorenzo identify the location of the penthouse of the former as next door to Shylock, with its lower floors a residential mystery and the most important gap in the play needing filling, as Arthur Miller very likely knew. Assigning it to Antonio will instantly, powerfully, change his relationship to everyone in Shylock's house.

Shylock, of course, "hate[s Antonio] for he is a Christian" and for his "bring[ing] down The rate of usance here with us in Venice," so that if he can trap him, "I will feed fat the ancient grudge I bear him" (1.3.37, 39, 41). What this ancient grudge is we are not told, but from their being neighbors, and likely ancient ones, it would date back to the time when Antonio could pop in next door to visit Shylock and his wife, a wife who is now absent from that household, where she once provided easy access to her husband's unmarried brother, with ships at sea and much time on his hands and Shylock off at the Rialto. Some critics believe she is dead, though we are never told she is, and there is not a shred of drama in her being so. The only information we have is supplied by her absence—and by Lorenzo's touching on Jessica's bastardy when he says that she may be "issue to a faithless Jew" (2.4.37). One kind of faithless Jew obviously is a converso.

Launcelot holds her out the hope that "your father got you not—that you are not the Jew's daughter" (3.5.9–10), an innuendo with substance since it is spoken by Antonio's neighbor, who would have been on location to witness Antonio's "brotherly" visits. Nor is the idea the exclusive property of Launcelot: driving the point home with a bitter attack is Solanio, who taunts Shylock with an allusion to Jessica's complexion, which is evidently lighter than Shylock's. Shylock is immediately defensive and calls Jessica "My own flesh and blood." Indeed, he peppers his speech with calling her "daughter," and has called her such so often that street urchins have picked it up and repeated it (2.8.24). But Solanio responds with biting innuendo: "Out upon it, old carrion! Rebels it at these years?" And this allusion to Shylock's being rank, corrupted flesh would have put some in Shakespeare's audience in mind of St Paul's warnings and hence alerted them to Shylock's own carnality (which will appear more fully later on). With dogged insistence, Shylock repeats himself, "I say my daughter is my flesh and blood" (3.1.26, 30–32). But we notice that he now backs away from specifying Jessica, which supports our looking elsewhere for his daughter. Salerio backs up Solanio's charge with bitter taunts that "There is more difference between thy flesh and [Jessica's] than between jet and ivory; more between your bloods than there is between red wine and Rhenish" (3.1.33–5).

Of much importance to these three passages is where they occur. Lorenzo's occurs on the street. Launcelot's occurs privately within Shylock's house; Solanio's and Salerio's occur publicly on a Venetian street, as do the voices of the mocking street urchins. Together they show that a story about Jessica's paternity is widespread in Venice, and given how intensely private a person Shylock is, this fact must sting him badly. Solanio has an inflexible belief that Jessica is not Shylock's daughter, and the attack finally overpowers Shylock's defenses, who then says nothing. Or rather, what he now says offers lengthy, oblique, embarrassed evidence that he has been cuckolded, for in his controlled anger he replies, "If you prick us, do we not bleed?" (3.1.56).[6] The verb "prick" is as close as a wounded Shylock can come to an outright admission of what he seems to have endured. And the blood-producing wound would have come from a rival's horns over a mate, and sounds like a rich and complete allusion to a cuckolding. It obviously includes important psychological and physical elements. Cuckolding, needless to say, is rich in relationships (which have long been the very stuff of drama), in this case involving four persons. Without the cuckolding, Shylock, Antonio, Leah, and Jessica are shallower characters and lacking the primary inter-relationship that cuckolding provides. It is even richer if done by a brother to a brother. Better still, it makes for powerful drama. If it is true, it means that originally three persons knew the truth, the cuckolder, Leah, and Shylock. Neither Leah nor Shylock would have a reason to broadcast the story. But the cuckolder would. The act and the leak would inflame Shylock as few things could, and they would certainly qualify in his mind as an "ancient grudge." Shylock has a basis for directly accusing Antonio of "the shames that you have stain'd me with" (1.3.134), and Leah has good reason not to be in Venice: Shylock would have thrown her out, or made life impossible for her staying, in either case a very human reaction, especially after a cuckolding. She seems to have removed herself, not to another Venetian area, but to a rival and poorer city, Genoa. This is suggested by Jessica's going there—daughters affirm relationships by bringing boyfriends home to mother—and spending a large, undesignated sum (3.2.95–96) in a place where a likely impoverished mother could use it. (One doesn't hear of Shylock or Antonio giving her a penny.) The renunciation implicit in her removal accords with Harold Jenkins' noting that "[t]he repudiation of a woman by her husband . . . is a central situation in at least half a dozen of Shakespeare's plays."[7] That central situation appears to operate in this comedy, as well. And a cuckolding will easily explain the ancient grudge that Shylock bears Antonio.

In bruiting about such a conquest, the cuckolder would intend the humiliation of Shylock: few things match a cuckolding for humiliation. For the comedy of the matter, your victim should be as sensitive as his cuckolder is insensitive, so as to achieve maximum embarrassment of and triumph over the other party. The bragging rights that go to the conqueror give us a strong reason to look carefully at the famous bond (which animates the court scene) to see if Shylock's revenge somehow matches the humiliation Antonio seems to have made him suffer.

The ancient grudge represents Shylock's anger at Antonio, it fuels his desire for revenge, and his revenge, at moments, may intend the legal murder of Antonio, though Shylock prefers a "pound Of your fair flesh, to be cut off and taken In what part of your body it pleaseth me" (1.3.144–46. Emphasis mine). Cutting off a pound of flesh strongly hints at a cuckolder's genitals. James Shapiro sees this, but he thinks Shylock is responsible for the change in the bond.[8] If this is true, Shylock would be primarily murderous. But if Antonio is responsible, the change is amusing and creates laughter.

The comedy of the matter is that Antonio would rather have his heart cut from his body than lose his one pounder and presumably the active life that comes with such a dazzler. Specifying the mere weight involved here strongly suggests that Shylock has been repulsed by Antonio's sexual swagger and its insinuation upon Shylock's size and skills. Shakespeare repeatedly deals with swagger in codpiece humor along with the non-gratuitous cuckoldry jokes that garnish the end of this play, and that he and so many playwrights of the age cannot resist: but Shapiro ignores this machismo in favor of using the matter as evidence that "Jews were aliens, they were a separate nation, racially set apart, and, most ominously, they secretly desired to take the knife to Christians in order to circumcise or even castrate them." Worse yet was the "insidious threat Jews posed to the . . . sexual . . . life of the nation."[9] A comic Shylock who wants only to act the mohel and take a little off the top is a threat not just to naval types armed with one-pounders, but a threat to the sexual life of the nation?! Who amongst us, in Shylock's circumstances, wouldn't want to spike Antonio's canon? Shylock should hate a brother Jew who has betrayed his hospitality and enjoyed his own wife in his own bed, and who parades as a person of superior Christian morals. But both men are caught up in a comic relationship, and their antics are consistently laughable, until we ignore their obvious bearings.

The bond provision is a masterpiece of comedy and is one of the greatest comic situations in all of dramatic literature. But some readers make it into a vicious case of Christian villainy to Jews. They have misidentified Shylock as one well-known type, the cuckolded victim, as a Jewish monster intent on the ritual murder of a Christian, and Antonio as another well-known type, the cuckolder, as his Christian prey, and their author as an anti-Semite. Well, when the wind is southerly, perhaps. And yes, there is a monster in the play. But it isn't Shylock. Rather it resides in Antonio's loins, and it weighs a full pound—a veritable butter brick of a tool. The scene is a triumph of comedy that shows Shylock nursing his wrath (to keep it warm) for about twenty years when the great moment comes. Shylock not only wants his unlimited choice sworn to before a notary; he wants Antonio to "Give him [the notary] direction for this merry bond" (1.3.167–68). Antonio, not Shylock, is responsible for the language in the bond, an important point that Shapiro misses.

But Antonio obviously loves his monster, so that in court the bond has been changed to involve a very specific area, "Nearest the merchant's heart" (4.1.231). This change suggests that Antonio couldn't bring himself to direct the notary to allow Shylock lower access. Our assuming that Shylock intends to ignore the change and cut off the offending organ, that seems involved in his humiliation to begin with, is valid because he tells the Duke (4.1.41) he is after "A weight of carrion flesh" (in OED 1 sense 3b s.v. carrion, "The fleshly nature of man, 'the flesh' in the Pauline sense.") He still has enough anger to want to cut out his heart, since that is all the bond will allow: but it plainly is a second choice. What stops him from humiliating Antonio, of course, is Portia's shrewd interpretation granting him his flesh, but not a drop of blood.

For Shakespeare to connect Jessica's paternity with the unnamed hatred between Shylock and Antonio makes brilliant comic sense. Antonio is a Christian with an ethnic Jewish look. He is a Christian who appears to have slept with a Jewish woman, the wife of a Jew, and probably in her very bed—why wear out his own sheets? He is a Christian who knows and shares the society of Shylock's (Jewish) friends and enemies (3.1.57–8)—and who would presumably be known to a brother who could then cool the one and heat the other (3.1.49–50)—a brother who would also know not only Shylock's ghetto neighborhood but the very house, and thus be a Christian with a decided appreciation of Jewish relationships and a desire to sustain them. As a smug, intolerant, self-righteous hypocrite who likely lives in his old community, Antonio is deliciously amusing. And his famous, mysterious melancholy is partly explainable as the result of his loss of status among his old community of friends, where, except for his own tight circle, he has encountered rejection—"I am a tainted wether[10] of the flock" (4.1.114), and he surely has lost access to Shylock's home and to Jessica as well. His circle's siding with Shylock would make him sad: it's depressing when friends can't see the truth of your obvious superiority. More depressing still would be living next door to a daughter who doesn't recognize the truth of her very identity and doesn't even see what others can see, that she is too light of skin to be Shylock's. Shylock reminds Antonio of Laban's (i.e. Shylock's) claim to the parti-coloured lambs (i.e. Jessica), and this loss is apparently very bitter to Antonio (1.3.66–85).

The inferred ironies that Antonio provides us are matched by a fine example from Shylock, who also appears to have played the cuckolder, a matter to which Shakespeare devotes the whole of 2.2 in a spirited dispute between Launcelot and Old Gobbo over whether the boy is young master Launcelot (the young man's contention) or plain Launcelot (Old Gobbo's claim). The vigor of Launcelot's insistence contrasts the forbearance, delicacy, and gentleness of the old man's counter stand. Shylock also supports Launcelot's suspicions in saying that "The patch [Launcelot] is kind enough, but a huge feeder!" (2.5.45), which plays on patch, the badge that Jews were forced to wear. Launcelot also, therefore, appears to be a Jew. This identification seems to be confirmed at 3.5.54–62, when Launcelot respectfully declines putting on his hat at dinner, but wants, in an apparent show of Jewish embarrassment, to cover the pork being served. Thus, if Shylock fathered Launcelot, Launcelot would enjoy a kinship with him that gives him his right to be regarded as young master: otherwise, he is plain Launcelot. He thinks he is master Launcelot because "my father did something smack, something grow to, he had a kind of taste"(2.2.14–15), which more easily describes the raunchiness of Shylock than the deference of Old Gobbo.

Much of this scene's humor occurs when the old man returns with a dish of doves—a forgiveness offering for Shylock[11] (which is rich in irony and pathos if Shylock bedded Margery, the old man's wife), the ironic offense being that Old Gobbo chose departure with Leah over remaining with Shylock, and now needs to return to his former post, probably because Leah is too poor to pay his wages. Just as Leah and Jessica have fled Shylock's house, Launcelot intends doing the same thing. And just as the ladies fled to escape Shylock, so too does Launcelot. Of course, what beckons him so strongly is carnival week, a new master's livery, and new freedoms that will later include his impregnating, as a chip off the Shylockian block, a Moorish girl (3.5.34–5): Launcelot too has "a kind of taste." What holds him back from leaving immediately is his title of young master—and his conscience, which tells him to honor his father and stay. Making this matter richer in irony is Launcelot's age: he appears to be older than Jessica, which makes Shylock's offense against Leah older than hers against him.

Yet Leah appears to have forgiven him, only to have herself succumbed when Antonio would seem to have capitalized on his access and her vulnerability; and she violated the double standard, allowing an unforgiving Shylock to drive her from his home. In any case, being cuckolded gives Shylock an excellent moral reason to hate Antonio. Antonio's chutzpah, which makes great comedy, is sustained by his apparent total dismissal of Leah after his conquest. She has the look of a trophy to feed Antonio's ego, and he dumped her once that purpose had been served. But he also lost her along with Jessica; and his life, like Shylock's, is characterized by important losses. We see Shylock's unbegrudged and uncomplaining generosity in caring and paying for Jessica's upbringing. These inferences brighten the character of Shylock and darken that of Antonio. To miss these relationships is to produce criticism that weakens the drama and makes it look incomplete. But this surface incompleteness shows the drama at work constantly requiring the reader to think so as to supply what is missing.

Old Gobbo hints at a very rich part of the untold story, in that his return means he is broke and needs reemployment. His astonishing atonement to his cuckolder suggests his apparently total ignorance of having been cuckolded, or else that he swallows his pride even though he is the outrageously offended person. Reduced as he may be, he comically enriches the occasion with an atoning present of doves. Launcelot atones for nothing, but his conscience deeply troubles him over his plan to leave Shylock. Their consciences suggest that Shylock has been good to each one. Jessica's conscience doesn't trouble her. Rather, she swiftly leaves the same man, who has uncomplainingly cared for, raised, and loved her as best he could, for close to twenty years. But there is more to her behavior than meets the eye because Jessica absconds with Shylock's money after Old Gobbo's returning for his old position. This likely suggests to Jessica her mother's own destitution. Jessica justifies her leaving with the splendidly comical reason that her life is tedious and she doesn't like Shylock's manners (2.3.2, 18). She who abandons him, steals from him, and marries a Christian, objects to his manners! This is great chutzpah, and it suggests her being a chip off the block of Antonio, whose setting a pretty high bar doesn't keep Jessica from strongly contending. But all six of these people are much more than simple characters, by virtue of the careful relationships that the play establishes for each one of them. They concentrate Shakespeare's efforts directly on his treatment of Jewish life and contribute powerfully to the comedy underway.

The minor characters, in short, play important roles, but directors have assumed they are so minor that they can easily be removed (as editors do with Salerino). The good sense of impressarios in not removing them should teach us that we remove or ignore them with disastrous results. We can no more expect to understand a Shakespeare play by attending only to the major characters than we could expect to produce great sound, indeed any sound worthy of his work, with a Stradivarius, made up of the large pieces of wood in the top, bottom, and neck, playing a Ninth symphony from which many minor passages had been scrapped.

Consider young Solanio. He is almost as keen in his attacks on Shylock as his friend Gratiano, but, as with Gratiano, anti-Semitism offers an unlikely explanation. To begin with, Solanio and Salerio know exactly where Shylock lives, and while hatred will contribute to explaining this fact so, too, will love. Their being Christians in the ghetto and at Shylock's house to begin with suggests they were once co-religionists with the other inhabitants. Sharing Shylock's shuttered shadows is "amorous Jessica" (2.8.9). Hormones make an ill match with avarice, but hers have attracted more than Lorenzo, as we learn from Shylock himself. When Jessica elopes, he directly accuses Solanio and Salerio almost of complicity: "You knew, none so well, none so well as you, of my daughter's flight" (3.1.21–22). This supports the idea that their relationship with her was an amorous interest, which Shylock has thwarted: Jessica herself is nervous about Shylock catching her talking even to Launcelot (2.3.8–9). Thus, if Shylock has frustrated Solanio's interest in her, Solanio's intense anger at Shylock probably resulted from a rejection. His bitterness looks like a still active resentment against his thwarter, not anti-Semitism, and if so represents, along with Shylock's protective impulse, unresolved feelings. And let us not miss Shakespeare's deft work establishing a triad of pursued women—Portia most, Jessica next, and Nerissa least.

And this brings us to Portia, restless, bored, sardonic, clever, scheming, generous, headstrong, and almost totally without relationships.[12] The lottery plan seems doubly calculated to frustrate her headstrong will and curb her choosing for herself, while at the same time frustrating avaricious suitors. Her father's intent to protect her from her own flawed judgment seems to have failed because Bassanio is a prodigal who mortgages his friend's life for his own quest after the golden fleece and brings Portia nothing but his good looks, charm, and the heartaches (signaled by his broken ring-promise) which they will entail. But this aside, what has been his plan to keep Portia honest? The obvious answer seems to be Nerissa, which raises the question "How?" This is best answered if she is Portia's younger sister—a clear parallel to Launcelot, watcher of his younger half-sister Jessica, and her liason to Lorenzo—and therefore the one monitor the father can install and trust. The sistership of this pair is supported because, as mere maid, Nerissa would not be required to marry after Portia. But by virtue of being her younger sister with a holy rabbi for a Father, one who honored Genesis 29: 26—"And Laban said, it must not be done in our country, to give the younger before the firstborn," she would put her own marriage second, as Nerissa does at 3.2.208–212. What is further detectible in this "Holy Father" is that with a sharp eye on Portia's interest in Bassanio, he failed to see Nerissa's sharp eye focused on Bassanio's friend, Gratiano. In short, he failed to see that Nerissa had reason to be an advocate for the very man the lottery appears designed to foil. The father innocently built failure into his plan from the start.

But for Portia's subtle musical help, as various writers have noted of the background music sung with rhymes for "lead," Bassanio might have failed. Such cleverness deserves a closer look, since she exercises it also on her German suitor by tempting him to choose wrong with a glass of wine on an incorrect casket (1.2.88–91). Bassanio may not know of musical clues beforehand, but he seems to know something because he has assured Antonio that his quest "should questionless be fortunate!" (1.1.176), which we can take as self-serving exaggeration or as an informed statement. If exaggeration, the play receives only a momentary lift in dramatic interest. If the latter is true, the play gets a great and lasting increase in dramatic interest because Bassanio would know which casket to choose, chance would be avoided, Portia would actively ensure that other suitors before Bassanio choose wrongly, and the question becomes, who would know the right casket in order somehow to inform Bassanio? Is there more drama, more humor in Portia's rhymed tips or in Nerissa's scheming independently and somehow doing the job that will end with the arrival of Bassanio for the lady and Gratiano for the maid and Portia all the time thinking her rhymes have pulled the caper off? Much of Shakespeare's comedy is of this quietly delicious inner sort. And it comes from, as it were, the whole Stradivarius, not pieces of it, playing the whole score, not parts of it. And for some more exquisite music, the others who know the answer are Nerissa and the poet who wrote the casket verses. Portia is bound not to disclose the answer, directly at least. But Nerissa and the poet are not bound. Nerissa knows Gratiano, and Gratiano knows Bassanio. As for the poet, the play has Morocco use rhymes (2.7.74–77) along with Lorenzo, good friend to Gratiano and Bassanio, and he makes rhymes as we see at 2.6.58–9 and 3.2.226–27, and is moreover a bountiful quoter of classical poetic passages and knowledge, which he recites in Act Five. He even appears with Bassanio and Gratiano in 1.1. And he speaks poetically at 2.4.12–14 and especially at 5.1.54–65, 70–88. Since a Moroccan prince hasn't hired himself out, we are left with Lorenzo, who could have gotten the job because Portia would mention the matter to Nerissa, who would mention it to Gratiano, who would know just the man. And this neatly helps to explain why Bassanio spends a small, loaned fortune so that Portia will take a penniless prodigal for an important suitor who "guesses" correctly, and why Gratiano is wild to accompany him, even to the point of forswearing his wildness and wearing prayer books in his pockets in order to be invited to go. So, who tells? Rather, who doesn't? Each of the three has a solid reason to tell, and this explains why Bassanio will "questionless" be fortunate. Portia clues him, Gratiano tells him, and Lorenzo tells him, and Bassanio uses thirty-four ruminating lines to pretend he makes an honest guess. He could have phoned it in. Portia is the only anxious one in this event, despite the tell-tale music she has chosen to be sung for the occasion. And her anxiety betrays how much she wants him to win. This in turn points up their having met earlier (1.2.104–6) when apparently they fell in love, together with Gratiano and Nerissa. Nerissa and Gratiano now simply await the inevitable, to announce they, too, are going to be married and may they join their master and mistress in taking vows? And we should note the great acting opportunities given each of the principals in this scene, along with the directors who often feel the need to infuse "freshness" into the play by dressing the characters in modern or unisex garb, instead of seeing what the language allows or requires us to see. Surely, we all can see that modern costuming is like plasticizing a Stradivarius, or adding sunglasses to the Mona Lisa?

Viewed simply as we see her on the surface of the play, Portia vies with Horatio as the Shakespeare character who best displays Arthur Miller's description of a mere character, for she stands visibly alone, except for a maid, and without relationships to Venice and its habitants, except through a lottery. But if Miller is right about the importance of relationships in a play, then so important a character as she is must have powerful relationships we don't see, and above all to Shylock and Antonio. She must have them because relationships are crucial to drama in that by binding characters together, they serve its essence by increasing tensions and conflicts so as to elevate dramatic intensities. This elevation occurs because Portia's father, a virtuous holy man (who was probably a rabbi, given the overall Jewish context we are dealing with), seems related to Shylock and Antonio (men his own age) as, say, a brother. This supposition gives us another threesome, of the sort the play is already so rich in, that is, structured in descending values, as in gold, silver, and lead, the threesome of elders (the virtuous man, Antonio, and Shylock)—all of them Jewish, and the first of them being so called to conceal his being a rabbi. Naming him a rabbi would identify Portia as Jewish along with Bassanio and require too many other clarifications. But he and his never-appearing wife give Portia alliance with Bellario, a doctor of civil law, with a degree of intellectualism to which Shylock can only aspire and Antonio miss by a wide measure.

These three are so rich a combination that they illustrate the kind of comedy Shakespeare writes, which, as I understand Shakespeare, requires us to figure things out from minimal clues so as to take in the history of the characters and their families, and sometimes events beyond both first and final curtains. This is the exact opposite of what academic critics have been demanding for the last two centuries: assume as proved our guess that Shakespeare personally endorsed the idea that we are to adhere rigidly to the surface of the text and that he recognized nothing and no one else beyond the surface, and assume as proved our further guess that he personally endorsed something like Aristotle's unity of time so that we are allowed to deal only with the play's visible timeline. These twin pillars of modern criticism are, as regards Shakespeare and a few others, wholly wrong. My basic assumption is that we are meant to devise answers to the great questions Shakespeare's text poses and that guesses have a place in such work, judging from the fact that all those who oppose guessing have been great guessers in a long line of guessers who were skilled at concealing the fact. For all the unanswerable cruces, I offer guesses that fit the requirements of the individual crux. Thus, instead of expecting Shakespeare to do what the scholarly consensus thinks proper—those, including myself, who have no experience writing for his company or any other stage— try to study his efforts to see the rules and laws that he appears to use in his work. Thus when I find no visible explanation that may settle the issue of the ancient grudge, I guess, which is exactly what everyone does while trying never to admit it. (An extraordinary doctorate thesis could be written on the guessers who camouflage this truth while berating others who don't).

Shakespeare provides no explanation of the relationships among this trio of elders. But it is clear enough that Antonio allies himself with the virtuous qualities of the unnamed brother and splits Shylock off from them, the better to vilify him as a double cuckolder to Antonio's single lapse. Antonio's egregious superiority may also result from his believing it to be one thing to cuckold so deserving a person as Shylock, but morally outrageous to cuckold a rabbi. Moreover, the virtuous father is not a native of Belmont, which seems to be borne out because, suitors aside, Portia and Nerissa apparently know persons only from Venice and Padua, Padua being the city to which Portia's mother likely went after leaving the virtuous man: presumably her mother lived there together with a brother whose son became a doctor of laws useful to Portia when Shylock pressed his case against Antonio. The virtuous man, therefore, appears to have abandoned Venice for an unknown reason, presumably to get away from his tormentor, who would be Shylock. The former can't have left because he found a better place in Belmont, that being of no dramatic value to the play. Dramatic values grow thick when we notice Portia's expressing respect but no paternal love, showing her to be a soul mate of Jessica. Her withheld feeling makes her possibly a bastard, and cuckolding could well have caused Portia's father to leave Venice, as Leah had also left it. Symmetry suggests that while Jessica stayed in Venice with her "father", Portia left it with her "father." We further notice that the virtuous man's "paternal" attempts to circumscribe Portia's choice of a husband are similar to Shylock's virtual (and unsuccessful) imprisonment of Jessica. Caskets are used to circumscribe her choice because she has fallen for a prodigal who loves a lavish lifestyle made possible by money. Since the "father" is dead and she is his heir, he clearly had some money which has apparently attracted suitors much more interested in it than in her. Caskets weed out opportunists, starting with Bassanio, a handsome, penniless prodigal who needs all the help he can get. And just as Jessica and Lorenzo inherit a good portion of Shylock's money, so too do Portia and Bassanio inherit her "father's" money—along probably with Antonio. Such symmetries are carefully crafted, not accidental. Shylock, in my scheme, pays a penalty for having a lady who, judging solely by the mere symmetry of things, would have been Leah's older sister. But the only thing certain about her is that she would have lived somewhere in the ghetto—a mere two and a half block area—with her virtuous husband, so that Antonio, who has long waits before his ships return, could have slipped next door to his sister-in-law's bed upon seeing Shylock steal away to tryst with their brother's wife. (One naturally wonders where Shakespeare's brothers lived in Stratford.)

The closeness of Antonio and Shylock to each other, physically and fraternally, explains as nothing else can their intimate knowledge of each other. They can't escape knowing about each other, and on a daily basis. Shylock complains that Antonio "hath disgrac'd me, and hind'red me half a million, laugh'd at my losses, mock'd at my gains, scorned my nation, thwarted my bargains, cooled my friends, heated mine enemies—and what's his reason? I am a Jew" (3.1.56–60). This is a list of exceptional knowledge, unless the two men are brother neighbors. For his part, Antonio has not only spit on, spurned, and called Shylock a dog, but anticipates repeating this behavior (1.3.121–26).Their physical proximity (by my scheme) makes all this very easy. To bring these things about, Antonio need only step outside his front door, await Shylock's appearance, and spit away, scorn him, or call him a dog, driving deeper the thorn that he is in the side of his next-door brother, whose house is hell. Shylock cannot escape him. More important, proximity gives each of them a perch from which to note leavings, especially Shylock's liasionic comings and goings. Antonio parades his Christian, moral superiority over Shylock from a belief in his own righteousness. (Righteousness, of course, comes easy when you lack a wife and your brother has one whom you can seduce, when you lend without interest, and when you are not a breeder of metals.) Such prides endow him with his grand contempt for Shylock, who makes the mistake of regarding Antonio the seducer to be morally inferior to Shylock the seducer. That Antonio has seduced Shylock's wife appears to be (to him) the merest of trifles. Antonio's extraordinary sense of feeling justified in punishing Shylock appears to result from a belief that Shylock's cuckolding of their virtuous brother costs him all right to decent treatment. So great an antagonism demands an explanation, and we can now address it.

The explanation involves the crucial fact about Antonio: his not having a wife. The answer obviously is not that he is attracted to men, though such an interpretation is the one attempt we possess that addresses the matter. There is no evidence that he has a sexual interest in Bassanio, for whom he has an obvious need of some sort. Having seduced Leah shows his interest in women to be normal. His trust in them is another matter. And this points to the possibility that he fears marriage out of knowing in effect that "Woman, thy name is frailty," Shylock having twice taught him their frailty and he having confirmed it with Leah's for him. As he apparently sees them, these infidelities warn him only about women, not men like him; and the fear appears to date back a long time, perhaps about twenty years. It represents, I believe, his possessing the castration-anxiety myth that Freud popularized as the "vagina dentate." The court scene dramatizes the matter a third and final time. Shylock's cuckolding their brother and then a servant seems to have been the psychic wound which has kept Antonio unmarried because he believed that his sister-in-law married to a holy man proved that even gold would rust, making it certain, in his view, that a woman would deceive him. But Antonio still had his male necessities, which included women and family. Hence, his visits next door. Then Shylock sealed off access to either by driving Leah out and entombing Jessica. Thus, when the son of a family friend turned prodigal and needed financial support, Antonio was fully receptive to the young man, who filled a deep void in Antonio's own broken life. The repair he sought over the years was to try to break Shylock's life as well, making Antonio the second man in the play wanting revenge, and Solanio the third. How twisted Antonio's thinking had become is seen in his revenging himself not on a woman (the true "cause" of his fear) but on a man. And for Shakespeare to choose this matter as the very first subject to address in the opening lines of the play shows how clearly he has worked out much if not most of his story, and how supremely confident he was at thirty-five or so to take on such a nuanced and psychologically mature matter with which immediately to challenge audiences and readers by means of Antonio's unnamed sadness.

Shylock counters Antonio's campaign of revenge with the dignity that comes with standing on the principal that two wrongs don't make a right. (The ironies involved in all this are luscious.) But in any event, the working out of the complexities I have briefly sketched shows that Shylock really has a daughter, but because she apparently is not Jessica, the possibilities are narrowed to Portia or Nerissa. The play receives little dramatic intensity if Nerissa is that person. But Portia would represent an enormous gain in drama for the play, being a perfect choice in every way, starting with her almost matching him in commanding stature and confidence, stunning us by her adjudicating between her plaintiff-father and defendant-uncle. If there ever was a case for recusing oneself, this is it. She is the perfect person to urge mercy upon Shylock, for in the possible scheme I am proposing he has cuckolded two men, one a virtuous brother and the other an honest servant, and he is in a poor position to exact a pound of flesh from anyone. Portia's own headstrong will and illegitimacy apparently have made her a maid not vendible, except through a lottery, and thus may have exposed her condition—and her father's—to the amusement of the mongering part of Venice. All this is possible, and surely known to Portia since some of it is notorious, in part, even to street kids. Her solution to the strife between Shylock and Antonio is to enforce Antonio's request that Shylock be made to convert. Antonio would be a poor one to impose this sentence, since he could hardly be impartial. But Portia is illegitimate and aggrieved, and her adjudication is pragmatic and reasonable: the hell his house has become is seen in his using his son as a servant; he is also willing to kill Antonio after having indirectly been involved (apparently through off-stage arrangements with pirates [4.1.348]), in pushing him over the edge of bankruptcy and wanting to humiliate him beyond what he has suffered. Portia alone can resolve this matter and reunite the warring parties in this play. Moreover, comedy itself must involve a resolution of its problems. Conversion does just that, giving Shakespeare a great enduring dramatic success, which is perhaps all he ever wanted from his work. Jews will naturally be testy about this resolution, but there doesn't appear to be a better one available. In a play where Shylock, a greater offender and a member of a minority group, obviously wants far too much revenge—a court-sanctioned in-court death of a member of the majority group—he is certain to be brought up short. He gets strict justice, nothing more, and the decision gives Lorenzo a good portion of Shylock's wealth, Antonio a smaller portion, and Shylock, the greatest offender, the smallest portion, but still a portion. It is not a sop. And most important, he is emotionally exhausted and content (4.1.392) perhaps because, weighed carefully, it offers him peace and, in a play that arguably brought Leah a visit from a daughter, may symmetrically bring Shylock a visit from a son who has a genuine conscience and will have a grandchild that may even bring Shylock joy. And why not? this being a comedy after all, where concord ultimately reigns when a competent writer, let alone a genius, knows what he is doing. And if Old Gobbo represents anything at all, he represents love, hatchet-burying, and a lesson that Shylock will have learned if he buries a couple himself, one with Portia and another with Antonio. Shakespeare, of course, neither shows this nor says it, so that for the saying, at least, we must rely on those who have gone to school with him. Arthur Miller did, and he produces for us the bedrock of drama in saying, "I regard the theater as a serious business, one that makes or should make man more human, which is to say less alone."[13] This means that characters need relationships. But none of my ideas are written in stone, and we are free to offer an infinite number of other solutions for each of the matters I discuss.

Comedy shows humans less alone through the medium of reconciliation, and Shakespeare has begun it with Old Gobbo's dish of doves. The continuation occurs when Shylock asks to have the deed sent after him for signing—that is, at his home. Portia then sends Nerissa to have him sign it while she awaits her, perhaps at the monastery (5.2.18). By sending Nerissa to Shylock's house, Shakespeare has constructed the natural bridge that can be used to reunite Shylock and Portia, and that this has likely happened is a missing part we are meant to address. When we do so, we find that although Portia says she and Nerissa will be "a day before our husbands home" (4.2.3), they have been delayed because they return at the same time Bassanio and Gratiano arrive, so that Portia has spent a day somewhere else. Where can she spend that day for the spending to provide the play with an absolute maximum of drama? We are given a clue as to where this might have been because within earshot of Shylock (4.1.399) she has declined the Duke's invitation to dinner and later Bassanio's, which Gratiano delivers to her at 4.2.7–8. The Duke will be dining alone, but the trio of Gratiano, Bassanio, and Antonio will likely be dining together, probably at Antonio's place. This leaves the symmetrical trio of Nerissa, Portia, and Shylock, at dinnertime, hungry, and without arrangements, and Nerissa at Shylock's house with a deed for him to sign, Portia having let him go home without signing it. He has every expectation that Portia herself will show up because she had promised him that "Thyself shall see the act" [of the law denying him a drop of blood] (4.1.312). Moreover, she must realize her obligation to deliver on her word, and that permits us to realize that she will remember her word, follow Nerissa to Shylock's house, knock at the door of Hell with its lone inhabitant finishing up with Nerissa (Leah having left long ago, then Jessica, and finally Launcelot), where she will show him the act, and he will invite Mercy and her maid to dinner. What they will dine on has been anticipated by Old Gobbo's gift of a transgression offering of doves,[14] which in a triadic system will make three portions, the first being eaten by Shylock. The two remaining portions will be available for Portia and one other. Old Gobbo's transgression against Shylock can have only been leaving him unservanted until young Gobbo grew into the role, thus identifying Launcelot as that person. Portia then is the person most transgressed against, Launcelot is right behind her, and Old Gobbo trails them distantly. And this triad is the most important and powerful one in the play, being the most transformative because it achieves forgiveness, unlike that of the residences, which produces offenses. And it is at this point that the triad shows its extraordinary power, for we have had two reconciliations, those of Old Gobbo and Shylock, and Shylock and Portia, and we need a third. There must come a knock on Shylock's door because Bassanio has sent Gratiano after Portia with the ring and instructions to bring old Bellario's surrogate "Unto Antonio's house" (4.1.452). That house being next door to Shylock, as Gratiano knows full well, what else has Shakespeare done but prepare us to see that Portia will either step next door, having Shylock with her, or go herself and bring Antonio to him, placing the hand of the one into the hand of the other as she converts hell into heaven. Shylock has been made more human: having twice declined (1.3.32, 2.5.35–6), he now eats. Triadic necessities show that he will dine this time, desirous of sharing life by being "less alone." This will become the great moment of reconciliation and the explanation of why Portia returns home to Belmont at the same time as Bassanio and Gratiano, all parties having broken bread, reunited, and rested. The alternative is that Shylock will brood alone with his hatred, while a few feet away Antonio will smolder with his contempt, and Shakespeare will simply have thrown away the obvious conclusion to all his masterful arrangements, that conclusion being the reunion of Portia and Shylock, Shylock and Antonio, and Shylock and Gratiano, and the reigning words will not be hatred and contempt but love and shalom.

Shylock's invitation reflects love. His reunion doesn't strike me as necessarily a tearful one, but one that reflects his condition in a house drained of people and money that he now can fill with love and harmony. The love so begun will increase. Portia has made it possible, indeed brings it about and makes reunion reign, for she is an extraordinary woman who sees in Shylock a human being who has left a huge void in her own life and is not a monster; and being a woman of his stature because she is his daughter and unafraid of him, she hasn't turned away, and has refused to let him do so, but rather said, "Tarry, Jew" (4.1.344), then lays down the law, and in so doing elegantly devises a way to call on him, for so much more than showing him a text. After the Duke trumpets what he thinks is the natural grandeur of his own spirit, it is Portia who asks Antonio "What mercy can you render [Shylock,] Antonio?" (4.1.376). What prosecutor has ever sought mercy for a litigant who, in open court, wields a knife against his enemy? For Antonio to show mercy at this moment will require humility, too. She exemplifies that the quality of mercy is not strained. What she does is nothing less than to repeat that speech for Antonio—and for Pride itself, the Duke—by compressing it into her example.

In treating Shylock as a human being, Portia asks Shylock's mercy for Antonio, which Shylock refuses to give. But her speech asks mercy from Antonio and the Duke for Shylock, and, as we all know, each one gives it, though in triadic degrees, the Duke giving the least. This means that a third person must be merciful to him. Portia's speech marks the turning point where Shakespeare changes the dramatic nature of the play from darkness to light—from something almost tragic to something more than comic. Up to that point, all the stresses, which their author has so carefully arranged, have accumulated unchecked, casting a deepening shadow upon the play. Shylock's knife is literally in mid-air ready to remove Antonio's heart in a sanctioned act of judicial murder that is but a few seconds from completion when Portia instantly replaces hate with mercy, and love as the defining character of the play. She addresses the black hatred and revenge and offers mercy as the light that leads to love and peace.

She is the third person who is merciful to him, and she makes the happiness of every-one possible. But the enormous power of the speech has yet to be recognized: it lies in its silent truth that Shylock has cheated her out of a father, and still her mercy for him drops as the gentle rain from heaven. Has comedy so powerful ever been written by anyone else?

The powerful triads of the concluding scene give us pure, lyric beauty even as they reveal another gap for filling. By eating a portion of Old Gobbo's dish of doves, Shylock became its first eater, leaving a remainder on hand when Portia calls and Shylock, after having his eyes opened followed by his heart, will offer it to her. She, then, becomes its second partaker, and must save a bit for a third party she has in mind. At her home in Belmont awaits her half-brother Launcelot, whom Shylock has offended and whose spirit is overtopped by his. The tidiest way to conclude this triad would have been to have Launcelot accompany Bassanio back to Antonio. But doing so would still have involved the youth in an unwritten event with Portia when she gives him the last of the doves, but would have cost Shakespeare the sustained handling of Lorenzo's nervous response to Launcelot's talking with Jessica and in-forming us of Launcelot's having impregnated the Moorish girl. What we get instead is another triad, that of Portia's—and Nerissa's—gifts from Shylock, a letter for Anto-nio announcing the recovery of his lost ships, a deed for Lorenzo to Shylock's estate, and, if I am right, the remainder of Old Gobbo's dish of doves to Launcelot. There is something inexpressibly poetic about how much forgiveness is accomplished by this single dish of doves, so reminiscent of the multiplying power of the loaves and fishes. The confirming touch for the latter gift is Lorenzo's exquisite summary of the ladies' presents, which he calls "manna you [Portia and Nerissa] drop in the way Of starved people" (5.1.294–95). From his father Launcelot would have gotten food (thanks to Portia), which "droppeth as the gentle rain from heaven," as she earlier said and as she now has brought about. In a play of great and many offenses, there must be great and many turnabouts. If Shylock has been much on Portia's mind, he has also been much on the mind of another woman—Leah. In the final scene, Lorenzo summarizes the precious events that have suffused their essences "In[to] such a night" as this, and he tells Jessica that then "Stood Dido with a willow in her hand Upon the wild sea-banks, and waft her love To come again to Carthage" (5.1.9). In this passage, Dido is argu-ably Leah (separated from Aeneas as Leah is from Shylock), sea-fronted Carthage is sea-shored Genoa, and Dido-Jessica's love is Aeneas-Shylock. The much-noted magical beauty of the first twenty-two lines of this scene bathes the conclusion of the play in such bliss as can be comprehended only when we recognize that the gift of money I earlier assigned to Jessica had been construed by Leah as from Shylock himself, probably with Jessica's help (daughters don't usually pour forth ducats and identify them as stolen from putative fathers, and mothers don't want to think of a daughter as a thief). Leah would respond with a wafting of love back to him, a greeting and an invitation to visit her, thus accounting for his absence from the final scene. This surmise gives us Leah and Shylock as making the third and final reunion after those of Antonio and Gratiano with Shylock. Lorenzo identifies and creates such pervasive harmony in the first twenty-two lines of the final scene that only Shylock's forgiving his attackers and their forgiving him will justify the total peace that bestows such sweetness upon the final night that Lorenzo feels and celebrates—with a bit of license, since Lorenzo's references, beyond the record of the play, confirm what we otherwise would not know, the Genoa reunion. At the end of Act four, what appears as a dispersal of people to far corners is, instead, a complex convergence of the principals upon Shylock's home.

Involved in this total peace is, of course, Bassanio, whom everyone identifies as a prodigal son without seeing that this likely makes him a Jew. Nor has anyone, to my knowledge, identified his father, who in the Bible prepares the fatted calf and goes forth to meet his son for their reunion. That identification remains as the final puzzle I hope to shed light upon. Bassanio needs then a little attention. This is a crucial matter because with Shylock reconciling with Antonio, the emptiness in their lives is filled, but Bassanio, joined with Portia, is removed from Antonio's life though still not reunited with his own father. So we have one important triadic necessity remaining, that of the three children who are reunited with their fathers, Portia with Shylock, Launcelot with Shylock, and Bassanio offstage with an unknown person.

This identification has three requirements. The person must be of the proper age, must be rich, and must be desirous of reuniting a child and father. The one person who perfectly fits these needs is Tubal, Shylock's wealthy, same-aged friend, who uncomplainingly does Shylock's bidding to find and return Jessica (and Lorenzo) to Shylock, and who "often came where I did hear of her, but cannot find her" (3.1.72–3). (Failing with her, means of course that he will succeed with his own child.) Tubal would be the perfect person to go looking in Genoa, because he likely has some feeling for Leah, since she must attract a third after Shylock and Antonio. Tubal would likely also give her money since she would need it. He would complete her triad of givers, after Jessica and Lorenzo. And he would also buy back Leah's ring from Antonio's creditor who exchanged a monkey for it, and return it to Leah, who would then return it to Shylock when love wafts him back to her, thus completing the important triad of rings that women return to their husbands.

But along with all of these beautiful things, Tubal must report his bad news to Shylock and then listen to him kvetch in one of the comedy's funnier moments. To the father of the prodigal Bassanio, the son having turned to Antonio for money that he won't unbend to ask from an abandoned father, Shylock ignores paying his expenses—but with what, since he's cleaned out?—ignores thanking him for his obviously pro bono work, and ignores asking about Bassanio in favor of the important matter, bemoaning his own misfortunes, which, he wants it known, are of a very high order: "Why, thou loss upon loss! The thief gone with so much, and so much to find the thief; and no satisfaction, no revenge! Nor no ill luck stirring but what lights o' my shoulders; no sighs but o' my breathing; no tears but o' my shedding." Tubal certainly has known much ill luck, has done more than his share of sighing, and surely has spent tears on Bassanio, but says only, "Yes, other men have ill luck too" (3.1.81–86), and mentions Antonio, saying nothing about himself or Shylock's flagrant ironies.

The greatest of these ironies has to be Shylock's possibly borrowing money from Tubal to make up "the gross of full three thousand ducats" (1.3.50–1) to loan to Tubal's son (by my interpretation) Bassanio, without saying a word to Tubal. Shylock sees before him the proof that Bassanio has turned to Antonio and from Tubal in the matter. And Shylock does absolutely nothing to heal the rift he can see between his friend and his friend's son, but instead uses it as his own opportunity to hurt Antonio. (Indeed, Shylock would have to know he intended hurting not only Antonio, but accepted hurting Bassanio and Tubal as well.) Shakespeare has powerfully contrasted here the striking differences between these two friends. But he hasn't made Shylock into a villain, only a human being who has been humiliated by his brother and treated with contempt and abuse for twenty years or so, and then been unable to turn from the temptation confronting him when Bassanio needs money. Tubal's actions are preferable, but he has not suffered Antonio's abuse. The ironies between Tubal and Shylock are not only massive, but dizzying. The opportunity for the actor of Bassanio to register Shylock's reference to his father as having the force of a body blow joins the opportunity for the actor of Shylock at this moment to turn his totally impassive eyes from Antonio so as to lock them upon Bassanio's visible, silent shock, and each is my imagined response that supports Hazlitt and James in their belief that Shakespeare's plays are unactable (that is, incapable of bringing forth their true content), being plays of enormous substance.

In the tiny ghetto district, everyone had to know about Bassanio's rupture from Tubal in favor of Antonio. But Tubal has only sympathy for Antonio's reverses. The contrast between the father Bassanio forsakes and the man he turns to is powerfully strong, and stronger still when we see that the two dining groups at the end—of Antonio, Bassanio, and friends, and Portia, Shylock, and Nerissa—must be completed by Tubal and Bassanio on a fatted calf, the latter completing the trio of animals in the play, of old Dobbin, the monkey, and the calf.

The above treatment of Tubal, to say nothing of every other character I have touched on, shows him to be another instance of Miller's observation that characters in a play are really a set of relationships. Tubal's "character" is a very simple affair that begins when Shylock speaks of his wealthy friend (1.3.51). which establishes his age and standing: he participates in the triad of lenders, along with Shylock and Antonio. As soon as we join these facts with his report on Jessica in Genoa, we see that he is the third man with a more than casual interest in Leah after Shylock and Antonio. His account of his search for Jessica shows his deep concern in reuniting her with Shylock: his traveling across the entire width of Italy to help reunite Shylock and his putative daughter, and at his own expense, creates his sustained and further relationship to the story of the father of the prodigal son, which so beautifully underlies his own suffering and humility as underlined by his relationship to the Biblical account. And Shakespeare's use of the matter, having Shylock seriously offer himself as a contender against Tubal and his silent paternal sufferings is beyond praise and beyond the reach of any other comedy I may ever read. Tubal's final relationship then to Bassanio deepens the misery he has experienced beyond that of Shylock and Antonio, in the triad of suffering fathers. We should notice, too, that triads produce highly controlled assembly, bit by bit, in units of most, less, and least, and immediately establish proportions and placement, allowing us to see the triad's odd manner of creating what, for want of a better word, we call character, much fleshed out by our imaginations.

Finally then, we see all this narrative extension when we supply a relationship for three elderly, male characters (Shylock, Antonio, and the holy man), who are without a visible one, in a play with the anomaly of Jewish and Christian characters running about the Jewish ghetto, making almost every character in the play a Jew.[15]

Shakespeare gives us Gratiano's residence right next door to Shylock and with its lower apartment available for another occupant who will supply more conflict; Miller gives us their need, as characters, of relationships and each other; Baron gives us historical facts of Venetian conversos associating with their old friends and family members; the OED gives us the Pauline meaning of flesh; the play gives us the hints of and allusions to paternity; the time gives us badges, patches, and conversos; and I give the suggestion that the three men are brothers and that the operating dynamic in their relationship is conversoism and cuckoldry, raunchy Shylock being the chief offender in the latter, Antonio runner-up cuckolder but foremost converso, and the virtuous third a virtuous victim, out of all which comes forth the quite clear irony that Shylock has no right to a pound of Antonio's flesh (as his daughter would know), to say nothing of the other point, namely, that Shakespeare remains a superlative dramatist—the 1600 Quarto heads every page of its text "The comicall Historie of the Merchant of Venice"—and that we need to look elsewhere for an anti-Semitic play. He has written a great comedy, and published it as a comedy, and his company included it in the Catalogue of Comedies; and he did it by working out next-door living arrangements for two principals at the beginning of the play and reasons to have them all meet again at the end, in houses right next door to each other, when they must reconcile simply because, with their anger exhausted, reconciliation is the necessary resolution of a successful comedy. As soon as he "saw" the two connected ghetto buildings, he saw most of the main matters I have discussed in detail. If this summary is correct, it would seem to be the first printed view of Shakespeare's overarching creative architecture at work that anyone has ever produced, made possible by the work of Miller and Felheim, a playwright and an academic, both Michigan men (I am proud to say). Beckoning us against doing so is the standard dismissive response to conjecture, even when scientific and intuitive. Adopting it is very easy because it leaves the play exactly as it appears, a surface without an extended narrative; and this is so sterile and attractive because it is so safe.

But adopting the theory of extended narrative gives us both the surface and the extension, and the surface is always untouched by and visibly unconnected to the extension, so that the surface remains absolutely safe. But a surface intact is a surface with its mysteries, its questions, its gaps in drama, and there is no denying them. It may not be a perfect solution, but it may be the best one we have, to listen to Miller and "constantly try to supply what is missing." His prodding only carries on that produced by Shakespeare's questions themselves. Those questions, moreover, fully concern the least of the characters that appear or are merely mentioned. Until we regard the entire work that a great writer produces, we can never advance beyond the surface of the work and major characters who appear to be without relationships to the minor ones, as Portia's "Holy Father" demonstrates in half a dozen ways regarding Bassanio, Shylock, Anthony, Portia and Nerissa. An extended narrative gives us great drama because it supplies the relationships that offer a solution to so many of the mysteries and problems attending the mere surface, and thus bring the real constructive and dramatic aspects of the play so powerfully before us that we are allowed to see the play as a series of problems present to Shakespeare's mind. And that is where we find ourselves when we try solving them. We are next to that mind, studying the case he presents us with, and as we select and fashion answers, we find ourselves closer to the writer than we have ever been. That experience is a very precious one and worth accepting the extension for because we are made co-authors, the play's surface is safe, the drama is visible and felt, and the experience becomes powerfully human and ennobling. And it is arguable that the only way Shakespeare could present so beautiful a study of a community of Jews was to hide it from a disapproving state.

3

Horatio, the "Ghost", and the Danish Succession

Niels Bohr's insight about problems in theoretical physics—"'Every great and deep difficulty bears in itself its own solution. It forces us to change our thinking in order to find it'"[1]—may offer help also for the question of the authenticity of Hamlet's "Ghost." Hamlet certainly qualifies as a great and deep difficulty, made so in part by supposedly being a Christian "Ghost" who "returns" to Elsinore in a holy season with the bloody demand that Hamlet kill Claudius. Not to question the authenticity of this "Ghost" is to further the dumbing down of Shakespeare begun by Tate, D'Avenant, Dryden, and Garrick. They helped to transform Shakespeare's great intellectual mysteries into general, unmysterious entertainment. Shakespearean drama came to be regarded as satisfying curiosity instead of exciting it, and nowhere more clearly than in *Hamlet*.

Our incuriosity has grown so that today the "Ghost" no longer seems to challenge scholars as an enigma. From having been a complex mystery, it verges on becoming a simple lucidity and seems but a precursor to our modern irrationalities—alien kidnappers, extraterrestrials, angels, and various spirits that "cross over." Failure to recognize the "Ghost" as a challenging puzzle in turn has led to our failure to identify the succession-question as central to the focus of the play, there being a revenge theme only because of a collateral succession theme. Indeed, no one has ever placed the "Ghost" in the context of Shakespeare's inherited Hamlet story that, as we have seen, traces itself back to Beowulf before Saxo's additions. Because Amleth outwits a court that plots to dupe and kill him, Shakespeare may consistently give the "Ghost" a duping function, too.

The "Ghost" challenges Hamlet, and us, as to what it is and what it claims. Ghosts are still unauthenticated realities that fly in the face of objective human experience. Having given up on explaining the "Ghost," we accept its enigmatic early battlement appearances in armor and its final appearance in nightdress, as seen by Hamlet but not by Gertrude; and we have even invented a reason for the latter conundrum—that ghosts can make themselves invisible to anyone they do not want to see them. Because Gertrude claims she doesn't see it, scholars assume she is telling the truth. That makes our denying the "Ghost's" reality with textual evidence very difficult work. But the great impediment to the reality of the "Ghost" is its armor. Being mere spirit, a ghost needs no armor. But armor would be appropriate for, say, an actor pretending to be a ghost before edgy guards expecting an attack from Norwegian invaders. A pike-thrust delivered to a man covered by a sheet could be fatal. Because the "Ghost" is debatable, we may easily deceive ourselves if we accept its armored appearance as the supernatural return of old Hamlet to Elsinore. Our deception is tied to Gertrude's denial. When it went unquestioned and when no convincing, discrediting arguments appeared, the scholarly community largely accepted the "Ghost" as real by default. I want to reopen the case and argue that the "Ghost" is fake and perpetrated by Horatio with Gertrude's help. This would involve it in a plot. A plot is positive and can be proved.

Two opposed positions regarding the "spirit" have emerged, arguing not whether the "Ghost" is real, but what its nature is. Fredson Bowers believed the "Ghost" is beneficent.[2] Eleanor Prosser thinks the "Ghost" is malevolent.[3] W. W. Greg alone has argued the "Ghost" is Hamlet's private hallucination and also the objective experience of the sentinels and Horatio. These views have not generated much discussion, least of all Greg's belief that "towards ghosts [Shakespeare was] frankly skeptical."[4] Greg was joined by Northrop Frye, who argued in his classroom that "the Ghost's credentials are very doubtful."[5] And finally, Anne Barton is uneasy about it.[6] And she should be.

If the "Ghost" is a fake, it is up to something very worldly and obviously represents some kind of plot. The plot would also be an able one, and we may therefore usefully look at the least likely plotter in the play, since a plot from that person would be very able indeed. John Dover Wilson has invited us to "'feel we know Horatio so well that we never think to ask questions about him.'" This is the most dangerous assumption we can make about a character, but it is exactly how Horatio is usually treated. Wilson's belief in his transparency is self-supported: his quotation cites his own earlier statement about Horatio.[7] Wilson's influential assumption helped to make Horatio as ignored as the "Ghost" and, in a play thick with political intrigue, almost universally taken at face value. In this haze of uncritical admiration only Frank Kermode has recognized that Horatio is "a somewhat chameleontic figure."[8] An uncritical view of Horatio finds him to be honest, stoical, modest, diffident, and polite, of a skeptical turn of mind, and given to understatement and verbal minimalism. (His first words in the play, "A piece of him" (1.1.19), minimalistically describe a partially present and awake Horatio.) He is the Prince's fellow student and friend. He is the soldiers' confidant. He is a servanted servant. He is Ophelia's watcher. And if what these add up to as a function for him to fulfill is unstated, they only underscore his unclear role.

However unclear his role may be, his character emerges when we consider his treatment of other people. Wilson notes the contempt in his question to the guards, "What, has this thing appear'd again to-night?" (2.1.21).[9] Contempt comes easily to him twice again when he mocks Osric, "His purse is empty already: all's golden words are spent," and jeers "This lapwing [who] runs away with the shell on his head" (5.2.130–31, 185–86). Horatio's courtly demeanor does not convert this ridicule into politeness; it only aggravates the wound. Nor does Hamlet's verbal abuse of Osric justify Horatio's joining in. Horatio impugns his own honesty and belies his diffidence and modesty when, from an apparent belief that he has Hamlet's warrant, he drops his politeness and mocks. As literature's most skillful exposer of impositions, Hamlet may mock Osric in 5.2 in order to draw forth and expose Horatio's real nature as a chameleon adopting the color of his surroundings.

Similarly, when Horatio tush-tushes the sentinels' report, but suddenly becomes a converted believer upon seeing a figure in armor, he illustrates instantaneous conviction, not the skepticism that some readers credit him with and that armor should arouse. At the Globe, the shock of an armored "Ghost" had to raise suspicion because a ghost's being already dead and unwoundable must suggest to every thoughtful spectator in the house that the wearer may be very much alive. When Horatio tells Hamlet of the figure and says, "I knew your father, / These hands are not more like" (1.2.211–212), he is manipulating Hamlet into acceptance before he even sees the figure and strongly encourages belief, not skepticism. Given his earlier tush-tushing, Horatio's quick conversion bears out Kermode's describing him as a changeable creature.

In one important instance, Horatio has benefited from gender-partial criticism, since we dismiss some telling evidence against his character simply because he is male and Hamlet's presumably loyal friend. That evidence concerns his veracity. He obviously is older than Hamlet, because he assures the sentries that he twice saw Hamlet's father, once when he fought "the ambitious Norway," and again when "He smote the sledded [Polacks] on the ice" (1.1.61, 63). If true, Horatio would be perhaps fifty or fifty- five years of age and fifteen or twenty years older than his schoolfellow. Rather than recognize this story as Horatio's boastful imposition on common soldiers, Greg quaintly explains it as "imaginative rhetoric."[10] But in the similar case of Ophelia's saying her father is home when he isn't, some male critics employ a double standard and say she is lying. That Horatio too is lying seems clear when he changes his account of the old King to Hamlet, saying, "I saw him once," without specifying where or when, and further insisting, "I knew your father" (1.2.186, 211). His having seen the man hardly constitutes having known him.

A second anomaly about Horatio is his apparently having been at Elsinore for two or three weeks before greeting Hamlet. Having been there so long means that Horatio has avoided three things: a funeral, a coronation, and a marriage. He comes forth only to tell Hamlet about the "Ghost." Yet, with classic schadenfreude, Horatio neither condoles with him over the death of his father, nor commiserates with him over his lost election and throne. His much belated "Hail to your lordship!" (I.2.160) dismisses all his absences and omissions as insignificant details, so as not further to delay speaking of the "Ghost."

The third anomaly about him concerns his "attempted suicide." Calling himself an "antique Roman" (5.2.341), makes him seem eager to die with Hamlet. But he chooses the wrong "fatal" instrument. The emptied cup that killed the Queen and that Hamlet forces Claudius to finish off is an insincere effort. Neither its remaining film of liquor nor his inability to keep a dying Hamlet from wresting it away offers convincing proof that Horatio has much interest in death, as would his choosing one of the many, easily reached, truly lethal weapons that litter the stage. More important still, antique Romans fell on their swords.

Furthermore, Horatio, oddly, doesn't regard his unsupported gentleman's word about the "Ghost" as enough: thus two guards. Odder yet, although they saw a figure that was like the King, Horatio thinks he saw "the King your father" (1.2.191), whereas the armored figure exposed perhaps a two by six, twelve square inch window on its face. Sensing his own exaggeration, he then abridges the soldiers' report, adopts its color, and says the "spirit" was but "like your father" (1.2.199). Horatio, in sum, exaggerates as well as he understates.

And in grand manner. When Bernardo says the "Ghost" appears "In the same figure like the King that's dead" and challenges Horatio, "Looks 'a not like the King?" and Marcellus likens it to the late King, Horatio's reply elevates the figure to "the majesty of buried Denmark" (1.1.41, 43, 48), though the old King would seem not to have worn armor in Denmark's thirty years of peace. Skepticism has become extravagance.

A truly skeptical Horatio would report to his friend on the battlements' encounter and let him decide for himself, without manipulating him emotionally and planting an identification. Greg observes that "from the first the two soldiers have made up their minds that the "Ghost" is none other than the late king." Concerning Bernardo's identification when the figure reappears, Greg adds, "He is not making a fresh observation. As to the grounds of his belief we are in the dark."[11] Since Horatio plants the identification in Hamlet, he needs to have planted it in the two guards, especially since their discussion of the "Ghost" has involved only Horatio and we hear of them having been in no one else's company. Wouldn't Hamlet suspect that their confidence is second-hand? And wouldn't Horatio's contradictory responses be as apparent to Hamlet as to us. If so, how far should Hamlet trust his "friend"?

Not, it would seem, very far. Horatio figures in too many coincidences. He happens to be in Elsinore when the "Ghost" appears, so that Horatio is conveniently available to visit the platform and use that encounter as the basis for reporting it to Hamlet, the report being the unstated but real reason for his initial greeting of his "friend." Without that report Hamlet would not have met the "Ghost," nor would he then go on to imperil his own life by plotting against Claudius. When this ambulatory "Ghost" appears only to Horatio and the watch, but will not speak to either, by curious coincidence Horatio knows not only that the figure "will speak to [Hamlet]" (1.1.171) but, as is implicit in that comment, that the "Ghost" will reappear. And of course Horatio assures Hamlet that the "Ghost" will return, which it does, on time, and at the exact spot where Horatio awaits it.

Another coincidence occurs because Horatio, the appointed watcher of Ophelia (who nonetheless drowns), meets an escaped Hamlet and takes him straight to the cemetery where Ophelia is being buried that day. Without his graveyard encounter with Laertes, Hamlet might have lived. True, Horatio tells Hamlet he will lose the match, but he doesn't act to stop him. Also, his noting that Osric and Hamlet "bleed on both sides. How is it, my lord?" (5.2.304) is a rather disinterested inquiry, along with its being an unusually disinterested confirmation of a clearly exposed and rigged match. But to stop the action so as to examine into the treachery would interfere with Hamlet's pursuit of Claudius and instead keep the King alive. Horatio's actions and failures of action affect Hamlet's life, along with Claudius's, and suggest he isn't much of a helpful friend.

Why Horatio wants to put pressure on Hamlet to kill Claudius grows clearer with a consideration of Horatio's paternity. A nobody with access to Elsinore in a virtual state of siege has clout. Hamlet's surprised greeting of him in Act I means that Horatio has independent access to Elsinore. Claudius, however, shows no surprise and needs no introduction on seeing him, but simply tells him once to give Ophelia "good watch" (4.5.74), and later has him "wait upon him [Hamlet]" (5.1.293). Horatio's access to court seems to be due to the King.

His knowing Claudius helps to explain why Horatio is accepted in two worlds, high and low, and can go everywhere. He visits soldiers on their battlements' watch. He assures a sailor he can take him to the King. He studies the King's face during the court entertainment. Though not manor-born, he explains for the watch the intricate thirty-year history—biographical, legal, and military—behind Denmark's war preparations. And he offers to explain the death of the entire court to Fortinbras. Such abilities and intimate knowledge of events and actors are strong evidence that Horatio is very well born. His access to both worlds, high and low, shows him having a foot in each. One answer to such a riddle is that Horatio is illegitimate. Elizabethan wits would have suspected this by the end of Scene 1, when Horatio bridges both worlds in taking two common soldiers with him to visit the Prince and again when he later takes a third person, a sailor, to the King.

What would mark his illegitimacy for a Globe audience would be that Horatio not only has a university education, but is schoolfellow-friend to the Danish Prince. In sum, Horatio is well educated and very well connected, as many illegitimate persons traditionally were. If such evidence suggests that Claudius is Horatio's father and sponsor, the connection adds to the drama of the play instead of deflating it (which occurs if we assume that Horatio's father is an unknown lord at Elsinore): Horatio becomes another claimant to the throne. Elizabethans knew that illegitimate heirs who make friends with soldiers during a political crisis bear watching. A claimant friendly with the castle guard simplifies addition.

If we accept the premise that Horatio is Claudius's son, then Horatio becomes what Hamlet is, the son of a King. At Wittenberg Horatio was simply Hamlet's friend; but with old Hamlet's murder the dynamics would have changed. Dynamics explain why he would want to manipulate Hamlet. Between Horatio and the throne stand Claudius and Hamlet; after the death of legitimate heirs will come those with lesser claims, which offers Horatio his chance. Horatio would not be the first claimant to find a crown more appealing than an old friend.

With Claudius's succession, Horatio could see a path to the throne. He seems then to have sent for the First Player and to have offered him a side job of sorts, namely impersonating the old King to the battlements' guards, so that after a couple of its appearances he himself could "accidentally" stumble upon the guards in their baffled state and offer his services in the matter. The First Player might argue the danger in such impersonation: a feared invasion makes nervous guards who, if they should strike at a sheeted, fake "Ghost," could easily end an impersonator's acting career. But not one in armor. Armor thus seems to be a provision against the death of a person who is very much alive, the First Player, who is also the most skilled impersonator in the play.

When, therefore, Horatio brings the guards to Hamlet, Hamlet would of course know Horatio's standing relative to the crown and, as literature's most skillful exposer of impositions, praise Horatio as one he holds in his heart of hearts. Showing that he is on to him would put Horatio on guard, make him more secretive and more distant from Hamlet, make him have Claudius killed and possibly succeed him. As long as he expects Hamlet to do the deed, Horatio can wait passively and in full view, thus allowing Hamlet to concentrate mainly on Claudius. Horatio treats as slow and ineffective a "friend" who neither turns on him, nor takes his eye off him. And Hamlet gives him a pair of veiled warnings. When Horatio pressures Hamlet to say what transpired with the "Ghost," which would really suggest what Hamlet might believe about the matter, Hamlet tells him they should part—"You as your business and desire shall point you" (1.5.129). Horatio cannot be sure how Hamlet uses "business," since Hamlet's usage verges on OED1 13 d. involving "A person's business," which is tied up with "ruin" and "kill[ing]". Business and desire are a nearly perfect characterization of Horatio's activity and motive: he is busily engaged in getting Hamlet to hand him the crown, which is his desire. In any case Horatio's missing or ignoring the warning but going ahead with his scheme shows him furthering his desire by more business. And that later brings on Hamlet's second veiled warning, that "'Tis dangerous when the baser nature comes / Between the pass and fell incensed points / Of mighty opposites'" (5.2.60–2). To Elizabethans, an illegitimate Horatio qualified as having a baser nature,[12] as seen in his steady intrigue bent on manipulating Hamlet. Horatio is a coward like his father, though he may think he poses no threat to Hamlet's life.

Helping us to see the opportunity that beckons Horatio is the weakened state of Denmark as the play opens. For all of Claudius's suavity, steady Fortinbras deeply shakes the Danish state. Obvious proof of how shaken Claudius is appears in the three passwords of the watch. "Long live the King!" "Friends to this ground," and "liegemen to the Dane" (1.1.3, 15) convert simple identifications into loyalty oaths dramatizing the King's fear of his soldiers' allegiance. Indeed, he rejects their allegiance in favor of paid Switzers (4.5.98). The great opening court scene dramatizes the state's turmoil over a neighboring Prince at the head of unpaid irregulars who support young Fortinbras as fully as the Danish people did their late, beloved King. It is Prince Hamlet—not craven Claudius—who enjoys the people's love, as Claudius's public attempt to undercut Hamlet for his "unmanly grief" shows (1.2.94). Denmark's political instability is Fortinbras's cue—and also Horatio's.

Shakespeare's audience stared at an amazing succession, one approved by a council that passed over the King's son in favor of the King's younger brother. Heirless Claudius cleverly tries to prop himself up and make his own toppling doubly difficult—for Fortinbras, Horatio, and Laertes—by the brilliant, Beowulfian, and meaningless fiat, before the assembled court, of having the "world take note / [Hamlet is] the most immediate to our throne" (1.2.108–9), a promise that is meaningless without a mechanism to make it binding on the next council, meeting in private, to elect the new king. By appearing to proclaim Hamlet his heir Claudius makes an ally of an antagonist. Anyone overthrowing Claudius must get rid of Hamlet too, who becomes a complicating, protective buffer. Loyalty oaths and Switzers aren't very protective when you hold the plum that tempts the hungry. And the hungriest persons in the play are Fortinbras and Horatio.

If this is the Danish political reality, then the "Ghost" is of interest because its command affects the Danish succession. Hamlet, we learn, has lost the election to Claudius (5.2.65) for reasons that presumably would still decide against him in the next succession, which the "Ghost" is urging him to initiate. By proclaiming Hamlet his heir Claudius may please the people, but not his counselors: a Denmark protected by a Prince immobilized by melancholy is a Denmark unprotected against an energized and ambitious Norwegian Prince heading a school of loot-hungry sharks. When, therefore, the "Ghost" orders him to murder Claudius, Hamlet is being told to remove the King that he probably cannot be elected to succeed. That means the throne will be available to other claimants. And Hamlet must know that to carry out the "Ghost's" command will position Horatio for the throne and himself, as has been noted, for hell.[13]

A fake "Ghost" makes Horatio a rich, political gambler, an heir seeking the crown by duping Hamlet into removing the King and himself. This is a dazzling, foolhardy bet that Hamlet silently accepts. A fake "Ghost" adds enormous tension and conflict to the roles of Horatio, Hamlet, the First Player, Gertrude, and the watch. A fake "Ghost" makes Hamlet extraordinarily dramatic. And because Shakespeare is a dramatist, he would want such political enrichments to character and drama, which also strengthens my argument.

Almost certainly, Horatio would have learned of the old King's death at Wittenberg, when a party from Elsinore would have brought the news to Hamlet. And since Hamlet left the university a Prince, Horatio could have surmised, if he had not been told, that Claudius had successfully pressed his own case and that Horatio himself therefore is in line for the crown—indeed, is next in line if Claudius can be removed. But doing the job himself would be tacky, virtual self-incrimination. His manipulating Hamlet to do it for him would be an elegant political solution because it would at once get rid of a King and compromise a claimant. Their long schoolfellow friendship was a history that probably yielded Shakespeare the reflection that Horatio would have intimate knowledge of Hamlet's hatred of Gertrude and love of his father, along with important knowledge of his character, his weaknesses, and how to impose on them. Thus equipped, Horatio need only hire the acting troupe, perhaps at the moment touring Wittenburg, and have the First Player precede his players by several weeks so as to perform a new role up on the battlements. Then he could slip away to rejoin them for an ensemble entrance into Elsinore.

That this is likely to have happened is suggested by the symmetrical structure of the play uncovered by Mark Rose. His study reveals that many tableaux and events in the play are flanked on either side by parallel symmetries.[14] A similar symmetry is apparent in the trio of preceders—the First Player who precedes his troupe in Act 1, the captain who precedes Fortinbras and his troop into the castle in Act 4, and Fortinbras himself preceding his troop in Act 5, the troupe/troop heads, First Player, and Fortinbras, flanking the subordinate captain.

Now Horatio would face the problem of how to keep Hamlet from exposing the hoax, which he would be certain to do if the "Ghost" appeared alone to him in the castle. Armor would have suggested a solution, as minimizing detection and possible injury, except that Hamlet could still question the "apparition" about matters that the First Player could know nothing about. Horatio appears to have kept the armor idea, but decided on having the "Ghost" visit the guard on the battlements instead of Hamlet in the castle. This arrangement would make it awkward for Hamlet to question a "Ghost" vouched for as real by the guard and Horatio. After the "Ghost's" second appearance to them, Horatio probably and conveniently "chanced," at watch's end, upon an agitated or arguing guard, to whom he would flatteringly offer his service. Drawing out their story, he could insist that they saw no "Ghost," thus prompting their challenge to see for himself by joining them the next night.

That encounter would "convert" Horatio into a "believer" and through his "belief" the guard, if they had any residual doubts. They witness an impressive interrogation of the "Ghost," replete with its classical formula, "If thou hast any sound or use of voice," "If there be any good thing to be done," "If thou art privy to thy country's fate" (1.1.128, 130, 133). This is polished acting, except for three bothersome matters. In the 1583 edition of *De Praestigiis Daemonum*, Johann Weyer cites Jacobus de Clusa, Carthusian author of the standard work on apparitions, who produces the same formula that Horatio uses, but calls for its being spoken by "four or five pious priests," not a skeptical, stoical layman. This is a telltale change because only Roman Catholic priests performed such rituals and ceremonies—for the entire religious calendar, for the sacraments, for exorcisms, and also for interrogating spirits—and performed them for about sixteen hundred years, apparently without sharing them with lay persons. Coming from a Catholic family, Shakespeare, along with every alert member of the audience, had to know this. This lengthy tradition surely meant more drama for any

Globe patron who could sense that some spectators seemed quite unaware of Shakespeare's sleight of hand, which makes us accept the way things don't happen as the way they do, as Henry James somewhere says.

Second, de Clusa says that because "[t]he spirit is now awaiting a state of reward or punishment [ie., is in purgatory, as is, supposedly, Hamlet's "Ghost"] . . . he cannot sin anymore,"[15] as a sinning "Ghost" does by the shocking command that Hamlet murder Claudius. It is amusing that many Globe patrons would believe this was a "Ghost" being purged of its sins in purgatory. Third and equally bothersome is the fact that Horatio skips a step. Priests were told to "speak thus: 'Spirit, we beseech you by Jesus Christ to tell us who you are, and if there is one among us to whom you would wish to respond, name him or point him out by a sign. Is it . . . [Name]? or . . . [Name]?'"[16] Conveniently, Horatio can't ask the "Ghost" these things because it leaves when the cock crows, after which Horatio divines that "upon my life, / This spirit, dumb to us, will speak to [Hamlet]" (1.2.170–71). This proves remarkably prescient, because the "Ghost" does want to address Hamlet, and once underway can hardly be made to stop. The "Ghost" addresses Hamlet simply because Horatio didn't await another of its appearances to make sure of the "Ghost's" identity, but sets off to persuade Hamlet to meet it and confirm what Horatio already knows without having questioned it. Skipping this step shows Horatio's eager complicity in getting Hamlet involved with the "Ghost." Horatio's show impresses the guard enough to assent to his suggestion that they report the matter to Hamlet and that they all watch together the next night. Contrivance is further suggested because Hamlet must be brought to the "Ghost" instead of the "Ghost" coming to Hamlet and because Hamlet has been carefully prepared to meet it—at one o'clock on a moonless night illuminated only by stars,[17] which adds to the difficulty of identification.

Horatio has a peculiar tie to the "Ghost"; he appears only after and because of it, which suggests connection as much as coincidence. Plainly visible is Horatio's causing the soldiers' to breach military law in reporting to him, who is not in their chain of command, instead of to their officer of the guard, who is. John Dover Wilson implicitly explains away this problem by promoting the sentinels to officers[18] (who supposedly need report only to themselves), and by saying that because a ghost spoke only in Latin the watch turns to Horatio as one who can address it. But Horatio is not needed to address an English- (i.e. Danish) -speaking "Ghost."

Moreover, on any occasion guard-duty is serious business. At a time of crisis and imminent invasion it is deadly serious business, and the last thing one should find on such a watch is a visitor to whom the watch first makes its report. He is the wrong person to report to. We also then need to know how they knew Horatio was even in Elsinore and how they had access to so great a lord: in the strict structure of military life; soldiers went through the chain of command and reported to their commander: they didn't approach great lords, even illegitimate ones. But illegitimate heirs have had a long-standing use for soldiers. When Horatio asks the guards' consent to acquaint Hamlet, "As needful in our loves, fitting our duty" (1.1.173), Shakespeare dramatizes their breach of duty in reporting an irregularity to the wrong person. And every person in the house would have seen the red-flag anomaly of an important lord asking consent from the commonest of common soldiers to join him in an unusual event, meeting and speaking to their Prince, as if commoners could decide such things for lords, who would bring them along for their testimony. Horatio, apparently, lets them suppose that no breach can occur when one King's son asks them to report the matter to another King's son.

Unless Horatio sought them out, as I have suggested, we have difficulty explaining this linkage. Night-watch soldiers sleep days, which is the reverse of Horatio's activities. Horatio's joining their watch further dramatizes their violation of duty: watches should be walked alone. The soldiers breach more military law by taking orders from him and asking, as one would expect of them, if they should strike at the "Ghost." And the "Ghost" moves fast to avoid a blow, being "here," "here," and "gone" (1.1.140–41). But this skipping about gives the game away, for an immaterial "Ghost" need not move. Only a fake ghost must avoid a clanging blow because if the armor can sound, its wearer can bleed: material armor is superfluous for an immaterial ghost.

Marcellus takes another cue from Horatio by noticing the "Ghost's" "majesty" after Horatio calls it "majestical" (1.1.143); and both men accept Horatio's idea of reporting only to Hamlet (1.1.168–170). Should Horatio report to Claudius, with corroborating soldiers in tow (the muscle in a coup), he might unmask himself. And if Horatio really thinks the "Ghost" has come back to warn the kingdom of some danger, he should report it to Claudius, to whom he has access. By not doing so, Horatio suggests to us that he knows the "Ghost" will urge the death of the King. Horatio could know this only by conspiracy, or by the "Ghost's" having confided in him.

Thus it appears that not Claudius, but first the guard and then Hamlet are carefully manipulated to believe in the "Ghost." Hamlet is under extreme pressure to believe because three other persons who have seen it vouch for its identity. It is an understatement to say that Hamlet is in an awkward position. Naturally, the "Ghost" seems to stagger him, and with something afoot—he doesn't know what—he appears to become an instant, agitated believer in it. Because Hamlet wonders only if it is a "spirit of health or goblin damn'd" (1.4.40), but not the third possibility, that it is fake, we set aside our skepticism. And since no one calls Hamlet's attention to the "Ghost's" earlier much emphasized eyes and beard, Hamlet apparently does not see these clinching identifiers. In their place is a figure that Hamlet now describes as being in "complete steel" (1.4.52). Steel becomes complete when nothing is exposed and the eyes are covered—as a Globe audience could have seen—thereby protecting the face from identification. This detail strongly hints at fakery. Moreover, Horatio plants the idea with Hamlet that, without words, the "Ghost" seemed "As if it some impartment did desire / To you alone" (1.4.59–60). Unless the "Ghost" silently mouths "Hamlet!" such an impartment is virtually impossible. But the "Ghost" must draw Hamlet away from the soldiers before telling him to kill their own king.

Hamlet is, and should be, wily, because a "Ghost" in armor is material, out of character, and anything but incorporeal. And incorporeality, the familiar state of being one of the "sheeted dead," which Shakespeare's mentioning at 1.1.115 means he knows is a spirit's usual costume, is what we have a right to expect of a ghost. In Saxo, Belleforest, and Shakespeare, Hamlet stays alive by foiling plots. If Hamlet foils a plot involving a "Ghost" whom he appears to believe, he acts in character with Amleth's actions in the sources. If his friend is an illegitimate claimant to the throne, who comes to court but associates with soldiers until making an astonishing report of having seen an armored figure that he claims is the "Ghost" of Hamlet's father, is Hamlet wiser to appear to believe or disbelieve the story? Hamlet's sources pit a wily Prince against a cunning usurper; Shakespeare, in parallel fashion, pits a wily Hamlet against a cunning father, a crafty son, and a good actor. In perfect character, Hamlet plays taken in. Assuming that Shakespeare desired intense drama, this arrangement provides it, especially if Horatio is "duping" Hamlet, who is duping Horatio along with the actor of the "Ghost."

If a hoax is in progress, the question, cui bono, points to Horatio as the originator: if he is Claudius's illegitimate son, he has the most to gain. The likeliest actor of the "spirit" would be the First Player, looking to gain a bit himself.[19] Collusion between these two persons appears likely because neither Claudius, Polonius, nor Hamlet has invited the actors to Elsinore, and the company cannot invite itself.[20] This leaves Horatio as the likely inviter. Moreover, Horatio facilitates the meeting of Hamlet and "Ghost" because, when the latter draws Hamlet off, Marcellus wants to follow. But not Horatio. He stays put until Marcellus finally and impatiently erupts against such stalling, urging Horatio, "Nay, let's follow him" (1.4.88–91). Horatio stalls, I believe, to retard Marcellus, for, should those two follow, Marcellus might hear the command to revenge and would be oath-bound to report the matter. But Horatio delays him long enough for the "Ghost" to get Hamlet away and issue its famous "commandment." Moreover, his being unafraid for Hamlet's safety here suggests that Horatio knows him to be in no danger, as he began by pretending, from a figure of undeclared motive.

When alone with Hamlet, the "Ghost" introduces itself to its "son," doing so, apparently, because Hamlet can't see its face or recognize its voice. Once "identified," it emphasizes only its other-world status, including the handy ban against telling secrets from the other side. In short, it offers neither proof that it is who it claims to be, nor evidence that it has come from beyond the grave. Any audience will accept a dividing curtain, but not a total ban against a detail or two from this or the other side. Without them the "Ghost" cannot unequivocally establish itself as the spirit of Hamlet's father.

The "Ghost" must be held to the same test that a séance "spirit" must meet—the knowledge of details about this world, which it could not know except by being what it claims to be. Its passing this test will remove doubt and convince a reasonable person. And this test the "Ghost" neither meets nor is put to. Stephen Greenblatt notes that "there is an odd sense in which Hamlet leaps over the questions that were traditionally asked of 'questionable' apparitions" (but Hamlet seems to know he is not the proper person to ask them) and that while the Mousetrap seems to satisfy Hamlet, "it notoriously leaves the question of the Ghost's origin unanswered."[21] Since, presumably, it shared thirty years with Hamlet, the "Ghost" strangely ignores every domestic detail, especially those involving its grooming of Hamlet for just this moment, when Hamlet should succeed his father. This strongly suggests that it doesn't know them. Mentioning just one shared event could instantly prove the speaker to be what it claims to be. But despite a supposed shared life, the "Ghost" avoids their common past in favor of commanding Hamlet to commit murder—and apparently in the Holy season, which insures his damnation. Absent is any mention of happiness when its own "flesh and blood" will occupy the throne—for the obvious reason that Hamlet's occupancy isn't its devoutly wished consummation. The argument that Hamlet seems content with the authenticity of the "Ghost" and doesn't feel a need to press it for confirming details can be made only by transforming him into a dupe instead of a duping exposer of plots.

The "Ghost" avoids details of its purgatorial life, of its former life with Hamlet, and of its court life, except for conventions and common gossip that any courtier would know. Greg calls its language mere rhetoric and "a frigid piece of academic declamation,"[22] but ignores noticing that, instead of offering shared knowledge as proof of its identity, the "Ghost" offers supposedly a merely "ghostly" sound and demeanor. But then, why offer more when the minimum seems to be working?

At court, everyone knows who is next in line. But Hamlet knows something else. He knows that while he enjoys Claudius's promise, Horatio (by my argument) enjoys Claudius's blood. Hamlet's delay is intelligent, which we miss seeing if we ask the question of secondary importance, why Hamlet doesn't kill Claudius, instead of the question of primary importance, who succeeds Claudius on an open throne if he does? Answering the latter question leads to an answer for the former. By delaying, Hamlet is not a procrastinator, but a quick-witted unmasker of Horatio and a shrewd assessor of bizarre visitations.

Hamlet reveals subtle suspicions about the "Ghost's" origin. The instant that Polonius runs in with news of the Players' approach, Hamlet replies "Buzz, buzz!" (2.2.393). Simple as this phrase is, it is simpler still in Q2 and F1, which produce it with a period in place of the exclamation point of modern editors. The words are usually glossed as "old news," which misses their important (though slightly modified) connection to the old source. As an onomatopoeic synecdoche for a fly, they reflect Saxo Grammaticus's text where a gadfly alerts Amleth to treachery,[23] because it represents a signal of danger. In the play "buzz," representing a fly, also represents danger: OED1 5.a defines fly as "A familiar demon (from the notion that devils were accustomed to assume the form of flies). b. transf., and with allusion to the insect's finding its way into the most private places: A spy (cf. F. mouche). c. A parasite, flatterer (cf. I. musca)." Each of these definitions will fit the context, since Hamlet has experienced a very questionable "Ghost," which has the look of a familiar demon, and since Polonius is the chief spy on Hamlet in the play, and is also a flattering parasite. Without the exclamation point, Hamlet's expression can also be read as the quiet, abstracted musing (prompted by but not addressed to Polonius) of a person suddenly alerted to a danger.

Hamlet is clearly suspicious, as we see in his promising a special reception to the First Player: "He that plays the king shall be welcome—his Majesty shall have tribute of me"—perhaps for an acting job bravely attempted. And when that actor enters with the troupe, Hamlet's welcome is very pointed: "O, old friend! why, thy face is valanc'd since I saw thee last; com'st thou to beard me in Denmark?" (2.2.319–20, 422–24). Literature's greatest exposer of impositions seems again to be at work. Of old, having seen the actor clean-shaven, Hamlet seizes upon the fact that he is now bearded, as the "Ghost" was reported to be. Further tying the "Ghost" together with the First Player is the tradition that the actor of the "Ghost" also doubled as the First Player.

Hamlet next sees the "Ghost" in the Queen's chamber. If it really is a ghost, it doesn't need a hiding place; if fake, it does. If it is real, nothing untoward should occur, since it can appear, or not, and thus control its collisions with reality. But if fake, something might go wrong. And something does. Gertrude cries for help, and Polonius seems to forget himself by crying out from behind the arras and giving himself away.

This act raises two questions: what causes the old man to betray himself, Gertrude's cry or his being startled on discovering that he is not alone back there? And does Hamlet know that it is Polonius behind the arras? Regarding the first question, Polonius seems to be startled by discovering he is not alone. Many at the Globe would have thought so too, for the reasons I shall momentarily suggest. Such an interpretation adds great drama to a performance as well as to a reading.

As for Hamlet's knowing that Polonius is spying on him, there is an unbroken causal line from "Buzz, buzz" to "How now? A rat?" making the first event directly connected to the second, with the Mousetrap intervening during which Polonius, not Claudius, rises with the order "Give o'er the play" (3.2.268). This order seems to indict Polonius as complicit in the death of Hamlet's father, and the entire developed line of events gives force, but not certainty, to the idea that Hamlet knows his rapier has not impaled Claudius. It isn't certain that Hamlet knows, but it is likely because Polonius brought him news that Gertrude wants to speak to him, which Hamlet agrees to and which Polonius replies "I will say so" (3.2.386). This obviously means that Hamlet knows Polonius will be in her chamber, even as he knows that Claudius will not be, having, as he goes to his mother's closet, past the praying King. This is powerful drama, which Hamlet's pretense of doubt before Gertrude sustains, for he cannot really alert his enemies that he has intentionally removed one of them.

If the "Ghost" is real, it can materialize wherever it will; if fake, it needs what Polonius needs, a convenient hiding place, and the Globe offered it an arras. The Globe spectators would have seen this arras occupied before, at (3.1.43), when the King and Polonius stepped behind it to spy on Hamlet and Ophelia. If in the unlikely case Shakespeare wanted to give the game away, what the spectators would see now would be a king's "Ghost" step behind it, soon to be followed by Polonius so as to spy on Hamlet and Gertrude. Otherwise, the "Ghost" would have entered the arras from behind, out of view of the audience. In either case, an earlier seen toe (according to stage tradition) and a later heard cry alert Hamlet to his twice being spied on. The balanced symmetry in these matters is no accident, when we consider Foakes's work on the doublings and Rose's work on the visual symmetries so evident in this play. Rose brilliantly notes that "[c]onfronted with a formal or intellectual problem of any kind, the natural tendency of the Elizabethan sensibility seems to be to construct a symmetrical pattern."[24] And from the start of the action forward, every discerning Globe spectator would have realized that the play involves Danish and Norwegian uncles occupying thrones that presumably are the rightful possessions of their nephews. Here was the first of the symmetrical designs that would have prepared them to assess the reality of the "Ghost."

If therefore the "Ghost" is arrased, awaiting the moment to emerge, when Hamlet is turned away from it, and Polonius steps into it in order to conceal himself, too, then Polonius will gradually grow aware that he is next to someone else. Such a realization would represent a genuine surprise, indeed fear, that erupts into the call, "What ho," and his alarmed cry "help!" (3.4.23). One common reading, which is deficient in drama, assumes that a senile, confused Polonius echoes the Queen; but most actors speak the words as anything but the alarmed commotion they appear to be. Polonius's cries cost him his life and suggest alarm and distress. The Elizabethan audience might well have seen the curtain move and flex as if from engaged, if not scuffling, bodies. Such a possibility is charged with drama—and with an interpretation denied to modern audiences. If the arras is behind Hamlet while he berates Gertrude, Globe audiences could have seen the "Ghost" emerge from the spot where, moments earlier, Polonius had entered, became agitated, and cried out. Thus, on the additional possible basis of performance and symmetry, the Globe audience could surmise that the "Ghost" is fake. I say additional because, three scenes earlier, Hamlet, alone, musingly emphasized *"The undiscover'd country* from whose bourn / No traveller returns" (3.1.78–79. My italics). Any Globe spectator who believed this statement would be prompted to ask how the "Ghost" got in the Queen's chamber and how ghostly it was.

Another matter of interest is the "Ghost's" appearance in nightdress. Presumably Hamlet and Gertrude are twenty feet downstage when, from the curtained rear and beneath the somewhat concealing "shadow," the "Ghost" appears. While a nightdress suggests less concealment, it still limits a spectator's view of the "Ghost's" body, and therefore is similar to armor in this regard. But it can now be worn, because as a believer in the "Ghost", Hamlet would no longer be thought a threat: he himself assured Horatio that "I'll take the ghost's word for a thousand pound" (3.2.285–86). But we should still imagine the First Player's state of mind when Polonius's cry is followed by Hamlet's lunge delivering his sword within a foot or two of that actor. (Those readers who argue the superiority of performance over closet are denying more drama than they ever acknowledge.) In any event, Hamlet can now see the "Ghost's" head, but probably not its famous eyes; for the actor, I believe, would lower his lids or otherwise obstruct eye contact. In any case, Gertrude helps out: her soul chooses this moment to fight with itself, thus creating a convenient diversion that allows the "Ghost" to direct Hamlet's gaze away from itself to her. For twenty-two lines Hamlet questions Gertrude, trying to confirm what he—and we—see, thus permitting the figure the chance to turn and leave through a nearby rear-stage exit that does not require its passing next to Hamlet downstage. Occupied with Gertrude, Hamlet cannot study the "Ghost" on the Globe stage, except from the corner of his eye. This suggests that (3.4) showed the Globe "Ghost" upstage, at a distance, hoping to conceal its true identity. And in shadow: the Globe stage faced north, shadowing the players but lighting the galleries.[25] In sum, Shakespearean symmetry and staging could have subtly cast doubt on the "Ghost," to heighten the drama.

If the "Ghost" is a hoax, we believe in it in part because Gertrude says she doesn't see or hear it. But once we recognize Horatio as Claudius's illegitimate heir and see the "Ghost" as discredited, then Gertrude's denials quickly suggest that she is lying. This study of Horatio and the "Ghost" deepens Gertrude's character and allows us to see that because her lies help Horatio in his plot to topple Claudius—indeed to have Hamlet kill him—she clearly loves neither the King nor her own son, her "only way of dealing with men [being] seduction," as Alvin Kernan notes.[26] Her "compulsive ardure" (3.4.86) apparently now burns for Claudius's would-be successor, Horatio.[27] This conclusion is perfectly in line with a crucial characterization in Saxo, where the mature Scottish Queen desires young men: ". . . for wedlock with the old [i.e. the king of Britain] she [the queen of Scotland] utterly abhorred, and desired the embraces of young men,"[28] a crucial quality that Shakespeare appears to use in shaping Gertrude's character and first perhaps adopted from Wealhtheow, who also favored young men.

Our catching Gertrude in bold-faced lies raises the important question of her motivation for turning on Claudius. Besides Shakespeare's splendid instinct for the dramatic (which is often ignored or underestimated), what will explain her throwing over a King for an upstart? An answer appears, I believe, when she coldly watches Ophelia die without helping her, for it follows a scene in which Claudius twice calls the young lady pretty. Ophelia sings him a Valentine's Day song about a young lady "tumbled" but not married by her tumbler. The royal rift and Gertrude's coldly watching Ophelia drown suggest that Gertrude believes Claudius has been sexually involved with a rival, Ophelia.[29] Jealous revenge would thus become Gertrude's motivation.

This suggestion is neatly alluded to by Hamlet's hints about Ophelia's possible pregnancy,[30] an idea sustained and reinforced by the priests' refusal to bury her in holy ground. That refusal would have followed their having given extreme unction to her wet body with its adhesive clothing that could have revealed a pregnant condition, making her death appear to have been a suicide.

Gertrude's imaged confession of "black and [grained] spots" (3.4.90) corrupting her soul refers to symptoms of the black plague and theatrically registers her sense of moral contagion. Her willingness to trash Hamlet for Horatio and even possibly drive him to believe himself mad displays her malevolence and the real malignancy of her black and grained spots. And her failure, as Virgil Whitaker points out, ever to investigate Hamlet's charge that old Hamlet had been murdered[31] exposes her indifference to what should be an astonishing matter. Let Claudius but hear that Hamlet is love-mad for Ophelia and he immediately asks, "How may we try it further?" (2.2.159) Murder mattering so little to Gertrude suggests her unblinking familiarity with it and her acceptance of it as a solution, as in her witnessing the drowning of Ophelia, her natural rival. Ophelia must be doubly hateful to the Queen as the "metal more attractive"[32] to her son and as the "pretty lady" that attracts her husband's eye.

Horatio's intrigue would succeed, but for Fortinbras's final effort to force Denmark to acknowledge his unstated claims. Fortinbras comes to demand his long-standing "rights, of memory" (5.2.389) in the kingdom, rights symbolized by the crown, rights that antedate Claudius's coronation, rights that Hamlet endorses with his dying, elective voice, and rights that also connect Fortinbras with Hamlet and old Hamlet. Unless the drama is a fairy tale of a neighboring Prince, who, just happening to be passing by, can pluck so great a prize without a murmur of dissent from anyone in the assembled court, including two Princes, what Fortinbras is relentlessly pressing upon Denmark would seem to be his blood-claim to the kingdom. This in turn suggests that the single combat between old Hamlet and old Fortinbras had had cuckolding as its cause. The play dramatizes the active political attempts of two claimants—Fortinbras, and Horatio—to gain the Danish throne. We can also see that although Horatio, being by my argument descended from the reigning King, has a slenderly better claim than has Fortinbras, the Norwegian claimant will win, in a second odd succession, when the son of the present King will lose to a son of the last King because the latter son is a clear leader who gets the crucial support of Hamlet and, presumably later, the council. Horatio has to know that courts, given a whiff of a plot, were ruthless in tracking it down. And this outcome can be neatly underscored by a performance plainly presenting Bernardo and Marcellus among the spectators of the duel, who, as Hamlet speaks his words, might innocently, noddingly smile a greeting to Horatio, if not offer themselves as among the unsatisfied.

The reporting requirement seems sure to double the unsatisfactory matters placed before the court. Hamlet's dying moments are extraordinary for their dual character, his dying while at the same time exposing and outwitting another opponent who has tried, unsuccessfully, to dupe him. In open court for all to hear, he tells Horatio, "Report me and my cause aright / To the unsatisfied" (5.2.339–40). This complicated cause involves a "snake-bitten" father whose death, putting Claudius on the throne, had made mortal enemies of Claudius and Hamlet and left Hamlet feeling "benetted round with [villainies]" (5.2.29). Also, Shakespeare inherited a Hamlet whose role requires that he repeatedly outwit his benetters. Horatio, to whom Hamlet's daring re-mark is made, is one benetter, which shows him indeed to be his father's son, villainy running in the family. There would be unusual interest in hearing Horatio present Hamlet's cause aright to the unsatisfied, Horatio himself heading this group because the throne is passing to Fortinbras. Hamlet's thus obliging Horatio to report his cause aright would be enough to turn a chameleon a metallic, ghostly white. The obliga-tion will expose Horatio's witnessed and reported earlier appearances to him. These guards also witnessed the "Ghost's" next appearance to Horatio and Hamlet. Report-ing Hamlet's cause will connect Horatio to the "Ghost" in Act one, and to Bernardo and Marcellus, all of which would require a very delicate narrative, especially because the guard can affirm or deny what Horatio claims. And to report this entire matter to a sober court, including Fortinbras, would be to report the matter to persons not "distracted," as Hamlet pretended to be, or was, persons not easily imposed upon or easily swayed in their judgments, and therefore likely to unravel the imposition as a damning exposure of Horatio. This is duping with a vengeance.

The "Ghost," then, appears harmless as long as we follow Dover Wilson's example and ask no questions of Horatio. But when we adopt the strategy laid down by Niels Bohr, then we indeed find that the great and deep difficulty of the "Ghost's" reality and role bears in itself its own solution and forces us to change our thinking and for-mulate a different theory in order to find that solution. Such a theory is only a theory, but it deserves consideration along with all other explanations, and not least because we can then see that Kermode's description of Horatio as "a somewhat chameleontic figure" is too thriftily accurate and that Hamlet exposes him as a person taking the color of his surroundings as he plots a crafty usurpation—the idea is on his tongue almost from the moment he steps onstage (1.1.46)—by means of a fake "Ghost" who orders Hamlet to kill Claudius for him. As Claudius's son, and claimant to an heirless throne when Claudius dies Horatio's role as claimant gives him, for the first time, a genuine, dramatic, villainous function in the play, a plot against his father with the aid of the Queen. The skill with which these matters are mathematically revealed deserves an audience of physicists and mathematicians who are familiar with the symmetrical and intuitive abilities the skill entails, and of literary critics intimately familiar with Beowulf.

4

The Poisonings in *Hamlet* Reconsidered

The overarching triad in this chapter is the triad of the poisonings formed by the poisoning of the old king, the poisoning of Hamlet by Claudius and Laertes, and the poisoning, as I shall argue, of Claudius and Osric by Gertrude. I shall present evidence that Gertrude is successfully poisoning Claudius through the agency of Osric. Some readers may believe that if Shakespeare meant to have Gertrude poison Claudius, he would have forthrightly shown it. But he could not have placed the matter in plain view. Lord Burghley and the court had no scruples about censorial prior restraint and would not have tolerated such a play for fear of its inciting unrest in those wanting to plot against Elizabeth, even if the Roderigo Lopez "plot" were not fresh in the minds of the audience. Such a poisoning could only have been advanced under a cloak even heavier than that masking the long-known satire aimed at Burghley and son (through Polonius and Laertes), though that satire would have alerted many in the audience to take nothing at face value, certainly not the health of a king without visible heirs, nor the innocence of an incestuous Queen, whose husband plans the English beheading of her son. Since dramatists could suffer being jailed or forced into hiding, having their plays prohibited, their passages cut, and their theaters shut down, they devised of necessity many different ways to deal with proscribed matters, beginning with the veiling achievements of irony, imagery, and correspondences, and, for dangerous material, triadic structuring. These methods offer safety for the writer, since the ideas produced existed not in the text but in the minds of discerning spectators and readers.

Members of the audience who understood such realities could catch and admire subtleties that eluded the censor. Censors saw one story, alert audiences another. The story of Hamlet being a very complex affair, most characters present questions and problems that expand and enlarge their nature and activities. Ophelia's deplorable burial, for example, suggests that she has committed a mortal sin offensive to the Church. A reasonable working hypothesis is that hers was a grave sin of the flesh. Hamlet's treating her as a whore suggests what she has done, though not with whom she has done it. But since Gertrude promotes Ophelia's wretched death by coldly watching her drown without in any way helping her, without even calling for help (as she does for herself in 3.4), Ophelia has at least the appearance of being an eliminated, triangular rival, and it becomes possible to look for a link between her and Claudius. Such a link logically means, moreover, that a relationship between them must be as veiled as that of Gertrude's poisoning of Claudius, which, out of jealousy, it would precipitate.

The Hamlet legend displayed a heart of broad mystery centuries before Shakespeare dramatized his life. The oldest reference to it occurs in eight lines of verse written by the Icelandic poet Snaebjorn, anthologized by Snorri Sturlason, and handed down by Saxo Grammaticus.[1] His mysterious, folkloric lines have an important share in the general legend and name Hamlet along with giant, seed-gathering, meal-grinding maidens who in ages past ground his meal, too. These maidens seem to be cultic figures involved in Nerthus-like fertility rites, and as such they lead us to reexamine important medical aspects of this play that bear upon its great—and largely ignored— theme of poisoning. The broad legend produces Pryth and Ermutrud as Gertrude's fierce, vengeful, incest-stained models.[2] Reexamining such matters will show that, in emotion, intellect, and spirit, Gertrude's role as Claudius's imperial jointress gives her a larger role than Claudius himself can claim. This role will justify Claudius calling her the "imperial jointress of this war-like state," and it will allow us to see that Wealhtheow (cup-bearer to Hrothgar/Claudius and Beowulf/Hamlet) is indeed her literary forbear, though of course a paler version that Shakespeare enlarged and strengthened. Gertrude is a co-antagonist, and she dwarfs Claudius. The oldest, best-known reference to the early Danish tribes, including Hamlet's, appears in Tacitus, who says the people were members of the Nerthus cult.[3] These people were vegetation and fertility worshippers, the northern European equivalent of the southern European Ceres/ Demeter cults. This Nerthus cultic influence on Hamlet, first noticed by Kemp Malone and recently by John Grigsby,[4] is intact and imparts medieval atmosphere to the play. Hamlet lives in an unweeded garden gone to seed, possessed entirely of things rank and gross in nature, where he likens Gertrude to Niobe, fertile mother of fourteen, and later tells her not to compost the already choking, noxious weeds.

This background is important because vegetation cults have always been highly knowledgeable about poisons, such knowledge going hand in hand with the study of vegetation. Laertes' unction, an unavailing cataplasm of simples, and Claudius's hebona and poisoned chalice, are probably vegetative alkaloids. Shakespeare not only gives poison unusual prominence in his drama (Saxo and Belleforest failing to mention it in any form), but presents it as Italianate plotting, which suggests great subtlety. How surprising is it then that Claudius, cast as the crafty Italinate villain, devises clumsy poisonings, which bring down their practitioner. Two modern medical writers, Avrim R. Eden and Jeff Opland, believe that for the orchard poisoning Shakespeare drew upon Bartholomew Eustachio's "exciting new discovery [1564] of the auditory (eustachian) tube,"[5] which makes the old king's death state-of-the-art work. These writers, however, ignore the curious final poisonings in Act 5 and say nothing about two other possible cases of poisoning, which medical literature helps to clarify.

Apparently responding to the Ghost's claim that the poison worked very quickly, Eden and Opland argue that old Hamlet has a "bilateral conductive hearing loss resulting from large subtotal tympanic-perforations," despite the old king's hearing—to say nothing about the "Ghost's"—apparently being normal. To account for the poison's swift action, the writers suggest the unlikely case of tympanic perforations in both ears. Having then to explain how such perforations occurred, they note that while "there is no direct or indirect evidence in the text of the play to suggest that the king had chronic otitis media, chronic otorrhea was not uncommon in Elizabethan times." But did the old king suffer from it?

The authors are on more solid ground when they suggest, I believe accurately, that the curious poison hebona derives straight from fiction.[6] Hebona seems intended to dazzle the groundlings and, as a fiction, would probably allay the fears of Court and Stationers' Company at a time when England was especially nervous over the "plot" of Lopez, Elizabeth's personal physician, who was executed for attempting to "poison" her. Real poisonings, of course, were dangerous matters, because the English successional question, like that in Hamlet, lacked an obvious heir. A fictional hebona, involving a buried king instead of a sitting one, would allow Shakespeare to include cultic contextualizing so as to deal with genuine poisonings where officials least expected them. This would keep state censors at bay while appealing to the interests of the pit and the galleries—the groundlings and the wits. The actors would have played to the groundlings' love of hebona poured in both ears, played to their hissing Claudius as a poisoner identified for them, played to their love of poisoned swords and to their feeling flattered at being let in on a secret royal poisoning plot of king and courtier against Hamlet. The wits would have enjoyed the more subtle, detailed craft and poetic veiling that we are examining, especially because it eluded court censorship: every generally undetected hit at state matters and figures would have amused them and sharpened their minds for more.[7]

They would have paid close attention to Claudius's health because although he carouses with his lords in Act 1, he cannot elude a dying Hamlet in Act 5, who forces him to drink off a cup the king himself has poisoned. All he need do is leave the room, shut the door, and await Hamlet's death from the poison that the king knows is fast-acting. Or if caught, he need only push the cup away and spill its contents. Because Claudius does neither, despite the urgency of self-preservation, it is fair to suppose that they are more than he can do. Also, it is fair to believe the king's lacking the strength to save himself means he lacks strength-giving health. His legs apparently are so weak that he cannot evade a stricken Hamlet or fight him with a sword, but must beg his court to defend him, when he need only spill the drink. Such vividly emphasized weakness needs an explanation. Earlier, Gertrude protected Claudius's physical debility when she interposed herself and effectively held off a threatening Laertes, so that Claudius had twice to order her, "Let him go, Gertrude."[8] (By not letting them grapple, Gertrude keeps Laertes unaware of Claudius's weakness and her handiwork; so that self-interest, not love of Claudius, will explain her interposing.) Moreover, the king apparently has an unspecified illness and is receiving a doctor's care, as we know from Hamlet's telling Rosencrantz and Guildenstern to inform the king's doctor about his present "choler" (3.2.291–94). Although we never meet this doctor, we have Hamlet to thank for pointing out that he figures in the king's life.

Shakespeare clearly emphasizes the king's ill health: Claudius's praying, Hamlet says, "prolongs [his] sickly days" (3.3.96). In a poetic drama involving poison, sickly days can suggest more than a degenerate reign; they can refer to vomiting, which is a symptom of a stomach disorder. Hamlet also calls Claudius the "bloat King" (3.4.166), and bitingly repeats this point when he alludes to "your fat king and your lean beggar"

(4.3.23–4). (Claudius as "fat king" contrasts Hamlet as "lean beggar." Claudius's puffiness is further detailed in Hamlet's likening him to a swollen or "mildewed ear" (3.4.63). This "bloat" may well result from something other than food. Food gives strength: Claudius is physically weak.

After his reported rouse in the first Act, Claudius's entire physical activity is limited to once dropping to his knees in prayer and later lifting a stoup of wine to his lips. Pharmaceutical accounts illuminate such debility. Weakness in the extremities, "the legs [being] more severely affected than the arms,"[9] is a symptom of arsenic poison. (Such weakness is on the king's mind when he gives Laertes "much unsinewed" (4.7.10) reasons for not proceeding against Hamlet's threats: Claudius would have been physically unsinewed against Hamlet in a confrontation.) Pharmaceutical literature also relates bloatedness with arsenic poison. From arsenic "[t]he liver may enlarge," and "[e]ventually cirrhosis may occur from the hepatoxic condition"[10]. In small doses arsenic may produce "an occult edema, particularly facial, which has been mistaken for a healthy weight gain"[11]. Arsenic therefore appears to explain the mysterious royal malady for which the king would need doctoring.

Arsenic, of course, was well known in antiquity, thanks to Egyptian and earlier metallurgical efforts, which produced it as a by-product in the smelting of various metals. Alchemists also knew of arsenic, as Chaucer's "Canon Yeoman's Tale," l. 798, shows. Indeed, Chaucer was the best available literary chemical manual from about 1393 on, and may have served *Hamlet*, *The Alchemist* and other plays as a kind of primer on some chemical subjects.[12] Arsenic imparts special significance to health, illness, and revenge. The first two are themes revealed by the imagery that Caroline Spurgeon analyzed (in 1935), and these two themes, as we shall see, greatly enlarge the theme of revenge and make Kyd's efforts in this direction those of a novice. All three themes add to the state rot—the moral sickness in the souls of the characters and the physical sickness afflicting some of them. At the start of the play Shakespeare imparts thematic significance to illness by means of "impotent and bed-rid" old Norway (1.2.29) and then by the unwell Player King in the Mousetrap, both of whom are heads of state whose physical decay provides analogues for Claudius. Each one parallels the Danish king (living, the Player King may also represent Claudius; dead, only old Hamlet). Sensing that his sickness is terminal, and expecting shortly to die (3.2.164, 206), Gonzago prophecies a second husband for the wife he urges to remarry. She counters with cold protestations of undying love and leaves shortly before Lucianus enters to poison him. In this Italianate analogue, the subtle point may be that she leaves as a cue to Lucianus. I am suggesting that the Mousetrap is a larger analogue for poisoning than has been generally recognized. It appears to represent the double parallel of Claudius's poisoning of old Hamlet and someone else's poisoning of Claudius. If so, the Mouse-trap exemplifies yet another doubled pair of the kind R. A. Foakes has reported on.[13] Claudius's twelve detailed references to disease reveal a man unusually concerned with health: he even uses health as a metaphor in a letter to England (5.2.22). Most of these references appear in Act 4 and suggest that his health has obviously worsened. They take two forms, those associating poison with others and those associating illness with himself. Those in the first group are often taken as unconscious, ironic betrayals of a poisoner's imagination, as when Claudius asks Hamlet's school fellows to open Ham-let's affliction to "our remedy" (2.2.17–18) and when he hopes that slander will trans-port "his poisoned shot . . . [and] miss our name" (4, 1, 43). Unconsciously, the king sees himself as a target of poisoning. If he is being poisoned, one form of a poisoned shot has not missed. The second group exposes some of the thoughts of a stricken man. In a passage meant to display his closeness to Gertrude, he speaks of her as "My virtue or my plague" (4.7.13), thus letting escape his sharply divided thought about her. This suggests something unwell in their marriage, since one wants, of course, to be rid of the plague, not to keep it. Even his saying that "She's so conjunctive to my life and soul / That, as the star moves not but in his sphere, I could not but by her" (4.7.14–16) unconsciously, ironically shows not only their separation, but his acknowledging his relatively lesser intellectual importance: in the Ptolemaic system motion starts with the outer sphere and works inwards, so that the turning of a larger outside sphere—in this case Gertrude—against a smaller inside one—in this case Claudius—imparts a motion to it (as God does to the outer sphere in Giovanni di Paolo's "The Creation of the World and the Expulsion from Paradise" c. 1445 at the Metropolitan Museum of Art). Adjacent spheres were eternally separated; but more to the point their en-cased bodies never touched, and even their alignments were rare. Further irony marks Claudius's decision to send Hamlet off: "Diseases desperate grown / By desperate appli-ance are relieved / Or not at all" (4.3.9–11). Desperate appliance may suggest the king's doctor is using a radical procedure to treat Claudius. The king appears to exemplify the imposthume that inward breaks and shows no cause without why the man dies.

If Claudius wants to be rid of his plague, Gertrude appears willing to be parted from him. John Russell Brown speaks of a rift existing between them, as reflected in Gertrude's ignoring Claudius at 4.1.27, 37, and 39:[14] and Maurice Charney notices some of Claudius's disenchantments with Gertrude. Neither writer offers, however, a satisfactory explanation of her behavior, though Charney points out that Claudius's heart isn't in his warning her not to drink from the cup.[15] Unlike Hamlet who wrests the cup from Horatio, Claudius's sotto voce merely warns Gertrude not to drink. His not simply reaching over and graciously taking the cup from her may suggest an arm and spirit too weak to do so. And right here, we have the further correspondence of Claudius's weakly bestowing, as it were, a liquid death on the Queen which balances her bestowing a liquid death on Ophelia. Obviously, his love for Gertrude seems limited.

Limited too has been the study of the play's famous Italianate side, which has never enjoyed much more than a general notice. Elizabethans abhorred Italianate villainy because the true villain, often a poisoner, escaped detection through consummate Machiavellian ruthlessness. As exemplar of such villainy in *Hamlet*, Claudius makes a highly curious case. A consummate villain isn't captured in a Mousetrap, caught off guard at prayer, and finally humiliated like an amateur and forced to drink his own dose of death.

Claudius's amateurishness is also underscored by the blundered outcome of the duel scene where Gertrude exposes the poisoned wine and Laertes the mechanical matter of the unbuttoned foil. But if Gertrude dies without realizing this latter treachery, the whole court witnesses the anomaly of a scratch killing their prince, the revelation of which damns Claudius. Apparently, the king believes the court will not connect him with the treachery: his own vanity blinds him to exposure because his plan focuses sharply on tricking Hamlet—and one other person. By saying that "even *his mother* shall uncharge the practice [in the match]/ *And call it accident*" (4.7.66–67. My italics.), Claudius acknowledges Gertrude's acute sense of knavery. Her craft, he believes, is of a very high order, though vanity makes him think that his scheme, which includes the poisoned cup, will outfox her. But it does no such thing. Unlike Hamlet who must be told he has been poisoned, Gertrude hardly drinks of the cup when she diagnoses accurately and cries, "The drink, the drink! I am poisoned" (5.2.263). She deserves our acknowledging that she has earned the imperial jointress role which

Claudius proclaims for her. She further deserves our nomination as the real Italianate poisoner in the play. Without knowledge of poisons, she could not diagnose with such accuracy. Poison is difficult to diagnose, and uninformed persons would not suspect it. Her knowledge makes her a likely poisoner, too, because women favor poison as a supposedly non-violent means of inducing death. Moreover, Gertrude is well versed in vegetation, for she names each of the plants comprising Ophelia's garland and, more important, also supplies their folk nomenclatures (4.7.142–43). Vestigially, Gertrude's vegetative acts of strewing flowers and being identified by Hamlet as a gardener whom he charges not to "spread the compost o'er the weeds / To make them ranker" (3.4.142–43)—rank weeds being those made stronger, more potent—are medieval touches. And Gertrude also has reason to desire a medieval-Italianate revenge on Claudius. Claudius's compliments and behavior toward Ophelia suggests a triangular royal rift. Before matronly Gertrude, he asks young Ophelia, "How do ye, pretty lady?" (4.5.40), an adjective never applied to the Queen, by Claudius or anyone else. Ophelia's reply is an ambiguous, threatening, Valentine Day's song, about a man who let in the maid that out a maid never departed more. This elicits his second notice of the "Pretty Ophelia—" (4.5.56), which actors usually pronounce with a patronizing, falling intonation. But a more accurate reading would linearize the stressed words to express the sibilant alarm that one person hisses to a second so as to warn the latter about saying any more that would inform a listening third. The Folio, moreover, gives the phrase an exclamation point.[16] This little drama suggests that Claudius's one-time warmth toward Ophelia has brought forth Gertrude's coolness and her Niobic jealousy. In the Ribner-Kittredge note on the passage, the song is identified as "the ancient custom by which the first girl seen by a man on the morning of St. Valentine's day was considered his Valentine or true-love," a custom Gertrude would likely know. The passage is neatly tied to Hamlet's associations of Polonius with Jephthah, judge of Israel (2.2.404, 411–12), who in exchange for victory over his foe promised the Lord to kill the first person to come through the door, and thus killed his only daughter. That Polonius sacrifices Ophelia to the king's gratification and appetite is revealed by a correspondence: the person who comes through the door preceding Ophelia's song is none other than Claudius (4.5.36.s.d.).

The king thus is designated as her Valentine love, which Gertrude would also know, which she would have hoped to end by her marriage, and which, by my argument, she would be avenging. Hamlet relentlessly, obliquely accuses Claudius of having dallied with Ophelia and scholars just as steadily have denied and ignored the charge. Hamlet reviles Ophelia as a common whore who should enter a nunnery, that is, a brothel, though most readers prefer reading the word literally, despite priests who refuse her the burial given one who dies in a state of grace. Critics who deny the brothel implication also ignore its equally important corollary, namely that "fish-monger" Polonius (whose one displayed court talent is prying into Hamlet's love-life and getting it wrong), treating Ophelia, as Rebecca West suggests, as his commodity, has sold his fish to Claudius for status and position.[17] Hamlet (who is "too much i'th' sun" [1.2.67], (i.e. burned by the royal beams) warns the counselor about Ophelia's conceiving from walking in the sun (2.2.186–87), i.e. being touched by the life-giving, impregnating beams of the corrupting, seducing king, in a passage that sustains the motif of Denmark's infecting rot. Seventy years ago a writer pointed to Claudius as Ophelia's seducer, but was condescendingly dismissed,[18] and I have found no one since who has paid much attention to Hamlet's charge. But the fact of her "maimed rites," which (Claudius's) "great Command" has apparently forced on them (5.1.214, 222), means the priests believe her to be a virtually certain suicide. Since the Church seldom wanted to humiliate important families and went out of its way to give them the benefit of any doubt, what reason was there to deny Ophelia such a benefit? Our refusal to believe this unsavory court arrangement may be overcome by recognizing the great dramatic power of Gertrude's reporting the event to the young lady's brother, as her stunned Valentine Claudius stands listening. We seem to be witnessing a queen in the intentional act of serving cold the dish of revenge, thus giving her actress a great occasion here, especially since the play is a drama of revenge. Just as Claudius sent Hamlet over the water to his death, Gertrude returns the favor by the important correspondence of, as it were, sending Ophelia over the water to hers. In short, Gertrude repays Claudius for the loss of her incestuously illicit love by making him suffer the loss of his illicit love—and the symmetry suggests tit for tat intention. It would be worth the price of the ticket to see the look she would give Claudius—to say nothing of the look he would give her. When pulled from the water, Ophelia would seem a likely suicide because a priest had to have been sent for, who, on administering extreme unction to a wet corpse, would have seen any tell-tale swelling as evidence of pregnancy, suggesting she had been distraught enough for suicide. Uncritical persons in the audience would have laughed at Hamlet's mocking Polonius about Ophelia, but those who were sensitive to subtle drama could have gotten the jokes and their bearing.

Contrasting Claudius's radiant friendliness are Gertrude's tart, veiling, mocking ironies: she hopes Ophelia's "good beauties be the happy cause / Of Hamlet's wildness. So shall I hope your virtues / Will bring him to his wonted way again, / To both your honours" (3.1.41–44). Later, a cold queen stands by and, without calling for help, let alone saving her, watches Ophelia drown. When the girl fails to surface, the queen simply returns to court to report her death.[19] Gertrude herself foreshadows this behavior. Told that she should speak to Ophelia because the latter is saying things that "may strew dangerous conjectures in ill-breeding minds"[20] (4.5.14–15), the queen speaks a crucial aside that is a perfect gem of foreshadowing:

> To my sick soul, as sin's true nature is,
> Each toy seems prologue to some great amiss.
> So full of artless jealousy is guilt,
> It spills itself in fearing to be spilt. (4.5. 17–20)

Apart from the Mousetrap's rhymes, this is the play's most extended verse passage, and it points up the important confession of her words. They are a prologue to the "great amiss" of Ophelia's drowning. The passage, moreover, ties the sickness of Gertrude's soul to the young lady outside. So great is the queen's guilt that she likens it to a brimming liquid that exceeds the capacity of its vessel. The sin and guilt that sicken Gertrude's soul suggest deadly thoughts.[21] And nestling there within the image is the cause of the power of such thoughts over the queen, "artless jealousy"—jealousy that she finds uncontrollable. Her overflowing jealousy is tied to and foreshadows the brook water that will overwhelm and drown Ophelia. The anomaly of Gertrude's cold, brookside detachment dissolves when we realize that Ophelia is a double rival, who has attracted the incestuous queen's husband and her son, Gertrude's violent feelings spilling themselves because of her incestuous attachment to each one. For Hamlet also prefers Ophelia's person to Gertrude's, as "mettle more attractive" (3.2.105). The attracting metal would appear to be the king's golden gifts, gifts and giver later stinging Gertrude to absolute inaction: her reporting Ophelia in the water as "one incapable of her own distress" (4.7.150) reveals, ironically, a Gertrude even more incapable of distress for the girl. Gertrude's refusal to help her explains the queen's brutal passivity as jealous behavior. It ensures the death of the pretty rival preferred by the queen's two incestuous loves.

Passively involved in Ophelia's death, the queen appears to be actively involved in the declining health of her husband. Indeed, her superior craft, prowess, and motive, along with Claudius's illness and debility, remind us of one other Italianate matter, the deadly female poisoner, a la Lucrezia Borgia, and prompt us to recognize that Gertrude"s avenging herself on Claudius with poison makes her the "plague"—the instrument of his death—that he senses she is becoming to him. In a revenge tragedy, a queen who poisons a faithless husband enlarges and strengthens this important theme. Moreover, Hamlet's accusation shocks Gertrude into the reply, "As kill a king!" (3.4.29), which dramatizes her momentary uncertainty as to which king Hamlet might have in mind, old Hamlet or Claudius. All the eyes watching Claudius at the Mousetrap missed seeing a Gertrude who might have wondered if she were one of its targets, which gives her actress a rich opportunity for voiceless facial drama. Expressing shock as a challenge of Hamlet's charge concludes her recovery, and it is a great, intense moment, revealing her extraordinary control subduing her sharp alarm: the king's counselor is listening behind the arras so as to report to the king. And we should remember that following the Mousetrap, she immediately sends for Hamlet. She does this, it would seem, not to protect the king, but, as my argument suggests, to test Hamlet's knowledge and protect herself if necessary by parrying his possible suspicions.

Gertrude shows the toll of so much treachery. She seems weary of her wretched life, because she drinks from a cup that she probably knows is poisoned. The Hell panel in Hieronymos Bosch's painting of "The Garden of Worldly Delights," c. 1505, offers illumination. It shows the fallen figure of a dead knight, in armor, a gold chalice just above one outstretched arm, and a pearl inches from the chalice rim. This event makes use of the orient pearl that is put into a victim's cup as a prize for drinking. Without the pearl the knight could be merely drunk. The pearl clarifies the death as a poisoning, and therefore would have contained the poison.[22] Painting and drama deal with the theme of combatants tricked into drinking wine poisoned by a hollowed-out pearl. As a skilled poisoner who would know various methods of introducing the deadly dose, Gertrude could hardly have been fooled into thinking Claudius's pearl harmless: such a trick has the look of an old chestnut. By drinking from the cup, she suggests she is weary of her life. She may even attempt to redeem herself by saving Hamlet from drinking. Whatever the case, Claudius's stolid response to both her peril and her cry (the cry exposing the poisonings afoot), displays how large their rift has grown: she would hardly expose the game unless she believes he wants her dead. And let us note that while many in the pit would have loved the poisoned cup, sword, and falling bodies, alert viewers would have enjoyed the masterly performance of Gertrude, the truly Italianate villain in the play. And they could have noticed something more as well.

William G. Wall has argued that Osric is Claudius's agent in the "duelling match".[23] Wall finds Osric curious because he appears so late in the play. This is half right. What Wall misses is that Osric exists only for three purposes: to entice Hamlet to duel; to be the vehicle which gets the greatest poisoning scene in dramatic literature underway by presenting the foils to the duelists so that only Laertes can "choose" the poisoned one; and then to supervise and judge the event once it begins. Osric is Claudius's choice, and we would be naive to believe he is an innocent, ignorant referee. If Gertrude is truly worthy of Claudius's implied praise, she should go him one better in villainous, Italianate cunning and use his own agent against him.

A bit of curious evidence suggests that Osric has a double role as Gertrude's agent in poisoning Claudius. Wall, and Dover Wilson before him, miss an important subtle matter. When Hamlet is cut and Claudius is killed, Osric says nothing. Yet when Gertrude falls, he interrupts the bout to command the assembly, "Look to the Queen there, ho!" (5.2.256). On this lone occasion, he lapses into understandable, ordinary English and voices alarm through his plain order. These examples of intensity, "the Dramatist's all-in-all,"[24] point to Osric's regarding Gertrude as personally important to him. Moreover, to Laertes' unusual admission, "I am justly killed with mine own treachery" (5.2.260), Osric shows no surprise. An innocent person would be horrified to learn he has been an unwitting agent in the deaths of his prince and Laertes. But Osric cares only for the fortunes of the queen, as he would by reason of her need to have out-promised Claudius. Self-interest explains the curious detail of Osric's solicitude for Gertrude. If she dies, he loses his pay-off.

Both the groundlings and wits would have been taken with Osric, the groundlings as a fop to despise and the wits as an amusing dupe to piece together, identify, and explain. For Osric is a type, the cony, and he has gull written all over him. But no evidence shows him as Claudius's actual poisoner, only an argument: he has the crucial thing, opportunity. Gertrude remains unconnected with an occasion to lace the king's food with small doses of poison. But Hamlet's poetic hint says that, thanks to his land and wealth, Osric has a place at the king's table (5.2.88–9). His being trusted opens up the ironic possibility that Gertrude has been having him slowly poison the king at the royal table. Such an addition to the story may get little appreciation nowadays, when story is dismissed as fare for the simple. But wits knew the greatness and the difficulty of devising a fine story, and they would have applauded the greatness here. The case we are considering fits the circumstances, explains them, reveals drama and poetry, and shows us the human dimensions of the characters. Failing to appreciate these things, avoiding them, or cutting them (as Garrick did in prettying up the fifth act),[25] produces shortsighted criticism. But a Globe audience would have expected subtle treatment of dangerous subjects and been well prepared to join Gertrude's skill and motive with Osric's opportunity through his access to the king's food. Osric has a smug, supercilious vulnerability unmatched in the Shakespeare canon; and the wits would have been fascinated by the implied story of a gulled agent unfolding before their rapt eyes. But Osric should not feel very crafty, since by my argument Gertrude would have access to him.

Poisoners' agents live short lives. Once they have served their purpose they are dispatched, thereby minimizing evidence, removing a dangerous tongue, and saving a final payment. We meet a dying Osric. In a play emphasizing poisoning, offensive breath is a symptom that deserves attention, but not on the weak and undramatic score of personal hygiene. Hamlet's noticing Osric's "more rawer breath" is an important detail[26] because "[o]ther signs and symptoms that should arouse suspicion of arsenic poisoning include garlic odor of the breath"[27]. Helping us to recognize this is its triple emphasis: there is raw breath, rawer breath, and more rawer breath. Such emphasis moves beyond foulness of smell to foulness of cause. A garlic-like smell suggests that Osric's rawer breath exposes his terminal condition. Also given unusual stress is Osric's refusal—for twelve lines—to wear his hat because, even though he agrees with Hamlet that objectively it is cold, he for some reason feels "very hot" (5.2.94–101; 106), so hot that he won't add to his discomfort by wearing even this minor article of dress. This seemingly trivial detail is important because other symptoms of chronic arsenic poisoning include "fever," "perspiration . . . and sweating," and "severe thirst."[28]

Chronic symptoms like these mean that Osric the water-fly (5.2.84)—so designated because living on water suggests his severe thirst and dependence on water—is dying, and that his death will follow the final curtain. Of course, we should consider the possibility that Claudius or Laertes is poisoning him, since each has a motive for wanting his mouth sealed. What tells, however, against each of them but in favor of Gertrude is that they are single-dose poisoners who choose the brute concoction that will overpower life quickly. Until the match ends, Osric is safe—from them. Once it ends, Osric is doomed. His dying by inches points to Gertrude, who prefers the tried and safe in the service of the subtle and patient. She is probably dosing him a little less than she is having him dose the king, so that he will last long enough to get the royal job done. Gertrude, easily able to watch someone slowly die (as her report of Ophelia's poignant, drawn-out drowning proves), earns her the black and grained spots tincting her soul. Afflicted with these moral equivalents of the deadly black spots bringing the Black Death to a plague victim, Gertrude is morally stricken. She is Claudius's plague and Osric's too, who for relief has resorted to the flattering unction that Hamlet warns her against (3.4.136). By dying after the play ends,[29] Osric will make old Hamlet's off-stage death symmetrical, as Mark Rose has described[30] the balanced elements in Hamlet: the group of deaths in the play proper will be flanked by an offstage death before the play opens and another after it ends. Osric's death will also confirm the count of that Irish wit, Stephen Dedalus, who claims that "Nine lives are taken off for his [Hamlet's] father's one",[31] which Gifford and Seidman assume—I believe erroneously—overstates the matter by one.[32] But Joyce, who was also a lover of symmetry, would have realized from his own research for the arsenic death of Bloom's father, that Osric shows classic symptoms of arsenic poisoning, and he brilliantly registers his insight to puzzle those who turn their thinking over to the author and expect to be told who is poisoning whom. Osric is one of the rank and gross weeds in Denmark's garden, adding strength to the theme of rottenness in the state of Denmark and to Shakespeare's theme of ill health. Regarding himself with self-satisfaction, Osric is only a sadly outwitted royal dupe. Gertrude is the clever one, for in true Italianate fashion, no visible trail extends from her victims to her.

Gertrude and Osric and Claudius and Laertes are the double pair of Italianate villains in the play, but Gertrude wins top honors, though each pair exemplifies anew Shakespeare's life-long interest in illusions and realities. She deepens the important subjects of illness and revenge in her cunning attempt to be revenged on Claudius. And just as that revenge must be heavily cloaked, so too must Claudius's involvement with Ophelia and the queen's jealous response at the brook, because the king's dalliance leads directly to his being poisoned. But in Shakespeare's hands Gertrude's villainy, once recognized, remains human and capable of being understood. Analysis of imagery, therefore (following Spurgeon), veiling devices, and the drama's details helps identify Gertrude as a poisoner. But for the masterly beauty of the case, nothing shows—besides the mystery and the detailed symptoms that Claudius and Osric suffer. Once we question Gertrude's brutal disregard of Ophelia's plight in the water and once Claudius admits that Gertrude is the craftier one, the incomplete narrative gives us just enough facts with which inferentially to flesh out and complete this part of the plot. Claudius's interest in Ophelia results in her apparent pregnancy that costs her a respectable burial; and signs of a growing rift between king and queen become clear concurrently with Claudius's displaying some of the classical symptoms of arsenic poisoning, from doses that Gertrude neither has nor wants the chance to deliver. Claudius as a crude and Gertrude as a subtle poisoner show Shakespeare's double genius, of appealing to both the pit and the gallery. Gertrude's counterplotting is a human act, and she deserves recognition for her subtle exercise of a cunning craft that makes her one of the main causes of the state rot, intensified by her mask of nearly absolute, innocent respectability. Gertrude's large, important role in the play has been minimized also because we have largely ignored the crucial details of the play, as probably did the pit; and because modern cinematic practices, pampering audiences by showing the poisoners shoes for two reels before panning up the body to the identifying face at the end of the third reel, teach us—wrongly—to expect that Shakespeare too must tell all by the fifth act and keep us from having to think. The matronly Gertrude who appealed to the galleries and the Italianate Gertrude who appealed to the pit are different characters.[33] Gertrude is a masterpiece of composition, and her few lines, of poetic brevity, establish her as one of the great tragic women in dramatic literature.

5

The Heart of Hamlet's Mystery

When Hamlet refers to "the heart of my mystery" (3.2.349–50), not every reader became a believer. T. S. Eliot thinks the mystery is only botched art that Shakespeare himself doesn't understand. Still, no one has ever answered Eliot's argument against *Hamlet*. The argument is that *Hamlet* is a failure as a work of art because Hamlet's expressed feelings have no apparent adequate cause:

Hamlet (the man) is dominated by an emotion which is inexpressible, because it is in excess of the facts as they appear. And the supposed identity of Hamlet with his author is genuine to this point: that Hamlet's bafflement at the absence of an objective equivalent to his feelings is a prolongation of the bafflement of his creator in the face of his artistic problem. Hamlet is up against the difficulty that his disgust is occasioned by his mother, but that his mother is not an adequate equivalent for it; his disgust envelops and exceeds her. It is thus a feeling which he cannot understand; he cannot objectify it, and it therefore remains to poison life and obstruct action. None of the possible actions can satisfy it; and nothing that Shakespeare can do with the plot can express Hamlet for him. And it must be noticed that the very nature of the donnee of the problem precludes objective equivalence. To have heightened the criminality of Gertrude would have been to provide the formula for a totally different emotion in Hamlet; it is just because her character is so negative and insignificant that she arouses in Hamlet the feeling which she is incapable of representing[1]

I agree with Eliot that there is no visible explanation for Hamlet's feelings about Gertrude. But I disagree when he argues that neither character nor author can understand or objectify these feelings. Eliot's argument, however, isn't met by saying, as C. S. Lewis did, that if Hamlet is an artistic failure, literature needs more such failures,[2] though the riposte was fatal to Eliot's case. Eliot's argument is met only by producing an objective equivalent for Hamlet's feelings about Gertrude.

Professor Avi Erlick comes closest, I believe, in his modifications of Freud. But Erlich and Freud are in the curious position of being able to read much of the phallic symbolism while lacking access to all of the triadic evidence. And, while the phallic evidence tells us a good deal, I believe that Freud was forced to deny expression to many of his insights because they could appear only hopelessly sensational without an objective literary method to establish them. Lacking access to all the triadically concealed evidence, Freud simply concludes that Hamlet incestuously loves his mother and hates his father. The play shows the opposite, that he hates his mother and loves his father.

If Hamlet incestuously loves his mother, as Freud argues, she would provide no objective equivalent for his feelings of disgust, since she does not cause them. Hamlet would have to be equally disgusted with himself. But he isn't; he is chiefly disgusted with her. The triad of his disgusts begins with Gertrude, includes Ophelia, and ends with himself. He represents the major difference here, which means he has most disgust for Gertrude, then for Ophelia, and least for himself. Literary critics and psychiatrists each think the other camp misreads the evidence. Triadic analysis may be able to help in this standoff.

Fortunately, as we have seen throughout these pages, mathematical evidence exists, and it is shaped by an objective form that disciplines all of the dramatic action. That form is the triadic structure, found everywhere, and equally at work within incestuous relationships. Shakespeare gives us a triad of periods in Hamlet's life—the period of childhood when he would have been available to Gertrude daily, the period of Wittenburg, when she could not have got at him, and the very limited period following Hamlet's return to Elsinore for his father's funeral. This triad tells a profound story. Childhood represented Gertrude's time of opportunity, Wittenburg her time of fast, and Hamlet's return her renewed chance.[3] "The seductive mother," as Erlich calls Gertrude,[4] has indeed been busy: to Polonius, Ophelia in 2.1 reports Hamlet's much disheveled and traumatized appearance when he comes to her chamber, his stockings at his ankles, doublet unbraced, hatless, pale as his shirt, knees knocking, "And with a look so piteous in purport / As if he had been loosed out of hell / To speak of horrors"[5] (2.1.82–84). If we were to describe a woman fresh from being raped, we could not improve on Ophelia's observations, physical and psychological. Such a description most likely vouches for Gertrude's ardor, ardor that exploded after having been pent up during Hamlet's school years away from her and carried forward from the only other time she could have fed on him, namely, his childhood. Moreover, his attempted rejection of Gertrude is one element in a triad of rejections, begun with Ophelia's rejection of Hamlet and ending with Horatio's bitter and unexplained attack on Osric for simply praising an absent Laertes in 5.2, which suggests strong jealousy and personal rejection.

Both Erlick and Rebecca West sense the sexual overtones of the episode in Ophelia's closet.[6] But both of them believe, as I do not, that Hamlet's relationship with the girl was carnal, and that the disarray in his clothing points to his having enjoyed her again. What happened during that visit is the story told by another triad, this one of the men that Gertrude physically struggles with. Hamlet tells us that "she would hang on old Hamlet" (1.2.143), and Claudius describes her grappling with Laertes (4.5.121, 126), making a third physical event necessary and fulfilled if Gertrude struggled with Hamlet just before he sees Ophelia in 2.1. An attack by Gertrude is the matter Hamlet would never breathe a word about. His shame would be far too intense to do so.

Without commanding the triadic structure, Freud and Erlich can not get at matters such as those under discussion. But also, Freud erred, I believe, in approaching the incestuous relationships (there are two others largely unaddressed in these pages) in classical fashion. That model gave him an adult Oedipus-Hamlet becoming the active adult lover and husband of Jocasta-Gertrude. Hamlet's time periods suggest, on the other hand, that Shakespeare is working with a pederastic model, which means Gertrude could have sexually abused Hamlet for perhaps ten to twelve years. Freud erred in giving the impression that their relationship was a mature one, and in suggesting, a bit vaguely, that Hamlet was the aggressor. The innocent child does not seduce its parent. One wonders if Freud saw the infantile character of Hamlet's relationship with Gertrude, but still regarded Hamlet as the aggressor.

Gertrude's sexual abuse of Hamlet as a child explains, as nothing else can, much of the rottenness in the state of Denmark. Her sexual abuse of her child can be offered as the objective correlative that Eliot sought and missed, perhaps because he allowed his energies to become so negative that he even endorsed the idea that Shakespeare was an immature artist whose substance was too vague for his expressive abilities to articulate. Editing *Criterion* might also have given him exaggerated ideas about his insights.

Triads offer us the intellectual proof of Gertrude's sexual hunger for her son. But the huge body of evidence comes from Shakespeare's emotional dramatization of that proof. Wasting no time whatsoever, Shakespeare begins the dramatizing with her first words to Hamlet. She tells him:

> Good Hamlet, cast thy nighted colour off,
> And let thine eye, look like a friend on Denmark.
> Do not forever with thy veiled lids
> Seek for thy noble father in the dust.

(1.2.68–71)

Hamlet alone is wearing mourning dress ("nighted colour"), and what these words tell him to do is to remove that clothing (but without telling him to change into some other attire) and in a naked state look upon her—for with Claudius, she too is Denmark—in a friendly way, instead of avoiding her eyes by averting his own. The passage operates as a stage direction, and suggests that Hamlet's shame and disgust keep him from meeting his mother's gaze. His shame and disgust likely arise from his having been an involuntary participant in her acts. Throughout this scene, the Mousetrap, and the fencing match, I believe he hardly looks at her.

The scene showing him meeting her eyes occurs in her chamber when he explodes with his long suppressed rage. Following the assault that Ophelia reports, he avoids even meeting hers. Though she apparently realizes that she fills him with disgust, she sends to have him visit her in her quarters (3.2.215), where ironically she may hope that intimate privacy will dissolve his aversion to her. But in the first court scene, all she could force from him was his courteous, formal, "I shall in all my best obey you, madam"[7] (1.2.120). Claudius's nervous pounce upon these words as "a loving and a fair reply" demonstrates his attempt to paper over a rift so strong that all present must feel it.

Hamlet is no sooner alone than his heart eases itself of its heavy burden. He almost prays for the dissolution of his "too, too solid flesh"—Dover Wilson reading "sullied" and Bowers "sallied" as a form of sullied unequally dividing the honors in this matter[8]—for Hamlet must indeed feel polluted and defiled. Such a feeling would explains his many thoughts about committing suicide. He would see Gertrude as part of the "unweeded garden that grows to seed," a garden where "things rank and gross in nature /Possess it merely" (1.2.135–37). It has become a commonplace that such feelings accurately reflect what sexually abused children feel about themselves and their victimizing parents, and they are unspeakable.

Perhaps Hamlet's most striking thought is expressed at the end of the soliloquy, when he says of Gertrude's remarriage,

> O, most wicked speed, to post
> With such dexterity to incestuous sheets!
> It is not, nor it cannot come to good.
> But break my heart, for I must hold my tongue.
>
> (1.2.156–59)

These words may carry a further shock in that even before posting to Claudius, she seems to have posted to such sheets with Hamlet, who then would know what he is talking about. He would have experienced Gertrude's dexterity in getting him between incestuous sheets, and watched her then going on to an incestuous marriage with her brother-in-law. Furthermore, as he implies to her, he easily believes her capable of having murdered her first husband, just as he seems also to believe she is up to something because of Claudius's need of doctoring. Because she has been capable of incestuous acts with her child, he apparently can easily believe her capable of murdering her husbands, it being clear that her love for them is suspect when she can commit incest with her child. These are matters he could never speak about and could only hold his tongue over. Hamlet can easily name its cause but must hold his tongue. Their author's accuracy in them is beyond praise.

Shakespeare masterfully dramatizes the complexities of this powerful human theme, For example, we learn that someone has objected to Hamlet's having "given private time" to Ophelia (1.3.92). This would not have been Claudius: kings don't object; they command. Women object, and the objection suggests that a jealous Gertrude has been secretly observing Hamlet and Ophelia. The queen's jealous prying would appear to be known to the girl, who calls Hamlet "Th' observ'd of all observers" (3.1.154), an expression that must aim at more than king and counselor (who are present when she makes the remark) because the queen will complete this triad. Moreover, by giving private time to Ophelia, Hamlet has less and less time to give to the queen exercising her voracious sexual appetite. When at court Polonius reports Hamlet's attention to Ophelia, he does it without revealing the source of his knowledge, apparently Gertrude:

> But what might you [Claudius] think
> When I had seen this hot love on the wing
> (As I perceiv'd it, I must tell you that,
> Before my daughter told me), what might you,
> Or your dear Majesty your queen here, think,
> If I had play'd the desk or table book.
>
> (2.2.131–36)

By mentioning the matter almost as an afterthought and thus minimizing the queen's interest in it, Polonius plays out his self-crediting story, whereas his earlier confrontation with Ophelia shows him acknowledging an unnamed informer. There, in private, he admits having been cautioned—and cautions accord with queens (1.3.91, 95).

Yet despite Gertrude's success in forcing him to avoid Ophelia, Hamlet manages within his constraints to inform Gertrude of his mature feeling for the queen. The Mousetrap gives him his opening. There, he pointedly refuses Gertrude's solicitation that he sit by her. He rejects her order and purposely offers himself to Ophelia: "Lady, shall I lie in your lap?" (3.2.104, 106). While this looks like a slap of his mother's face, the dramatic possibilities of this play endorse our sensing ambiguities in Hamlet's actions with Gertrude because in this instance his words must produce a jealous fury in her. His words depress Ophelia, who merrily pretends that Hamlet is merry, even as he notices how "merry" Gertrude pretends to be. Such subtleties and turns as we find here make this episode, among dozens of others, unactable, except on our mind's stage.

The triad, however, reveals two merriments to be false shows, masking depression. Gertrude's doubtless is the deepest of the three, because she would also be tormented by being forced to face Hamlet's rejection of her in apparent favor of a rival. But Ophelia is no rival, for, when she speaks about Hamlet's keenness, he mocks her pregnancy by saying, "It would cost you a groaning [a childbirth] to take off mine edge" (3.2.238). Is it doubtful that Hamlet speaks this so as to allow the queen to hear it?

Shakespeare's richest emotional dramatizing is saved for Hamlet's confrontation with his mother after the Mousetrap. Rose believes that "In Hamlet's eyes, his mother's essential failing is her moral blindness . . . ."[9] Hamlet suggests that it is her depravity. This rich drama begins when Hamlet approaches his mother's chamber, calling out "Mother, mother, mother!" (3.4.5) The brilliance of this line comes from the insight it displays. The victim of incest often "defends" against forthcoming and future attacks by public announcements of meetings with his or her victimizer and proclamations of their relationship, announcements and proclamations meant to induce restraint or fear in the aggressor. Gertrude prepares for the meeting in the opposite way, by sending off Polonius, thus securing intimate privacy for herself and her victim:

Withdraw; I hear him coming.

(3.4.6)

The statement suggests the image of her body being vacated by her counselor so as to be sexually available to her son. When she charges him with having "thy father much offended," Hamlet returns the charge: "Mother, you have my father much offended." The line rings with the unvoiced charge that she has also offended her son. Amongst other things, Hamlet may mean that she has broken her marriage vows with her husband's son. Her reply, "Come, come, you answer with an idle tongue," may remind him of cunningulus. Hamlet appears to understand her meaning, because he now consciously destroys the parallelism in their exchanges. He rejects her verb and substitutes, "Go, go, you question with a wicked tongue" (3.4.9–12).

More than mere formalism is at work in Hamlet's countercharge. It contains symmetrical accusations of murder and infidelities, involving old Hamlet and Claudius. To Hamlet's countercharge, she ambiguously questions, "Have you forgot me?" (3, 4, 14) (she obviously has forgot Hamlet) which demands that he see her as the third offended party because she seems to understand his insinuation that she is guilty of murder. In an ambiguously bitter line, Hamlet says, "You are the Queen, your husband's brother's wife, / And (would it were not so) you are my mother" (3.5.15–6). His parenthesis suggests he might desire a legal union with Gertrude. But child victims of sexual assault often seek protection through the talismanic reminders of their parental abusers' sacred relationships to them and to their other parent.

Hamlet's hatred is authentic (and so is his ambiguity), and it flashes forth as a residue from all of Gertrude's past sexual abuse of him. When he says he intends to wring her heart, "for so I shall / If it be made of penetrable stuff," she demands to know "What have I done that thou dar'st wag thy tongue / In noise so rude against me?" (3, 4, 36–41) and the demand seems meant to inflame his visual sense of some past erotic action on his part. To give us this glimpse into her possible strategy is to reveal a woman filled with a lust unblunted by the sight of the dead, bleeding body of her husband's counselor probably within five yards of her. She has no pity whatever for the death of Polonius,[10] no anguish for the incalculable pain she has caused, and is causing, Hamlet. Her lust seems to have deadened ordinary human feelings in her, and her insensitivity causes him to explode:

> Such an act
> That blurs the grace and blush of modesty;
> Calls virtue hypocrite, takes off the rose
> From the fair forehead of an innocent love,
> And sets a blister there; makes marriage vows
> As false as dicers' oaths. O, such a deed
> As from the body of contraction plucks
> The very soul, and sweet religion makes
> A rhapsody of words! Heaven's face doth glow
> O'er this solidity and compound mass,
> With heated visage, as against the doom—
> Is thought-sick at the act.

$$(3.4.40–51)$$

For all its force, the explosion contains no charge: Hamlet has not named the act. Twice he seems ready to name it, when he speaks of such an act and such a deed, only to specify qualities of the act and consequences of the deed, without clarifying the matter, once and for all, with a name.

In response, Gertrude asks a question, and it offers an important clue as to what Hamlet is driving at but veering from, and cannot bring himself to say:

> Ay me, what act
> That roars so loud and thunders in the index?
>
> (3.4.51–2)

She isn't sure whether Hamlet is talking about her and old Hamlet, her and Claudius, or her and him. Unable to name the unspeakable, he resorts to pictures. One is put in mind of the unthreatening indirection that figurines offer the modern child-victim:

> Look here upon this picture, and on this,
> The counterfeit presentment of two brothers,
> See what a grace was seated on this brow;
> Hyperion's curls; the front of Jove himself;
> An eye like Mars to threaten and command;
> A station like the herald Mercury
> New lighted on a heaven kissing hill;
> A combination and a form indeed
> Where every god did seem to set his seal
> To give the world assurance of a man.
> This was your husband. Look you now what follows
> Here is your husband, like a mildew'd ear
> Blasting his wholesome brother. Have you eyes?
> Could you on this fair mountain leave to feed,
> And batten on this moor? Ha! Have you eyes?
>
> (3.4.53–67)

And here, directed by his near rage, he dares to look straight in her eyes.

But here, fifteen lines later, Hamlet still has not answered Gertrude's question, "What act?" Eliot thinks this is failed art; I think it is supreme art, showing us Hamlet's scalding shame. But what the lines do is once more avoid the dreaded truth. To the qualities of the act and the consequences of the deed, he now symmetrically adds differences, the differences between Gertrude's sexual partners.

Hamlet seems to show pictures, miniatures perhaps, one in each hand, one worn by Gertrude and one by him, one of Claudius, one of old Hamlet, and he grows so strident about their differences, each one carefully named, that we gradually become aware that he is answering her question.

> You cannot call it love; for at your age
> The heyday in the blood is tame, it's humble,
> And waits upon the judgment; and what judgment
> Would step from this to this? Sense sure you have
> Else could you not have motion; but sure that sense
> Is apoplex'd; for madness would not err,
> Nor sense to ecstacy was ne'er so thrall'd
> But it reserv'd some quantity of choice
> To serve in such a difference. What devil was't
> That thus hath cozen'd you at hoodman-blind?
> Eyes without feeling, feeling without sight,
> Ears without hands or eyes, smelling sans all.
> Or but a sickly part of one true sense
> Could not so mope.
> O shame! where is thy blush? Rebellious hell,
> If thou canst mutine in a matron's bones,
> To flaming youth let virtue be as wax
> And melt in her own fire. Proclaim no shame
> When the compulsive ardour gives the charge,
> Since frost itself as actively doth burn,
> And reason panders will.
>
>   (3.4.68–88)

He holds before her two pictures, one left, one right, but what she sees are three persons, with Hamlet standing between the pictures, producing three powerful sets of differences, the triad of males on whom she has battened, two presented in paint, and the third in flesh and blood, flesh of her flesh and blood of her blood. When he goes on to speak of the "rank sweat of [her] enseamed bed" (3.4.92), we are made to consider the possibility that the child Hamlet has been brought to contribute to its enseamation. Eliot finds all this to be failed art; I find it unpraiseably great, superbly accurate art. I have quoted so much of the text here because it is so vitally important to our understanding that despite its length it represents the total failure of Hamlet, literature's greatest master of thought and word, to specify the act and name it. No matter how intricately or often he approaches the matter, an insurmountable wall stops him. He cannot pass through it, around it, or over it. His aversion to the subject is absolute. And the only matter I can think of that accords with such conditions is his having been his mother's victim, her repeated victim, and her forbidden victim. And what Shakespeare is doing then in so lengthy a passage spoken by so articulate a person is addressing the farthest reach of his character, the point at which there is no further possible expression of it. Shakespeare has carried his art to the point of its utter exhaustion, of itself and its vessel, thereby producing the farthest reach of his own art. It is the holy grail of the creative act. There remains more for his character to do, but no deeper or farther depth to probe. And there may be a concealed triad that deals with what she did to him, what he may have done to her, and what they may have done to each other. And exquisitely, Shakespeare shows Hamlet's limits, Gertrudes, and his own.

For me, this triad of pictures is the most stunningly brilliant in the play. The minor difference is that between the fair mountain and the moor. The major difference is that between those two eminences and the child she bore to the elder brother. The intensity with which Hamlet emphasizes the impossibility of any judgment stepping down from mountain to moor contains the logic accentuating the impossibility of such a judgment stepping down even farther, all the way down to a mere child, flesh of her own flesh. To make sense of her act, which sought and found sexual gratification of and domination over her victim, Hamlet resorts to an image drawn from a child's game. If Gertrude had been blindfolded and was playing with children, then she could have seized only a child. But she was not blindfolded, and she certainly wasn't playing the innocent game of a child.

Hamlet's indirectly accusing Gertrude of having gluttonously battened upon the brothers is probably a projection of his own experience of her having ravenously fed upon him. The passage helps clarify why Hamlet so loathes his mother's marriage to Claudius. As an incestuous union in a lesser degree, it seems to stimulate his jealousy while reminding him of her greater and ineffaceable sexual feeding upon himself.

Such sexual energy as we see imputed to the Danes in the play has been noted by R. N. Hodgkin in *A History of the Anglo-Saxons* where, in his chapter on the Vikings, he presents "points of contrast between the Norwegians and the Danes":

> [From] the history of the two peoples before the Viking age ... we may think that the traditions of the Scyldings, the Danish family which ruled at Leire in Zealand, were less darkened by tragedy and treachery than was the tale of the Ynglings, who established themselves as lords of Westfold at the head of the Oslo fiord. But the story of Rolf Kraki, the sixth century king who was the last of the Scyldings, was ended by a crime, and this story, like that of Hamlet, prince of Jutland, seems to have in it vestiges of genuine tradition. The English, in the epic of Beowulf, remembered the Scyldings for the magnificence of their hall Heorot, for the stateliness of their court and their lavish generosity; but in the Danish tradition they were handed down as a family doomed by its passions. Brother murders brother, father commits incest with daughter; and Rolf Kraki, the offspring of the incest, though raising Denmark to a short spell of empire over its neighbours, in the end by threefold treason—that of a sworn vassal to his lord, that of kin to kin, and that of the guest to his host—is brought to destruction; for the last scene in the hall of Leire, the hall in which Beowulf had fought with the monster Grendel, is the slaughter of Rolf Kraki and all his men save one in the dead of night by the hands of their guests.[11]

For Hamlet, Shakespeare appears to have had access, as I have argued in chapter 1, to Beowulf and to the Danish traditions that show this early ruling family to be doomed by its passions, for Shakespeare, too, produces a Danish story in which brother murders brother, a father commits incest with his daughter (Polonius with Ophelia, producing his hugger-mugger funeral, hers of maimed rites, and hints of pocky corpses), and rot eats at the land.

The rot is so open that Claudius even publicly boasts of his incestuous union with Gertrude by calling the assembled court's attention to "our sometime sister, now our

Queen" (1.2.8), just as Polonius boasts of his excessive feeling for Ophelia as "a daughter that *I love passing well*" (2.2.400. Italics mine). Not to be outdone, Laertes resorts to the extravagant gesture of jumping into his sister's grave and "covering" her, I believe, again. The act is ugly, not pure, but no stage direction exists to show the spectators being shocked by it.

Hamlet knows that Ophelia has been intimate with her father because Polonius proudly acknowledges his immoderate love of her to Hamlet, who tells her to have Polonius play the fool only in his own house, and within six lines urges her to marry a fool (3.1.132–33, 138), as she would need to do if his repeated talk to her about pregnancy is the hint vouched for by their marriage. Moreover, he is as brutally truthful about himself, as when he says, "I could accuse me of such things that it were better my mother had not borne me" (3.1.122–25), which seems to suggest his having a scaldingly shameful memory of pleasure with her, along with a hint at his having thought of murdering her, a fury that destroys the gentleness and sweetness of his nature.

The sum of all the matters Hamlet knows about Ophelia perhaps explains why he treats her as he does. And he may knowingly reject more than a pair of earrings from Ophelia (probably Claudius's gift to her), for she has one thing more to give him. Shakespeare arranges events so that two funerals, those of Polonius and Ophelia, straddle the gravedigger's mentioning burying pocky corpses. This arrangement suggests that both bodies were infected with a venereal disease. The sexton's noting that "we have many pocky corpses now-a-days that will scarce hold the laying in" (5.1.152–54) accurately describes Elizabethan venereal rampancy, and it can point immediately only to father and daughter, whose bodies the sexton has most recently handled. Polonius's having been infected with the pox, apparently in an advanced state, will explain why Claudius had him buried so quickly and secretly, and why the Church refused him a solemn mass. That he was accorded burial in sanctified ground, along with his daughter, with any rites at all, is probably due to Claudius's power of lay-investiture. The play's reality, as opposed to its illusion, casts a pall of deep melancholy upon it.

Hamlet's unexplained melancholy derives only in small part from the general rot affecting the entire state, and specifically from Gertrude's having sexually battened upon him to such a degree that his ambiguities even suggest his having found hateful pleasure in it, to his own unspeakable horror. Moreover, sexual performance would now seem to be beyond his ability, as it would appear, for the full triad, to be beyond

Osric and Yorick. Sexual bonding also would appear beyond him, since human sexuality seems to be but festering pollution in his eyes. What burns in his mind are his memories, which give him bad dreams, bitter thoughts, and a wretched life.

More rottenness, especially powerful, is triadically revealed during the fencing match. As Hamlet and Laertes duel, Shakespeare introduces a curious detail through Gertrude: "Here, Hamlet, take my napkin, rub thy brows." When he declines her offer, she then urges, "Come, let me wipe thy face" (5.2.274, 280). She means to wipe off his sweat. These two wipings, urged and attempted, are an almost completed triad whose symmetry probably involves brows, face, and groin. The other "sweat" that Gertrude would have wiped from her son would have been semenal, and this recalls for us Hamlet's nauseated reference to "the rank sweat of an enseamed bed" (3.4.92). Does Gertrude mean now to remind him of it to make him lose concentration, the match, and his life? Neither Hamlet nor life is for the squeamish, but one is grateful for a system able to present the unpresentable without becoming graphic.

If the heart of the mystery is Gertrude's incestuous abuse of her son, then Eliot is wrong in stating that neither author nor character knew what it was, leaving the play mere pretense and an artistic failure. I suggest that Eliot couldn't recognize what was under his very nose throughout the entire play. Not naming Hamlet's feeling is but another instance of Shakespeare's verisimilitude, and missing the point in a hundred instances all around him but a powerful demonstration of Eliot's inadequacies. Had Hamlet been able to confront the truth, he could have given his feeling a name, such as "abomination," the excellent catch-all term of the King James translators for various Biblical unspeakabilities. Gertrude also could have named what Hamlet avoids naming, but self-protectively pretends ignorance of Hamlet's charge.

With two who know what it is, symmetry requires that a third person must also know. And since between prince and queen we can recognize the minor difference, the well-born pair direct our search for the major difference that this person will supply. That difference is obviously between the high- and low-born. The low-born person who simply and humbly stands out is the sexton. He and Hamlet have a curious conversation at Ophelia's grave, and it is begun when Hamlet asks a question about himself:

HAM. How came he mad?
CLOWN. Very strangely they say.

HAM. How strangely?
CLOWN. Faith, e'en with loosing his wits.
HAM. Upon what ground?
CLOWN. Why, here in Denmark.

(5.1.144–49)

Three times the gravedigger, who is remarkably well-informed, evades answering Hamlet's question. And he isn't playing the buffoon, but rather the sensitive friend who knows a horrible secret and is protecting a friend who has already borne too much. He himself is nervous, very busy, and in my mind not able to return Hamlet's look.

The sexton has no trouble telling Hamlet he is digging a grave for "a gentlewoman" (5.1.21–2) whose death appears to have been a suicide. He also identifies the owner of a skull he pulls from the earth, and tells how long it has lain there. His having the answers to Hamlet's queries about Ophelia and Yorick means he should also know the answers to Hamlet's questions that he avoids answering. The triad Shakespeare is working with here concerns the sexton's knowledge of three persons. He wittily uses inoffensive humor as substitute answers to Hamlet's questions.

Why then does he avoid answering except out of respect, politeness, and an innate sense that the answer as to the cause of Hamlet's madness is shameful and offensive? Even repeating the common view that Hamlet grew mad when kept from Ophelia would be indelicate. But the greatest indelicacy would be to say that Hamlet grew mad out of his mother's sexually molesting him. This is what the sexton would have surmised if, long ago, he found the child in the graveyard, freshly parted from the queen, and seeking the one solace available to him, a visit to his father's grave. This surmise completes his triad of visits required once we find him at the graves of Ophelia and Yorick. Years ago, Yorick would have been with his friend, seen a shattered boy, instinctively resorted to his one therapeutic balm of laughter, and swooped down to swing him onto his shoulders. Then he would listen for laughter replacing numbed horror, but probably have heard only resisting sobs of agony which would have intensified his efforts until they broke through the boy's fighting against his countering efforts, and brought forth weak and then strong sounds of victorious; laughter that returned the boy to something like normalcy—until the next time. This effort completes the triad of Yorick's royal laughers—king, roaring bench, and royal prince. Each of these three elements is practiced hundreds of times, though this last one apparently even more often. No young prince would otherwise not need the therapy of the court jester repeated a thousand times (5.1.173). And such is Shakespeare's miracle that attaches itself to not a character so much as a skull.

This story is so touching, we catch our breath over it.[12] In the graveyard now, it is beautiful to see the sexton offer the old balm of humor for the sexually wounded psyche of his younger friend. The sexton's language, embarrassed and selfless, tender and human, seems meant to reassure Hamlet that his secret is safe with him. Moreover, the sexton returns tenderness for abuse, for Hamlet defensively protects his own awkward feelings by triadically calling the man fellow, knave, and ass (5.1.62, 72, 74). These terms are protective because, through them Hamlet pretends not to recognize his old friend. When earlier, Hamlet momentarily failed to recognize Horatio and Marcellus (1.2.160–65), he made a third and concluding such "failure" a symmetrical necessity.

The sexton understands Hamlet's edgy, embarrassed awkwardness and is not offended by his abuse but pretends ignorance, thereby completing the group of those who seem uninformed. Horatio kept him uninformed of the person being buried; the sexton keeps Horatio ignorant of his own friendship with the young prince. And Hamlet keeps Horatio unaware of his long-standing friendship with the sexton. Some measure of our love for Hamlet is traceable directly to his love for the sexton and Yorick and theirs for him. Hamlet's feelings for them has nothing to do with rank or status.

The psychological wounds carried by every person in this play make the tasks their actors face absolutely impossible to convey and extraordinarily difficult to know. Even Eliot didn't realize that Hamlet won't name the cause of his feelings because they are too shameful to address. He might have been dumbfounded to learn the play deals with a subject that has to remain unnamed, making it tough, brilliant, and mystifying. None of this means we should give up trying to mount the play. But it does mean that actors need to rethink the problems posed by the realities that come with attempts at representing the drama as the artistic success it is. We probably will never know how Hemmings, Condell, Burbage and friends carried out their work, and what Shakespeare was willing to tell them in answer to any of their questions; but all serious attempts need to continue because successes lie ahead, and really great things are in store for directors who think through various ways of lightly underscoring the play's objective triadic structure, and still more for the successful struggles of the actors who are blessed with the magnificent roles of Hamlet, Gertrude, and the sexton, to start with. Still more great things await those critics who avoid the blunder of assuming a master playwright has bungled the art required for a success in his obviously most carefully devised play. Niels Bohr's dictum will help us much more than T. S. Eliot's negative, baffled inertia.

6

"He Takes Her by the Palm": Heresy and Inquisition in *Othello*

The problem with Coleridge's beguiling phrase "motiveless malignity" really explaining Iago's hatred is simply that it enjoys no relation to reality as we know it. Hatreds are reactive and have motives, and by placing Brabantio's home squarely before us the instant the play begins, means, his likely connecting Brabantio with the cause of Iago's feelings. The economy is obvious as is the pleasure the solution brings everyone who enjoys a fine surprise in finding that the answer was before them from the start. Why Iago wants to antagonize the senator is one of the great cruces we are now to address.[1]

In *Othello*, Shakespeare once more treats, as he did in *The Merchant of Venice*, strong family themes concerning conversos, but this time studied not under the lens of comedy but under the enormous pressure supplied by the Inquisition and its fiery stake, the whole once again given narrative extension by the powerful tool of symmetry. In *Othello*, relatives feed victims to the Inquisition, Moor and Jew alike, by turning them in to the state as relapsed suspects, the inquisitional context adding intense drama and pathos to the tragedy.[2] Lodovico and Gratiano set us moving forward toward our goal.[3] Who they are and what they represent are mysteries. With Cyprus hardly secure, they no sooner arrive with a letter of recall for Othello than he plans to flee to Mauritania.

In greeting Othello, Lodovico betrays an ominous hint of his institution: "God save you, worthy General!"[4] shows him as a holy person interested in the salvation of Othello's soul. Moreover, on an island not yet militarily secure, Lodovico and Gratiano are unarmed, the clown being the only other member of this group of weaponless males. Their being unarmed explains why the former pair only fearfully listens without aiding Cassio, when he cries for help. Montano must later give Gratiano Othello's sword so that he can impose house-arrest on the Moor (5.2.239–41). Juan de Llorente quotes the decrees of the assembly at Toledo in 1498 which identify officers who greet in the name of God and are weaponless:" each tribunal [of the Inquisition] should be composed of the two inquisitors, one a civilian, the other a theologian. They are prohibited from inflicting imprisonment or torture . . . Secondly . . . the inquisitors should not allow their dependents to carry any defensive arms, except where their office obliges them to do so."[5] Lodovico and Gratiano appear to be fangless officers of the Inquisition.

Lodovico's letter offers further evidences that he is an officer of the Inquisition. Othello reads aloud its threat, "This fail you not to do, as you will—" (4.1.219). An inquisitor was empowered by the royal mandate issued for "the towns where the inquisitor would pass to perform his office, commanding them, on the pain of the most severe penalties, to arrest all the persons whom he should mark as heretics, or suspect of heresy, and to execute the judgments passed upon them" (Llorente, 24). Othello stops reading in the middle of a threatened and severe penalty.

Excellent evidence that Lodovico is an officer of the tribunal appears when he turns Iago over to Cassio: "To you Lord Governor, Remains the censure of this hellish villain. The time, the place, the torture—O, enforce it!" (5.2.367–369). This passage dramatizes Lodovico's zealous dedication and non-involvement in the execution of the sentence. The Church took scrupulous pains to disassociate itself from the carrying out of sentences against its victims: acts done by the state were not the responsibility of the Church. This famous strategy was the "relajacion al brazo secular." Llorente, himself a former member of the body, argues that the Inquisition's goal was the victim's wealth (xvii–xxvii). Whatever the truth, the state had effective rules for confiscation, which was sudden and total. Othello dramatizes this aspect of inquisitorial injustice, too, for Lodovico settles the Moor's estate in one summary sentence: "Gratiano, keep the house, And seize upon the fortunes of the Moor, For they succeed on you" (5.2.365–67). Whether the Moor has a living relative is immaterial to these officers. Othello's goods pass on to an officer of the Inquisition, and the episode ably illustrates Llorente's belief that the goal of the Inquisition was no more noble than confiscating its victims' wealth.

That the letter speaks of an inquisition of Othello is suggested by his exclaiming "Fire and brimstone!" (4.1.224), the phrase imaging the contents that he reads. The letter "command[s] him home, Deputing Cassio in his government" (4.1.225–26). The letter probably commands another and more serious matter. When a pair of officers of the Inquisition arrived in town, "The commander of the town [such as Othello] presented himself before the delegate [such as Lodovico], and took an oath to put in force all the laws against heretics" (Llorente, 24). The spectacular irony in this case is that the letter most likely makes Othello Lodovico's deputized intermediary against himself and his own wife.

Othello must know the real meaning of being recalled. He has already endured Brabantio's unresolved charge of witchcraft, and he now plans to disobey the command and flee, for Iago tells Roderigo, "He goes to Mauritania and takes away with him the fair Desdemona" (4.2.222–23). By returning to the land of the Moors, he would escape, as did thousands of Moors, the reach of a tribunal. Among some of its luckier victims, the Inquisition inspired two responses, flight or suicide: Othello illustrates both.

An occasional victim escaped by killing his persecutors. One such famous incident occurred in Aragon when an attempt was made to foil an inquisition by assassinating a couple of inquisitors. But the assassination failed because the inquisitor, Peter Arbues, "wore a coat of mail under his vest" (Llorente, 44). Shakespeare appears to use this story when Roderigo's thrust fails to kill Cassio because it strikes a "coat [that] is better than thou [Roderigo] knowst" (5.2.25). Cassio is referring to a shirt of mail which saves his life. Shakespeare alters the story in various ways, but the main dramatic features, an assassination foiled by a person wearing hidden armor, match the historical account.

From Cinthio, Shakespeare took the idea of the handkerchief; for its magic and witchcraft, he turned to a few of the great fears of the Inquisition. Othello is an absolute believer in the power of his handkerchief to render Desdemona faithful. And the Inquisition not only explains the dangers of the handkerchief's occult properties, but also the detail of its strawberry spots because for one of its tortures it made use of a piece of cloth offering us an analogue for the design. A victim, strapped to the escalero and tilted so that the feet are higher than the head, suffers "a violent and painful respiration . . . with intolerable pains in the sides, the arms, and legs. . . ." Then, when the mouth "is in the most unfavourable position for respiration . . . a piece of fine wet linen is introduced into the throat . . . and water . . . is poured so slowly, that it requires an hour to consume a pint, although it descends without intermission. In this state the patient finds it impossible to breathe, as the water enters the nostrils at the same time, and the rupture of a blood vessel in the lungs is often the result" (Llorente, 122–23). A poet's imagination could easily convert a blood-spotted piece of fine linen—for so the procedure would cause the cloth to appear-into a strawberry-spotted handkerchief. The Inquisition also helps to explain not just the armor and the strawberry design but Othello's famous reference to the fabulous "men whose heads Do grow beneath their shoulders" (1.3.144–45), a passage which makes some readers think Othello is naïve. But beneath the veil of the fabulous, Shakespeare may be concealing a historically accurate figure.

Where in his travels could Othello have seen such figures? One answer is Spain. At an auto-da-fe, some victims advancing to the stake wore a sanbenito, or tunic, on which was painted a large human head surmounting flames, causing the wearers to look like persons with their heads growing beneath their shoulders. Llorente (70–71) describes the garment, and Chaim Potok prints a drawing that shows the tunic as worn by victims at an actual auto-da-fe. So large are the painted heads that we may easily miss seeing some victims' real heads.[6] When that occurs, we are looking at figures whose heads indeed appear to be growing beneath their shoulders. Othello's fabulous account equivocates, and by telling some but not all of the truth may avoid a tribunal. He has witnessed or heard of autos-da-fe, and either one would account for his baptism. It is likely that Othello suddenly got religion, got baptized, and got out of Spain. Venice would then have beckoned him; it had a long history of importing condottiere, including Carmagnola on whom Othello is partly modeled.[7] Baptism would have allowed Othello to avoid a fiery stake and depart for safer shores. But baptism used as a passport to the Venices and Mauritanias of the world raised suspicions and often produced pursuit, like Lodovico's of Othello.

Since pursuit implies suspicion of heresy, Othello may be thought to have committed such an act. The first article of Manrique, the fifth Inquisitor-general, 1524–1539, concerns the heresy of those who "mingled holy things with profane objects, and worshipped in the creature that which belongs only to the creator" (Llorente, 131). Othello utters such injudicious words when he joins Desdemona in Cyprus. His cry, "O my soul's joy!" omits God. And he adds, "If it were now to die, 'Twere now to be most happy; for I fear My soul hath her content so absolute That not another comfort like to this Succeeds in unknown fate" (2.1.182, 187–91). His worshipping in her that which belongs only to his creator, his substituting her for the beatific vision as his soul's supreme happiness, and his calling the next life an unknown fate make this a damning utterance. Worse yet, his officer and the entire greeting party hear his avowal. I am suggesting that an informer—the next governor perhaps?—reports him to a tribunal that strips Othello of his command and causes him to plan to flee from Cyprus.

Another act of heresy occurs when characters read palms and tell one another's fortunes. When Othello tells Desdemona, "Give me your hand" and finds it "moist my lady," she says that "It yet hath felt no age nor known no sorrow", the irony is thunderous because her reader sees her future quite differently: "This [line?] argues fruitfulness and liberal heart"—fecundity and avidity that he will kill her for, when his distortions decide she has cuckolded him with Cassio—"Hot, hot, and moist. This hand of yours requires a sequester from liberty, fasting and prayer, Much castigation, exercise devout; For here's a young and sweating devil here [her other hand, also moist?] That commonly rebels. 'Tis a good hand, A frank one" (3.4.31–9). He studies her palm as a palm-reader might. And for her utterly silent part, she seems mesmerized by the reading. The tone of his words pulse with chilling and murderous energies, until he ends the reading favorably in ordinary fortune-telling fashion. By "reading" Desdemona's hand, Othello rubs against the occult, imperiling himself and her.

Shakespeare gives us a triad of women believers in occult arts that draw the veil from the future, Othello's mother being the second. Othello tells us that the strawberry-spotted handkerchief "Did an Egyptian [the third] to my mother give. She was a charmer, and could almost read The thoughts of people. She told her, while she kept it, 'Twould make her amiable and subdue my father Entirely to her love; but if she lost it Or made a gift of it, my father's eye Should hold her loathly, and his spirits should hunt After new fancies" (3.4.50–58). When the reading evinced the mother's concerns about her husband, the gypsy gave her a sybil-woven "magic" handkerchief to cure the husband's wanderlusting eye.

Iago reports a third reading when Cassio takes Desdemona by the palm (2.1.166) as she awaits news of Othello's safe arrival on Cyprus. In this simple act, we hear a woman crying out to hear of Othello's fate at sea, as Cassio takes her hand as if for an on-the-spot reading that will pronounce her wife or widow. To calm her nerves, she asks Iago how he would praise various ladies. His reply takes up fifty lines, each one confronting us with naming its real purpose. Individually and together, what do they dramatize? His amusing stories, which are tailored to her particular interests (and thus show him very knowledgeable of them and her) dramatize one of her favorite superstitions, her predilection for hearing fortunes told, of character-determining fate. Probably, therefore, when Othello took her by the palm, he believed she would be sure to hear his ominous reading as a warning against illicit passion.

Desdemona's favorite form of fortune-telling is Inquisitionally-proscribed chiromancy, the reading of palms. In its second article, the Inquisition declared that heresy was suspected "If the offenders only made use of natural and simple means of discovering the future, such as counting the lines in the palm of the hand" (Llorente, 21). Shakespeare shows Desdemona to be deeply affected by her sense of fate and fortune, and he wastes no time in dramatizing this: she no sooner appears on stage than she speaks of her own fated adversity as "storms of fortune." In another five lines, she talks of her "soul and fortune" (1.3.249, 254). She later refers to Cassio's "fortunes" (3.4.89), and of what has "fall'n between him and my lord" (4.1.215). His ill fortune powerfully, easily appeals to her desire to help him. She mentions "portents." She dreads what "my fear interprets" (5.2.45, 73). She feels that being called whore is "my wretched fortune (4.2.128). And on learning her handkerchief contains sibyl-woven magic, she becomes frightened and expresses shock, in hushed, doom-stricken tones—"Is't possible?" and "I'faith? Is't true?" (3.4.63, 70). Family and friends must know her as one obsessed with the future and quickly moved to forbidden, chiromantic means of discovering it. Cassio had only to tell her his problems to win her help—and doom—with Othello.

Brabantio would know of her hunger for fortune-telling, and therefore avoid pressing his charge of sorcery too hard for fear an inquiry would discover her superstitions. And it is precisely her susceptibility to matters occult that supplies him with his specific charges against the Moor, charges of spells and witchcraft, which Othello dangerously sharpens to drugs, charms, conjuration, and mighty magic (1.3.61, 64, 91–2), thus bringing the matter potentially into the Inquisition's purview. Othello's folly here obviously results from his relying on the belief that Venice needs him so much against the Turk at this very moment that the state wouldn't dare pursue Brabantio's hints for fear of a military defeat. But Othello, Brabantio, and Desdemona walk a very thin line here, and they guess wrong, as the final outcome tragically shows.

For her part, Desdemona seems to have made a similar bet that her father can't destroy her marriage because of the state's mounting military necessities. This game of psychological chess produces pure rushes of adrenalin in each of the three principals because they are dancing so close to the fiery stake. Othello gambles the most, followed by Desdemona, and trailed by Brabantio. Desdemona plainly lives vicariously through Othello's calculated moves, her very abode being the Sagittary[8] the sign of the archer warrior engaging an enemy. This sign probably also attracted her because it represents the zodiacal house of Sagittarius, which imprints its characteristics upon the occupiers of the house. Her being a "fair warrior" (2.1.179) suggests personal occupancy, which would be hers by having been born under the sign of the archer. Desdemona's character and what she believes influenced it help us to see why she is so drawn to Othello, who sees just the half of it. Besides accepting the archer's reign over the bed of her birth, she would naturally solicit its influence over the bed of her marriage, just as she has accepted it as a triumphant force and energy in her life.

We feel that energy as she proclaims to the court, "That I did love the Moor to live with him, My downright violence, and storm of fortunes, May trumpet to the world" (1.3.248–50). (Does her "storm of fortunes" hint that she has defied predictions of estrangement, a bad marriage, and death from a tall dark stranger?) And when Othello honors her spirit as "my fair warrior," the astonishing irony of this sovereign sign is that she sees it as a good omen, whereas Shakespeare shows it to be, from her point of view, the doom of death. Its power over the bed of her birth apparently doomed her mother. Brabantio seems obviously to have been unable to tell his daughter that her birth brought on her mother's death. The sign of the archer indeed brings death, dooming mother, child, and Othello. And we should note that autos-da-fe used archers to arrest attempts at martyrdom (Llorente, 270) The mother's death in childbirth means that the difficult delivery was likely the result of the birth of twins, in which one child died.

The Sagittary symbolizes Desdemona's second superstition, astrology, and it joins with her third, the dread she has of the magic in her handkerchief. Of the three, she favors chiromancy and astrology, but fears the magical third, perhaps from thinking that in breaking so great a spell she would doom herself by offending the infernal powers. The Inquisition, of course, inveighed against all three, but, according to Manrique's second article of denunciation, required Christians to declare if they "had studied judicial astrology to discover the future, by observing the conjunction of the stars at the births of persons" (Llorente, 132), as Desdemona had reason to do.

Since Desdemona's superstitions identify her as a person the Inquisition would carefully watch, Lodovico's orders would likely not only affect her but require Othello to judge her as a heretic and turn her over to a tribunal. Her greeting to Lodovico, "And what's the news, good cousin Lodovico?" betrays a slight tremor of apprehension that the state means to try her. As she dies, she claims that she, not Othello, is responsible for her death (5.2.124). There is no reason to doubt her claim, and no reason to suppose she has not taken poison, secreted when she began fearing a tribunal. Indeed, she answers Emilia's asking how she does, with "Faith, half asleep" (4.2.92). Her words would make stones weep and are among the most poignant in the play, allowing us to believe she has taken poison that is now ending her life. Emilia responds to Othello's coercive reminder that she heard Desdemona claim responsibility for her death by saying, "She said so. I must report a truth" (5.2.128), leaving us to see that there is more to her death than is apparent. Her end comes in three stages, from the poison she appears to have taken, enhanced by the botched doubled smothering he attempts, until finally the combination appear to ease her off, independent of his efforts. It is made all the more ghastly by Othello's characterizing it as "yet merciful' because he won't let her "linger in thy pain" (5.2.86–7).

Desdemona's being the daughter of a senator and the wife of a condottiere makes it astonishing that she is hunted down, and through the agency of her own husband, to whom the state is strongly beholden. Aretino's letters show us that many Venetian ladies amused themselves by "magic . . . mind-reading, prophesying, and fortune-telling"[9] (Arentino, 168, 325), but unlike Desdemona—and Othello—they suffered nothing at the hands of the state. The great question then is why the state fastens upon the principals in Othello? Part of the answer concerns Desdemona's being the wife of a disaffected Moor, whose intended escape marks him as such. The rest of the answer involves her being Brabantio's daughter and his being suspect as a Jew with a Moorish friend the state is employing.

With a great military crisis threatening Venice, the Duke lets Brabantio sleep. Unnotified, Brabantio is surprised by the news that the Duke is in council until an officer confirms it: "'Tis true, most worthy signior. The Duke's in council, and your noble self I am sure is sent for." At such an awkward moment, the officer is diplomatic, but offers no apology for the court's neglect. Except for the string of ominous naval reports, Brabantio would have slept the night away. His stunned reply, "How? The Duke in council? In this time of the night?" (1.2.91–4), shows his ignorance of even the crisis. At the war council at court, when the first senator announces, "Here comes Brabantio and the valiant Moor," the Duke ignores the senator for the captain: "Valiant Othello, we must straight employ you Against the general enemy Ottoman. [To Brabantio] I did not see you. Welcome, gentle signior We lack'd your counsel and your help tonight" (1.3.47–51). If the Duke didn't see him, he certainly heard him announced, so that he follows his face-saving lie with a clear attempt to make Brabantio the truant from his job by choosing to be absent. But Brabantio sees through the attempt and shrewdly says, "So did I [lack] yours," which parries the lie, causing the council to ask the curious question if Desdemona is "Dead?" which he doesn't seem to think odd, saying only, "Ay, to me!" The question is strange because a prominent, healthy young lady would die only if suspect and falling foul of the Inquisition. Upon this exchange a council of war is turned over to settling a family marital dispute, giving us a triad of the major state war, the father-daughter war, and the daughter's reciprocation. We watch excitedly as the latter pair move toward a total rupture, Desdemona saying, "I am hitherto your daughter" and Brabantio countering "God b' wi ye! I have done" (1.3.185, 189), each trying to leave the final break to the other. This is a double disowning and its triad is complete when we produce a third, as we shall shortly. The death question that immediately came to the common mind of the council, that Desdemona might be dead, therefore, must express their fear about a lady known to them to be vulnerable. And what would make her vulnerable would be her being a Jew, which of course would make Brabantio one as well. He, of course, may hope that his publicly disowning Desdemona will protect him from the suspicion of disaffection.

It is a desperate card that he plays here because all he has experienced so far are state humiliations. He must rise because his servants dare not challenge the bawlers under his window. There at home he asks Roderigo not who but "What are you?", as if certain whats have a right to taunt a senator. His warning to Iago, "This [scurrilous behaviour] thou shalt answer," is bluster, never made good. His order, "Call up all my people!" produces not one soul. His command, "Raise all my kindred!" gathers no one behind him. His charge, "Call up my brother," produces no Gratiano. No ally follows him to court. And even though "At every house I'll call I may command at most" (1.1.79–80), both in his encounter with Othello and then with the council, Brabantio leads only a "party" of a servant or two in his own pay. He has no political support whatever. The inference is impossible to ignore: everyone sees him as imperiled, and all are trying to separate themselves from a Jew fallen in favor.

At court, his luck remains unchanged. He declares that "The Duke himself Or any of my brothers of the state, Cannot but feel this wrong as 'twere their own" (1.2.95–7). But even this proves incorrect in the empathetic, supportive sense in which he means it, since Duke nor brothers do nothing for a colleague with a "voice potential— As double as the Duke's" (1.2.13–4). He must even endure Iago's presence as a mere ancient in a council of war, which speaks to Iago's curious standing despite his rank In that council, when the Duke promises that Brabantio can proceed in the bloody letter of the law against Desdemona's beguiler, this potent peer replies "Humbly I thank your grace" to the man who will break his promise. Contarini, who was one of Shakespeare's sources, speaks of the majesty of [the Venetian] Senate, "Address to the Reader." Does this unrelieved stream of abuse, slights, lies, disdain, insult, and humiliation suggest that Brabantio's fortunes plummet the moment his daughter makes a dangerous marriage? There is nothing else to tie the disfavor to. And the treatment of both of them is well explained if they are conversos, a group that Shakespeare has dealt with before in *The Merchant of Venice*. Salo Wittmayer Baron documents many cases of conversos holding high public office (IX. 285; XIII, 22, 30–1, 69, 72), among them Torquemada and Diego Deza, the first Inquisitors-general, who each had a Jewish ancestor (Baron, XIII, 43, 87). In Brabantio, Shakespeare offers us the dramatic spectacle of an apparently Jewish senator who, before our eyes, is insulted, demeaned, marginalized, and excluded outside his house, in the streets, and at court, before and by the Duke and others.[10] And scholars have said not a word! Brabantio has taken unsuccessful pains to avoid all of this trouble, beginning with Othello's visits to his home, when he carefully questioned him on "the story of my life From year to year . . . even from my boyish days To th'very moment that he bade me tell it" (1.3.29–133). An interrogation so precise and comprehensive seems meant to uncover whatever skeletons might make Othello personally dangerous to know. This questioning parallels a more rigorous interrogation, well known throughout Shakespeare's world:

Another custom of the Inquisition was to examine the prisoner on his genealogy and parentage, in order to discover by the registers of the tribunal if any of his family had been punished for heresy, supposing that he might have inherited the erroneous doctrines of his ancestor. (Llorente, 63)

Torquemada originated this type of inquiry in 1561. Valdes, the eighth Inquisitorgeneral revised the ordinances for his code of eighty-one articles. The fourteenth requires the recorder to "place each name [of every person known by the accused] at the beginning of a line, because this practice is useful in consulting registers, to discover if the accused is not descended from Jews, Moors, heretics, or other individuals punished by the holy office" (Llorente, 231). This law, establishing guilt by blood and association, probably explains why Othello is so reluctant to name his royal ancestors. The likelihood is that they include a person who would cause him great trouble with the Inquisition. The fifteenth ordinance introduced a refinement on this law:

When the preceding ceremony has passed, the accused shall be required to give an abridged *history of his life*, mentioning those *towns* [where] he made a considerable stay, the *motives* of his sojourn, the *persons* he associated with, the *friends* he acquired, his *studies*, the *masters* he studied under, the period when he began them, *if he had been out of Spain*, at what time and *with whom* he had quitted the country, and *how long he had been absent*. (Llorente, 231, my italics.)

By telling the court of Brabantio's digging into his history, Othello may be hinting that he is without blemish by virtue of having passed so careful a parallel examination. In short, he may have known exactly what Brabantio was doing and why he was doing it. But the Senator appears to have thought he was taking no chances in trying to identify any closeted skeletons in Othello's family, which could easily return to haunt a Jew-turned Christian friend. Clearly, Othello seems to have told him about his mother, who from a gypsy charmer got a doom-drenched handkerchief, since Brabantio's charges of magic and witchcraft strongly suggest he knows the story. Why Othello felt he could trust such dangerous matters with Brabantio may stem from his friend's apparent position: he is addressed as "reverend signor" [OED sense 2] (1.1.93) and "your reverence," (1.1.131) and persons deemed worthy of "respectful form[s] of address, now only used by the lower classes" are clergyman, OED, sense 6, which suggests Brabantio is a rabbi who has won Othello's trust. Brabantio himself, referring to Desdemona, recalls her shunning "The wealthy curled darlings of our nation" (1.2.68), a line rich with a triad of Jewish touches, "our nation" being the strongest and indicating here a reference to Jews collectively as it does when Shylock says of Antonio, "He hates our sacred nation."

Othello is not so naive as not to see that his old friend is friend no longer: Moors and Jews were allied, looking out upon the like oppressions of a common enemy from the same vantage point of a ghetto that confined both groups (Baron, X, 140; IX, 256). But he seems to hope that a Venetian senator's personal inquisition will protect a Moor from a tribunal's scrutiny. Brabantio's inquiry is treacherously prudent; he has learned caution. But it is a piquant irony that the form of the interrogation is itself modelled so closely on that of the Inquisition. It is chilling psychological drama to see those who suffer most from the miasma of the time absorbing it as a potent venom against fellow sufferers. Othello's one friend in the council is the apparent converso Brabantio who, to save his daughter and himself, turns on the Moor. Anyone familiar with the history of the Inquisition, or any other state persecution, knows how perfectly realistic this scene is.

Brabantio, of course, is simply protecting himself and Desdemona. No motive is given for his turning upon Othello, but this is the one that makes the most powerful sense. A converso was constantly watched for signs of a relapse, and relapse invited the terrors of the state, which Brabantio would know very well. He would also know that the most vulnerable marriage was one between two conversos, a Jew-turned-Christian and a Moor. Trouble for either one automatically meant trouble for the other. Desdemona's being of Christian faith but Jewish blood would offer her no protection should the Inquisition investigate Othello. Her alliance with him would make her only more suspect, since the tribunal suspected all conversos of relapsing into their former faiths. Brabantio seems to be trying to protect her by proudly proclaiming that she shunned her own kind (1.2.67–8), a striking argument showing him clearly hinting at her wealthy, curled Jewish suitors whom his equally Jewish daughter has avoided. The exquisite psychology here shows him trumpeting the amusing, implied notes that in his family Christians are preferred and Jews avoided, though instantly ready to disown her to save himself. Brabantio obviously either misread her affections or is inventing them. Nor did he suspect that a Moor had a chance with her.

The Inquisition knew better and enumerated, as Baron points out, "some typical actions considered indicative of Judaizers, such as "the changing of attire or of table and bed linen in honour of the Sabbath" (Baron, XIII, 36). Thus, when Desdemona has Emilia lay out bed linen and asks to be unpinned (4, 3.20), we can see Shakespeare not merely contextualizing the Inquisition even in such ordinary matters as changing bed sheets and dress, but dramatizing Desdemona's reversion to her Jewish faith, and completing the triad of her faiths—Jew, Christian, Jew. Presumably, the gown Emilia unpins is a garment superior to the one she wore aboard ship. She appears, therefore, to be honoring the Sabbath by wearing her best attire, as Rabbi Michael Rascoe has suggested to me. Linen and clothing, then, bear witness not only to Desdemona's return to the faith of her birth, but to her being a *converso* whose conversion was coerced and understandably insincere. Hers is a spirit that bent without breaking, and Venice has reason, according to its own twisted values, to be suspicious of her.

The predominant mood of Othello is suspicion. And joining jealousy in creating the shroud of suspicion mantling the play is the terror of the Inquisition. In such a climate, circumspection means life and indiscreet speech death (Baron, IX, 267). How wise is it for a Brabantio to open his house to a great Moorish *condottiere*, and trust his own inquisition into the man's life? And because the convert "certainly could not reveal his innermost thoughts without gravely jeopardizing himself and his family" (Baron, XIII, 65), how wise is it for the Moor, in public, to call Desdemona his soul's joy and absolute content before a lieutenant who helped him woo his Jewish wife, a man Othello shortly cashiers, and who stands in line to become captain and governor? How wise is it for Desdemona to defy fortune, marry the Moor, and from the floor of the Venetian senate trumpet to the world a love that most other persons might not dare whisper to friends? The triad of persons we are considering commit enormous pride-drenched indiscretions out of hubris and from a belief they are protected by being vitally necessary to the state.

Shakespeare found discretion endorsed in the first paragraph of Sir Lewes Lewkenor's translation of Gasparo Contarini's *The Commonwealth and Government of Venice*, 1599, "Address to the Reader," to which our eye is drawn by a summary in the margin praising "Wise and discrete speech." Cinthio gave Shakespeare the Moor and

Desdemona, and Lewkenor, hitherto thought to have afforded him but eight or nine minor touches, gave him, by implication, the connection of indiscreet speech with Venice, and thereby provided Othello with one of its greatest dramatic impulses.

The Inquisition singled out, for scrutiny and pursuit, chiefly two classes of people, Catholics showing interest in Lutheranism and conversos showing signs of relapsing.

Othello is one converso, i.e. a person who had turned to Christianity, but who now appears to be turning from it. Desdemona appears to be a second one, as Brabantio's daughter and the Moor's wife. Her marriage to Othello would make the pair especially suspect, because a marriage not between Catholics but conversos would reinforce each other's faltering faith. If one of Shakespeare's themes is to dramatize how the Inquisition treats its victims, its treatment of Jews is inescapable for a dramatist committed to his theme. And theme, powerful theme, infusing the entire drama of the Moor, whose entire joy comes from his wife, but who is brought to revile her as a "devil" (3.3.478; 4.1.43, 230, 234)—shows him regarding her as the Inquisition regarded the Jew (Baron, XIII, 194)—and then twice smothering her, who, in his mind, has changed from a loved person to a hated class. The very air of the Inquisition has infected Othello, one of its great tragic fictional victims, whose prejudice and hatred victimize his own wife.

In treating this strong theme, Shakespeare dramatizes one more superstition. The final believer in irrationality is identified from a consideration of a triad of the characters' names, Othello, Desdemona, and Cassio. After Othello's greeting of Desdemona, and her owning a proscribed, magical handkerchief, what is the last matter an informer could use to poison a tribunal against the Moor and his wife? An informer could point to the clear role of the diabolical in the lives of Othello and Desdemona because his name memorializes the word "hell" and hers the word "demon," making them an infernal pair. Once alerted to such "damning" evidence a tribunal could also, of course, spot "ass" in Cassio's name, though it might provoke smiles but no action. Thus, the final believer in superstition would then be the Inquisition itself, and its name for its own heresy was onomancy—divination by names (Llorente, 132).

And now we may turn to the best and toughest matter, namely Iago and his fitting into Shakespeare's spare structure of powerful themes. Iago belongs to the Jewish victims of the play as we discover upon hearing him implore "Good heavens, the souls of all my tribe defend" (3.3.175). Spain had been tribeless for a thousand years, but Jews then—and now—still refer to their tribes. As for his father, Shakespeare puts Iago on the very doorstep of his own family where, with a bit of work, we see his grievance and family emerge—his mother Barbary, his sister, and his senator-father, faithless to wife, daughter, and son, and we can answer the question why Iago hates him so much by recognizing that Brabantio, triadically needing three children, has an illegitimate son, has completely disowned him (well before father and daughter do the same thing), prompting Iago to do what many illegitimate sons did and enlist in the military. The likelihood is that Iago's mother identified his father for him and that the father had had access to her because she was his wife's maid Barbary (4.3.25). These inferences suggest how Iago knows where Brabantio lives. Moreover, Barbary also suggests Moorish country, which would make her a likely Moor (the second) and the solvent that would naturally bring Iago (the third [and half] Moor) under the command of Othello, who would trust Iago for his possessing Moorish blood himself. We will never know the truth of what I have just sketched, but the sheer economy and beauty of it speaks persuasively for Shakespeare as deviser of such exquisitely masterful work.

All that remained for Iago's return to Venice were Turkish threats against Cyprus to give the city need of a protecting condottiere whose bringing Iago along would return him to his natal city. Iago's prompting Roderigo's insults outside Brabantio's home likely comes from Iago's bitterness over being related to so great a man whose voice as double as the Duke had never spoken helpful words for his own son. Unfortunately, the best way to get back at Brabantio would be through hurting his favorite child, Iago's half-sister Desdenona, by interesting a Moor, along with Roderigo, in the great one's daughter and sitting back to watch as the Inquisition got fired up. Iago had a powerful and steady grudge against Brabantio and is jealous of Desdemona's standing with their father. But a couple of triads show us why Iago hates her so much. The first one identifies those who keep him from advancing—his powerless mother; his powerful, uncaring father; and his own unavailing half-sister married to the man who could advance him. The second triad makes Iago's bitterness clearer, namely Desdemona's advocacies. She twice advocates for Cassio. At (3.3.51) she beseeches Othello, "I prithee call him [Cassio] back." and at (3.4.83) she begs, "Pray you let Cassio be receiv'd again." Though unavailing, just her pertinacity for him must be galling to her half-brother. Her two separate appeals for the lieutenant require a third such appeal, and it most likely would have been made, but much less tenaciously, for Iago, since her position would have been weaker in his case. And finally, because Iago knows of her deceptive period with Brabantio when he did not side with her in her desire to marry the Moor: "She did deceive her father, marrying you" (3.3.206), Iago may have seen her treatment of himself reflected anew in her deceiving of their father. These matters positively establish a solid explanation for Iago's bitterness over his family's failure to help him as a much more likely reason for his own behavior than Coleridge's notion of his motiveless malignity. Moreover, and most importantly, the triad of persons whose deaths Iago is responsible for does not include Desdemona, but rather Emilia, Roderigo, and himself. Iago is not a monster but a petty person who tips off authorities to highly vulnerable people.

In the matter of those responsible for Desdemona's death, what seems clear is that we have failed to see how many contributors there are to it. But Shakespeare did, and he presents her complicated death as a result of the twists and turns of life itself. Desdemona is dying by her own hand of a poison she likely turned to Iago to get for her, assuming that his twenty-seven (by my count) health, pharmaceutical, and medical images suggest training in that field. She is the advocate for herself being allowed to go to war with Othello. She advocates for Cassio, and she likely advocated for Iago with their father, as her easy familiarity with Iago is shown throughout the play. By helping her, he completes the triad of those whose deaths involve him, Emilia's being the second and his own offstage torture causing him to poison himself being the third. Even at the moment Othello is trying to kill her, she is dying. Iago's supplying her with a fatal dose can be argued as a genuine kindness, considering the mercies of the Inquisition.

Her opponents seem without number, starting with Brabantio, who feeds her to the Inquisition so as not to be eaten himself. This powerful treachery gives us not quite the full measure of his cold-hearted disregard for others, which is helpful when we consider Iago's bitterness toward him and realize that Iago must have had an idea about how Brabantio treated Barbary, his mother. She completes the triad of those abused by Brabantio. Brabantio's rejection of Iago cheats him out of his birthright and overturns the reign of the theory of motiveless malignity that supposedly explains Iago's behavior. Then there is Iago in his plot to induce Othello to murder her. Then comes Michael Cassio in his pretending innocence as he tricks Othello into thinking him the General's cuckolder so as to gain Othello's double place as general and governor, which needs much more weight than it has been given, and all of this to facilitate Iago's handkerchief plot, which will bring Othello down for preferring Cassio before himself. Then there is the institution itself, the Inquisition. And all of this is a true and accurate picture of life, along with its infecting evil worm and its source in original sin.

And if all of this isn't complicated enough, Shakespeare gives us the additional touch of Desdemona being of "most blessed condition" (2.1.246–47)—pregnant—and representing not one death but two. And then as the final touch, Shakespeare arranges his achievement to produce one more triad, that of the deaths Desdemona brings on, which include her own, her baby's, and her mother's, in childbirth.[11] Not even the delta mud of the Nile is as richly fertile as Shakespeare's imagination.

We are now in a position to clarify how tightly knit the play really is, symmetry letting us see how exquisitely connected the parts really are. Because Othello had a brother (3.4.132) he needs an additional sibling as well, and who better than Barbary? She probably would have been able to introduce Othello to Brabantio so that the Senator could have advocated for him to the Duke for use against the Turks. Also, when Desdemona showed an interest in his story to Brabantio, the Moor would have sought the advocacy of Cassio, whose use crushed Iago's hopes to gain the open lieutenancy. Cassio bids well to have met Barbary and broken her heart, thus completing a triad of ruined hopes, Barbary's, Iago's, and Bianca's. This sketch also offers light upon the tight-knit family of military personnel of the time, a closeness that has always marked members of a regular army.

Shakespeare's audience would have caught many of the matters concerning the Inquisition that I deal with simply because that audience was sharp and informed, as they had to be regarding a political practice that had been imprinting on Europe for two centuries when *Othello* was written. The Inquisition was the news and talk of the Christian world every day of Shakespeare's life, and especially in 1588, the year of the Spanish Armada, when, but for a fortunate storm, it could have come to rule in England. With the execution, 7 June 1594, of Elizabeth's Jewish physician, Roderigo Lopez, for his so-called plot to poison her, thoughtful persons could see England succumbing to continental solutions—executions—for continental fantasies—Jewish poisonings of Christian leaders. The victims of the Inquisition aroused immense, exacerbated hatred because the Roman Catholic Church claimed moral and intellectual superiority over all other religions. Shakespeare was drawn to show, among other things, how little of either the Inquisition could claim.

Atrocities, however, seldom do more than encourage the rest of the world to avert offended eyes, it being a cardinal and honored rule of political life that "ethnic cleansing" and other such matters are the strict business of the "cleansers." Dramas, therefore, that examined the political affairs of other countries could be discouraged, lest they soon look into the court of Star Chamber at home. Claudius's questioning Hamlet about whether the argument of The Mousetrap contained any offensive matter reflects the censoring concerns of the Stationers' Company, which saw Essex-like dangers and rebellions in usurped Richards and melancholy Hamlets. With the Stationers' Company active and powerful, Shakespeare had good reasons for handling the Inquisition indirectly.

But his masterstroke may be his putting us on the wrong scent so that we focus on Iago instead of the real villain, Michael Cassio. Iago is after one position, the lieutenancy, but Cassio is after two, the General's rank and the Governor's control. The two men perfectly distribute the three elements of advancement, displaying proper proportions. Since Iago recognizes Cassio as "A slipper and a subtle knave" (2.1.238–39) and one who has outfoxed him for a coveted rank, it is clear that Cassio sees Othello as easy to fool and highly vulnerable, since almost the first thing Shakespeare dramatizes him doing, in 2.1, is imperiling Othello and Desdemona with extravagant and almost fulsome praise, which is almost certain to inspire the locals with dislike. As the "divine" Desdemona arrives, Cassio has just characterized her as "our great captain's captain," which has to appall the Cyprians, who are learning that she will be wielding power and making decisions through him. In short, they will be ruled by a Jewess. Cassio suggests that Othello's interest is not them, which they now can certainly believe, but her, since he wishes to "Make love's quick pants in [her] arms." And befitting her power, Cassio urges "Ye men of Cyprus, let her have your knees" (2.1.73, 74, 80, 84). He must know such announcements, to islanders expecting to be butchered by the Turk, do not reassure them that their protection is much the concern of their panting general, nor are they much inclined to bend their knees to a Jewess—a Jew awaiting an amorous Moor. Usually, it takes a couple of weeks to set back relations as badly as Cassio cheerfully does in two or three minutes. Here then is Shakespeare in one of his most powerful moments having Cassio tell islanders with stiff codes of female inferiority (and fear of powerful women) not just to submit to a non-royal-woman, but to a Jewish hand behind the governor's seat as well. These matters might even have the appearance of a catastrophe to them. As initial announcements go, they don't "blunder" much worse than this one. With a few carefully chosen words, Cassio instantly turns the island against its military governor. When then the island awakens to the nighttime clamor of a local bell, which they must easily take as a warning of the Turks' arrival, they discover it is not their safety that is uppermost on their General's mind but the slumber of a Jewess exhausted from panting. From this point forward, Cassio's subtle treachery brings Othello to his doom.

Manipulation is simply one of Cassio's oft-exercised skills. We see him at it again when he further betrays himself in talking to Bianca, saying, "I do attend here on the General And think it no addition, nor my wish, To have him see me woman'd" (3.4.188–90). This matter displays Cassio manipulating his sexual reputation. Not to be seen "womaned" is to give him the appearance of being exclusively available for and intent upon Desdemona. When we catch him in the act of editing the truth of a matter, apparently for Othello's consumption, we add to the evidence supporting Iago's characterizing Cassio as "a subtle and a slipper knave." Iago of course is also a manipulator, but on nothing like Cassio's scale, who shapes the opinion of the entire population of Cyprus and through it that of Venice as well. Whereas Iago moves single persons to act against Othello and Desdemona (who is almost as great and distinct a character as Gertrude), Cassio moves large numbers of people whose disfavor is surely reported to Venice where the real votes for governor exist. Therefore, when Iago urges Cassio to sue to Othello for reinstatement, Cassio's reply is disingenuous: "I will rather sue to be despis'd than to deceive so good a commander and so indiscreet an officer" (2.3.259–261). It also seems to betray what really is on his mind because "will" used where we expect "should" is decidedly emphatic and suggests will to power. Indeed, Cassio stumbles badly in the passage because the "indiscreet officer" refers really to Othello, not to Cassio, and constitutes a Freudian slip.

It once was an article of faith that at the end of his tragedies Shakespeare restored all to right order. Whether that is true or not has had to wait until this moment for what the triadic evidence shows. The triadic structure shows that at the end of Othello, the closing order is comprised of the real villain, Cassio, as governor and, Iago, the lesser villain, in custody and soon likely to take poison so as thwart being tortured;

A Greater Tradition

the officers of the Inquisition are undiminished in number or power; and finally the Inquisition itself is as deadly and secure as it ever was. This last point is delivered with grim realism because Lodovico turns Iago over to the new governor for "censure" in the famous act of "relajacion al brazo secular"—release to the seculat arm, the trick meant to keep the act of murder from staining the reputation of the Inquisition. This is the conclusion of Shakespeare, who, at the end of the play, is still as great a realist as he was at its beginning.

7

The Paternities of Ishmael and Ahab

Herman Melville had two great literary experiences before he wrote *Moby-Dick*, his formative experiences with Shakespeare and Dante, both masters of triadic structure. When Melville then created his novel with three captains, three mates, three harpooners, and a ship that was a converted freighter, further decked out in whalebone for a third appearance, we have evidence that he had mastered their structural method and likely was the first writer to use it in a prose narrative. This was a quantum leap in the history of prose narratives, and it relegated all that came before it and most that followed it to secondary and mediocre structurings. Strange things were then to follow. Henry James spent a lifetime avoiding ever directly speaking of Melville or his achievements and thus distorted, indeed deformed, James's critical account of the form and its practitioners, one deformity being arguably the self-serving, implicit ranking that his refusal ever to praise Melville promoted for himself as the superior writer. And then James Joyce did virtually the same thing. To understand better this profound silence, we may now analyze *Moby-Dick*.

The question of parentage is a recurrent theme in *Moby-Dick*, which Melville forces us to address because of certain important questions regarding Ishmael. What motive is strong enough to explain his signing onto a battered relic of a smallish ship, sailing from a declining port, for a 300th lay that won't replace the clothes he wears out on a life-threatening voyage, in order to be ever closer to a mad captain (after Pip, Ishmael being the only other person with such a desire)? What motive is strong enough to explain why Ishmael no sooner accepts being cheated in signing aboard, than he praises the very calling that is cheating him and declares his obvious pride in being a member of the fraternity of great hunters, Ahab being the latest and perhaps the greatest of them all if Moby Dick is the greatest of adversaries? And, finally, since Ishmael tells Captain Peleg that he is going a-whaling "to see the world" (NN M-D 71), we know he will see only a world of water. If you are serious about learning your identity, the last place to search for it would be aboard a whaler, which stops at no ports. So a whaler is the last place to find it, unless it is somehow the first, somehow connected to your parents. Ishmael's false reason requires two other reasons concealed from Peleg, which, as we shall see, would be to see two specific ocean sites. Ishmael never complains of a wasted voyage, so that we must ask how the water he sees can be so precious as to be worth all that he survives? Put another way, what motive is stronger than that of learning one's identity through the discovery of one's parents and one's roots? If this is Ishmael's motive, then Melville illustrates Henry James's contention that once an author has chosen his character's motive, "this motive is his ground, his site, and his foundation."[1] Ishmael appears to be on a quest, and the great question is, a quest for what? His unchanging focus is Ahab, even, as we shall see, before Ahab comes aboard. Ahab therefore bids fair to be somehow involved in Ishmael's quest. So important is Ahab to it that he no sooner dies than Ishmael ends his story. If Ahab wasn't the quest, he seems to be a large part of it. But Ishmael turns aside our curiosity and makes us decide what his quest is and who is involved in it. While remaining silent about his own quest, he shows much interest in learning Queequeg's history: in Chapter 11, an eager Ishmael "begged him to go on and tell it," which silently reminds us of his own concealed one. He also gives us the less essential information that Doughboy's parents were "a bankrupt baker and a hospital nurse,"[2] while further teasing us with a chapter entitled "Biographical"—pertaining to Queequeg, not Ishmael. Moreover, Queequeg's account says virtually nothing about his mother (NN M-D 55). These matters throw into stark relief the great blank of Ishmael's and Ahab's unknown, parental, familial, and identificational histories. They would really interest us, but they remain a blank that we are left to fill in. Though identity comes from such things, Melville withholds almost all these traditional sources of information for the central group of Ahab, Ishmael, and Queequeg. Such withholding has the excellent effect of stimulating us to work harder. Melville is a master; and mastery, in part, consists in inducing us to confront and fill in such glaring gaps. One response is to say the author has blundered. Another is to use his information and his system to supply symmetrical ways of filling them in.

At the end of "Loomings" Melville gives us a kind of epigraph for the rest of the novel. Ishmael becomes a second Noah, on a second ark, with "endless processions" of whales in twos and twos, replenishing parental pairs, as "the great flood-gates of the wonder-world swung open," and "wild conceits . . . swayed me to my purpose" (NN M-D 7). Ishmael's purpose is his forthcoming ocean quest, and since the ark image emphasizes endless parental whale pairs along with human progenitors, the Pequod looks symmetrically like a second parental vessel involving the family pair that gave him his identity and life. In Melville's world, one's family always involved a pair, and they would inhabit Ishmael's inmost soul, driving him on to find answers.

Mysteriously drawn to water and images in it, Ishmael says that Narcissus suggests to him the "same image we ourselves see in all the rivers and oceans. It is the image of the ungraspable phantom of life; and this is the key to it all" (NN M-D 5). This is a highly efficient image, uniting male and female, the key being hard, phallic, generating, and male, the water being reflecting, reproductive, and female, and Ishmael seeing his body only through its attachment to and connection with another body, that of the sea, the source of life, the source specifically of his life. If the sea is his double mother and also contains her, Melville has not overlooked Ishmael's parents. Rather, we have failed to give a necessary reading to his poetic handling of the idea. Since nothing is more ungraspable for Ishmael than his identity, his "wild conceits" (NN M-D 7) may concern his sense of the tingling possibility that he can relate to, and somehow be accepted by, his unnamed mother and father through the agency of water. The unusual emphasis on water in "Loomings" is more than poetic; it is even more than Ahab's element: it is capitalized and thus has the status of a character, a matter I shall analyze in the next chapter. Melville's emphasis on water gives it a group of three importances—for Ishmael's past, present, and future. Looming largest for him is the Pacific, and in the chapter of that name Ishmael says, on entering the great South Sea, that "now the long supplication of my youth was answered" (NN M-D 482). Such a fervent and unexplained youthful prayer may involve his conception and possible sea birth, since he exhibits the classic symptoms of an identity-less person— depression, rootlessness, homelessness, isolation, a vague past, and no visible family.

Paternity helps us understand Ishmael's unusual and intense interest in sailing not from wealthy New Bedford (from which eighty-three ships sailed in 1850),[3] but from Nantucket (whose mere fourteen ships includes Ahab's and which like his are lighter and less profitable than their New Bedford counterparts) and aboard the smallish Pequod, an obsolete, fifty-year old ship with a second set of masts, a new (i.e. third) look, a second chance at service beyond the usual 20–25 years, and an injured, returning, unfit Ahab.[4] It would be hard to emphasize more than this a voyage seeking knowledge, not wealth. Ishmael seems drawn to Nantucket because of the Pequod and to the Pequod because of Ahab. Ahab and Ishmael being dark-skinned (but not mulattoes as I once thought[5]) make it possible that, since Ahab is 58 years old and Ishmael is of unspecified but plainly far fewer years, Ahab is old enough and racially capable of being the narrator's father. But neither the Pequod nor Ahab will bring Ishmael needed money or any chance to see more of the world than he has already seen. The two things they do offer him, however, are chances to see Ahab and to share Ahab's life. This theory of Ishmael's paternity helps explain his driven, almost voyeuristic interest in Ahab. Ishmael's hiring interview begins and ends with his stated interest in meeting Captain Ahab. Once hired, Ishmael becomes interested in Ahab's quarters, as opposed to those, never described, of the other officers, which he also ignores. But most interesting of all, the ship is associated not only with death but, symmetrically, with birth.

Seven anomalous birth images (NN M-D 343–44) accompany Queequeg's rescue and delivery of Tashtego. These images act as a lens onto an old, necessary, and duplicate woman's birthing event. Symmetry produces the theory that Ishmael was conceived and born in Ahab's quarters, and in this study perhaps no idea will prove harder for Melvilleans to accept, who are pretty well convinced that if such a person existed, Melville would have told us of her. Of course he could have done so, but only if courting unthinking readers and being willing to reduce further the sales of this all too avoided novel. For the case that will now unfold is a bitter tale involving very mature subjects which would have cost him readers. But above all, the parenting question becomes a triadic necessity from "Loomings" onward, where the Pequod is cast as a vessel associated with doubled parents, cetaceous and human.[6]

We will never know the truth, but Joan Druett's study is helpful in showing that captains' children were often born in captains' quarters used as delivery rooms.[7] Of even more interest is "The Cabin Table," which associates the room with Ahab's second "family," of "little children," the group of three mates (NN M-D 150–51) who symmetrically balance a real family, and are also a group of three people. And because

Ahab shares his quarters with Pip, we have two blanks to fill to complete this stunning group of the sharers of his quarters. These blanks are filled if earlier and symmetrically Ahab shared them with a mother who then bore an infant, for the triad thus made displays proper proportional values—in this case values of age.

Melville treats the huge psychological void in Ishmael's life when in the narration of his desolate incompleteness he admits that his very name is problematic, and identifies himself as one given to "involuntarily pausing before coffin warehouses, and bringing up the rear of every funeral I meet" (NN M-D 3). At one level a joke, at another level these are the haunted, melancholy actions of a person doubly denied the burial of a loved one and with it, therefore, the closing of a lifelong grief. Such a grief seems stirred anew before the chapel tablets honoring unburied, sea-lost souls. Ishmael's identifying with such losses suggests his mother may be unburied. Moreover, he says that those who have buried a loved one "know not the desolation that broods in bosoms like these"(NN M-D 36), Ishmael's among them. His strong feeling requires expression, if only for surrogate strangers. The poetic power of the opening page deserves attention for its offering the reader the twin, contrasted fare of great humor yoked with deep pain and grief. So strong is Ishmael's melancholy that he seeks remedy for it in double sea duty, as merchantman and whaleman. These are his substitute for suicide by "pistol and ball" (NN M-D 3). But if Ahab is Ishmael's father, Ishmael's grief is clearly for his dead mother and himself.

Ishmael's apparently relived, first glimpse of his father (and our first glance at a boyhood home that contributes to his identity) occurs in "The Counterpane." He was a child of about four years when his stepmother punished him for "trying to crawl up the chimney" at two p.m. on June 21, "the longest day in the year" (NN M-D 25, 26). Why a child should specify only that one date from among all others may be explained by a symmetrically-derived inference that it is not a single but a double date, antithesizing his birth and his mother's death in giving birth to him. Melville is much given to showing that the same moment contains utterly antithetical events. Ishmael's date would have been the longest one not only as the summer solstice, but as psychologically commemorating the brightest and darkest of days at one and the same time. With so many things doubled in this novel, Ishmael's land home joins with and becomes symmetrical with the Pequod his sea home. In turn, his sea home is symmetrically doubled and tripled if he occupied it at birth and in adulthood, thus illustrating another doubling that extends to a tripling.[8] Ishmael's abusive punishment would have been highly cruel on his birthday, and doubly so if it cost him a visit from a barely known father returning from a three- or four-year voyage, a father the abandoned boy might be seeing for the first time (and the father seeing the boy for the second). If so, the unnamed place is probably Ahab's Nantucket because of its unusual bustle, "the great rattling of coaches in the street, and the sound of gay voices all over the house" (NN M-D 26). Such early afternoon activity, when most American houses enjoyed calm and rest, accords with housebound preparation to welcome returning whale men. The chief welcomer would have been the wife that Ahab had married and then left Ishmael in the care of, while he, Ahab, returned immediately to sea. The thwarted chimney climb suggests a child's admirable hunger to catch a rooftop glimpse of his returning father's ship (balanced by Ishmael's adult failure to get a glimpse of Ahab in port).

The figure that waking Ishmael apparently encounters at his bedside "sent a shock running through all my frame": "a supernatural hand seemed placed in mine." Ishmael is as much repelled by as he is attracted to the person: "For what seemed ages piled on ages, I lay there, frozen with the most awful fears, not daring to drag away my hand; yet ever thinking that if I could but stir it one single inch, the horrid spell would be broken" (NN M-D 26). The experience remained a "mystery" and a "puzzle" for Ishmael. But it describes the awe and fear that Ahab inspires in him and others. It seems also to suggest the psychological maelstrom affecting a boy drawn to a father who creates in him a "horrid spell." "[T]he most awful fears" that would repel a son from his own father would seem to involve the boy's having heard whispered bits of horrible sins. Thus, the man beside him could have attracted Ishmael as a father, but could also cause a vague, ill understood, horrible repulsion because God had punished him with a brand from head to foot. Such an explanation makes sense of Ahab's contribution to the "tornadoed Atlantic of [Ishmael's] being," (NN M-D 389) tornadoed being the precise word to express what he may sense as swirling about and tearing at him, the Atlantic being the place of his birth and his mother's birthing death, nine months removed from her Pacific conception. All the doublings involved here in "The Counterpane" show Melville's great power with Ishmael's attempts to gather up the shreds of his identity, but they do not warrant our following Harrison Hayford in mocking what he fails to recognize as Dante's strength-imparting structure, which should rather be acknowledged as one of Melville's greatest accomplishments.

Up to this point what we are given is Ishmael's birth on Nantucket soundings, then a period at best of a few days, until Ahab, ashore, sought out a lady with whom to leave his newborn motherless son, while he resumed sailing for perhaps four or so years when he returned and awoke his sleeping child only to horrify him while adding to his hunger to know the man momentarily at his side. These two periods, one of days and the other of minutes, require a completing third, months, which is precisely what the ship's voyage to the Line supplies, and which completes the triad of the time father and son spend together. The brevity of the first two periods explains Ishmael's quest and his signing aboard the Pequod.

Adding yet more intensity to Ishmael's feelings might be his mother's race. The paradigm for her giving birth aboard ship seems set up in "Cistern and Buckets." There a dead, black whale's head is metamorphosed into a birthing mother. (Hershel Parker notes Melville's use of such processes,[9] though he finds no instance of it in *Moby-Dick*.) The person brought forth is the Indian Tashtego, delivered by another person of color, Polynesian Queequeg. Conspicuously absent from these color-values is white, despite the ship's having a number of Caucasians. The event itself was what obstetricians call a breech presentation. That is, Queequeg first began withdrawing Tashtego when "a leg was presented; but well knowing that that was not as it ought to be," Queequeg reversed matters "so that with the next trial he came forth in the good old way" (NN M-D 343). It is hard to miss these obstetrical notes when Ishmael is there to say the whale's head "was doing as well as could be expected" (NN M-D 344). This grim, ironic joke, which glances at the dead agent, is, the symmetry seems to suggest, that Ishmael's mother delivered him in a birthing event that brought on her death, Ahab acting as midwife. And although whale and mother were dead, Tastego and Ishmael, contrastingly, lived. The human delivery apparently created the living bond that Melville seems to dramatize by Ishmael's obsessive interests in the Pequod and Ahab's cabin.

Melville completes the doubling of a black delivery in "The Counterpane," where Ishmael tried "to crawl up the chimney, as I had seen a little sweep do a few days previous." The outcome was that Ishmael's stepmother "dragged [him] by the leg out of the chimney"(NN M-D 25–26). This is careful work: a freshly cleaned chimney will easily represent a dusky birth canal clean enough to deliver, again by leg (a breech presentation of sorts), a soot-smudged, i.e. dark-skinned child, which suggests mother and father were both dark skinned.

What that child later comes to do aboard the Pequod seems to involve his search not just for his identity—since he seems to suspect his relationship to Ahab—but his attempt if not to meet him then to offer himself for horrified, but irresistibly attracted conciliation, should Ahab desire it. Superficially, the bitter, perhaps even blessed truth (since Ishmael may dread it as much as want it), is that throughout most of the novel Ahab gives no evident sign of a shock of recognition. But whenever Ishmael has the helm, is on deck, or is close to Ahab, his intense interest is obvious, and the corollary of Ishmael's watching Ahab so much is that Ahab could watch him in return. Melville's repeated modifications of first-person limitations are extensive and extreme enough to make Ishmael's account of Ahab voyeuristic. And one likely reason for such apparent narrative violations is that they allow Melville the important characterization of an Ishmael intensely fixated on Ahab. To a young man of no social standing, who had been a digger of ditches and other brutally hard labor, Ahab is a monumental figure. In Ishmael's eyes, he enjoys modern standing with the great whale hunters of antiquity. He is a person that Ishmael seems, contrastingly, at once proud and horrified to have as a father.

Ahab's dark character is abundantly discussed by critics who take it for a given and now seldom attempt to explain it. A fairly obvious explanation is implicit in what I have so far argued. Ahab's character may be considerably darkened by the confrontation he is facing with his own neglected drifter-son. We know that captains are given rosters and that he takes an uncommonly long time to appear on his quarterdeck, the likelihood being that he knows what awaits him. What the text displays, once Ahab appears on his quarterdeck, is a beautifully balanced account of his fiery excitement and Ishmael's interlaced chapters of unemotional whaling lore, which contrast Ahab's repeated fiery eruptions. Ishmael seems to use his various expository sections to mask his own inner turmoil and excitement as he begins staking out Ahab's quarters. But however well Ishmael may conceal his excitement at being so close to Ahab, his obsessive interest in him, matched only by Pip's, displays it. Still, we catch important glimpses of Ahab's emotions, which are out of all proportion to their apparent causes, as when Ahab threatens Stubb, later levels a loaded gun at Starbuck, and explodes intemperately at the Enderby's captain. Ishmael's presence appears to have a very profound effect on both men, which Ishmael's account suggests is more one-sided than it is.

Critics dealing with Ahab's softer side have the field pretty much to themselves. But Peleg insists that "'Ahab has his humanities!'" (NN M-D 79) They are apparent when Ahab tells the carpenter that Perth's soot "must be the remainder that the Greek made the African of: when [Perth]'s through with that buckle tell him to forge a pair of steel shoulder-blades; there's a pedlar aboard with a crushing pack" (NN M-D 470). Ahab obviously has a concern for this "pedlar." The two clues of identity, burden and maturity, eliminate the child Pip and leave the adult Ishmael. Ishmael may indeed be a runaway because OED sense 1 defines "pedlar" as "One who goes about carrying small goods for sale (usually in a bundle or pack)." In 1851, this description matched the infamous logos heading newspaper advertisements of runaways, as seen in illustrations which John Hope Franklin and Loren Schwenenger reproduce in *Runaway Slaves*.[10]

If Ahab's pedlar refers to Ishmael, then Ahab has seen him and may recognize the symbolic burden that he has forced him to shoulder. Moreover, in Ahab's wish to make the burden bearable, we see more evidence of Ahab's "humanities." To the question, has Ahab shown Ishmael this sign, the novel gives no clear-cut answer. But Ishmael has apparently been giving Ahab chances, as a hint in "Loomings" suggests: "I am quick to perceive a horror, and could still be social with it—would they let me—since it is well to be on friendly terms with all the inmates of the place one lodges in" (NN M-D 7). The shipboard horror is its captain to whom owners and mates imperfectly block Ishmael's access. But Ahab may be ambivalent about Ishmael's hiring, since he ostensibly doesn't want to "'up Burtons'" because of "'those miserly owners'" NN M-D 475, 474), whose chief, dramatized miserliness was swindling Ishmael. One can only wonder if Ahab is upset at Bildad and Peleg for signing Ishmael for so little.

In "Ahab and Starbuck in the Cabin", Ishmael cuts the distance between himself and Ahab. He is now outside Ahab's cabin, perhaps observing him inside as the first mate approaches to report oil leaking in the hold. When Ahab asks "'Who's there?'" but orders him "'On deck! Begone!'" and Starbuck answers, "'Captain Ahab mistakes; it is I'" (NN M-D 473–74), the mistake seems to be Ahab's mistaking Starbuck for Ishmael. Ahab appears to know that Ishmael is outside, and he seems to believe the footstep is Ishmael's, until Starbuck corrects him, the first mate being the third person outside. If Ishmael is pressing a meeting with Ahab, Ahab now seems either to be denying him or waiting for him to make the second move, too. Ahab could easily order Starbuck to order Ishmael below. But he does not do so. And his not doing so himself may suggest he wishes Ishmael success in a meeting, when the truth may be that Ishmael is drawn to the very spot where he was born and his mother died, Ahab serving as midwife.

Ahab's conversation with Starbuck may show at what cost he continues denying Ishmael. When told that the oil is leaking, oil-hunter Ahab oddly cries out, "'Let it leak! I'm all aleak myself'" (NN M-D 474). The passage involves another doubling, tear-shedding eyes balancing oil-leaking barrels. It thus suggests that Ahab has been weeping as Starbuck entered. And the confession is a crucial sign of Ahab's humanity and of his likely interest in Ishmael: otherwise, he has no reason to weep. You don't weep over an unknown seaman. But is he weeping at his own stubbornness or at Ishmael's? Whatever the case, it is powerful, psychological, human drama, made all the more powerful because Ahab, too, must be reminded of Ishmael's birth and his mother's death.

Moreover, Ishmael has forced the issue in a way that places a huge burden on Ahab. If Ishmael owes his life to Ahab, then, for the further symmetry of the case, Ahab should owe his to Ishmael. The one available episode occurred when Ishmael reports on fallen, injured Ahab in "The Leg." In "The Carpet-Bag" Ishmael also encounters a fallen person he calls Lazarus, freezing to death in a gutter outside the twin-businessed Spouter Inn (liquor and lodging), where inside the bartender "dearly sells the sailors, delirium and death" [NN M-D 14] and also drunkenness. Since this New Bedford gin shop teems with whaling crews, those crews would include officers. The only physically wounded person so far mentioned in the novel is the Captain of the Pequod, Ahab, who has a drinking problem. He would have been attracted to the inn as removed from the prying eyes of Peleg, Bildad, and Aunt Charity, the latter of whom stocks the Pequod with ginger-jub for the harpooneers (NN M-D 322), one of whom is Ahab.

Lazarus would appear to be Ahab's second Biblical name. Ahab needs another (since Melville's systemic doublings are binding on him), which Lazarus will supply, especially because, if Lazarus is Ahab, Ahab has arisen once from the dead when dismasted and again, now, after his unexplained beating. Moreover, both Lazarus and Ahab are found freezing at night, in winter, and prone (NN M-D 10, 463). Both are associated with a pipe (NN M-D 10, 129), which is Ahab's second "vice," along with drinking.[11] More important, Ishmael also links Lazarus with Sumatra and the Line

(NN M-D 11). These are two of Ahab's whaling haunts, especially the latter, the Pacific "sea [that Moby Dick] was most known to frequent" (NN M-D 381). And when Ishmael asks whether Lazarus would not "rather lay him down lengthwise along the line of the equator"(NN M-D 11), we can be almost certain Lazarus is Ahab, since if Lazarus is not, what need for a warm spot half way around the world, which Moby Dick favors? And symmetry requires that by interacting at sea Ishmael and Ahab do so on land as well. as they may do now

In the gutter and blue with cold, Lazarus has a powerful effect on Ishmael, whose "blubbering" (NN M-D 11) is not the response we would expect Ishmael to show a total stranger. But it is appropriate for a child seeing his fallen, helpless father. Ishmael's tears (doubling Ahab's) and poor eyesight—he needs the "'largest sized'" Bible available in Lima (NN M-D 259)—which doubles that of the whale's poor vision—probably prevent his noticing Lazarus's "sores" (Luke, 16: 20), the Biblical parallel to Ahab's wound as later described in "Ahab's Leg." But Ishmael's words and tears doubly pledge Samaritan help for the prostrate victim before him. On a running reading of the passage and its conclusion, we might suppose that Lazarus is a kind of prop, establishing the degradation and poverty of the place. Such conventional uses were probably less interesting to Melville than its psychological values.

We are not told what Ishmael does when the chapter ends. Surely, though, he could hardly blubber in pity and callously step over the man. The chapter ends with Ishmael's promise, which seems addressed to the guttered figure, that "we are going a-whaling, and there is plenty of that [i.e., weeping] yet to come. Let us scrape the ice from our frosted feet, and see what sort of place the 'Spouter' may be" (NN M-D 11). Symmetry means that Ishmael scrapes two sets of feet, for who does Ishmael's unroyal "we" include if not Lazarus? Also, the promise means Samaritan Ishmael will then take the man inside to a warm room for recovery—in short, that Ishmael means to book a double lodging—as he must later double up with Queequeg. But we learn that this inn has neither vacancies nor warmth. Ishmael, therefore, must take the man to a second place of lodging before returning alone to the inn: you don't scrape ice off the man's feet only to put him back in the gutter because the "Spouter" is full.

Where then would Lazarus ultimately have ended up? Where can an injured dark-skinned man find warmth, friends, and help? Obviously, in a black house. And by the bounty of Melville's provisions, there is one—a neighborhood church (making the neighborhood likely a black one). Ishmael thus would seem to have returned for a second time to the black church that, moments before he found Lazarus, he had left on his way to the inn. On its porch he had stumbled over an ash-box (NN M-D 9). That ash-box promises heat, and it serves the double function of identifying a sanctuary as at once free and warm. A freezing dark-skinned man would be welcome there, where a Samaritan could find a reverend second to join in saving a helpless man. These exquisitely symmetrical matters, supported by Melville's details, would occur in the interval between Chapters 2 and 3, where to all outward appearances nothing is happening. The narrative extension I am hypothesizing can be wrong, but its powerful basis is Melville's symmetry; and nothing can occur unless we utilize its balancing elements.

Long after Ishmael's gift of healing and well into his voyage, Ahab shows some signs of changing. His tears and his taking Pip into his cabin, and Ishmael into his boat (making Ishmael, after Pip, the second hand removed from Stubb's boat) are the acts of a man in the incomplete process of redeeming himself—incomplete because Ahab seems to be saying that if Ishmael wants to speak to him, why, then, speak up! Ahab's imperfectly reborn humanity suggests, however, his acceptance of his own non-white identity as he protects Pip from more anguish, while silently acknowledging the existence of Ishmael. Ahab has not so much reached out as he has looked toward his stalker: he alone has the authority to assign him a place in his own boat. (And we must note that he has chosen the least experienced hand aboard ship, the one who is making his first whaling voyage.) But the pattern of doublings shows Ahab doubly benefiting from Ishmael, commercially as well as emotionally. And in "The Gilder," the emotional kinship of Ahab and Ishmael is emphasized in an ambiguous passage: "'Where is the foundling's father hidden? Our souls are like those orphans whose unwedded mothers die in bearing them: the secret of our paternity lies in their grave, and we must there to learn it.'" The NN editors make this passage a quotation reported by Ishmael and thus apparently the speech of Ahab. In his edition, John Bryant removes the quotation marks, thus mirroring the original editions and allowing the passage in whole or in part to be ascribed to Ishmael, Ahab, or both (Leviathan, 9, June 2007, 97–98). The part of the passage I quote matches my reconstruction of Ishmael's early history and my designating his quest as one of identity by moving closer to his parents. But the passage, without quotation marks, can be applied equally to Ahab and I believe we are so meant to apply it, because he and Ishmael share a symmetrical case. Ishmael's thoughts are attuned to Ahab's for the powerful reason that they share so much in common, especially blood.

For our added bafflement, Ahab has taken Ishmael, the least financially rewarded and least experienced crewman aboard the ship, into his boat well before the end of the novel; though thanks to his cutting so many first-person corners, Melville is able to obscure the event. They help to persuade us to accept his handling of this narrative form as obviously loose. When, then, we read Chapter 117, "The Whale-Watch," we likely regard as pure license Ishmael's reporting on the midnight boat conversation between Ahab and Fedallah as they wait for the Pequod to find them, while the "boat's crew seemed asleep" (NN M-D 498). But to record the conversation, Ishmael had to be a crewman feigning sleep: he could not have heard much aboard the distant, invisible ship. And he had to be a boatman in order for Melville to double Ishmael's appearances in Ahab's boat, here and at the end, for the completion of this important symmetry.

Moreover, Chapter 116 deals with Ahab's killing a whale, and Chapter 117 treats his midnight whale-watch. The curious bitter-sweetness of the earlier chapter has a double source, the first being Ahab's hateful attraction to the whaling-ground where Moby Dick nearly killed him, and the second being his apparent attraction to the place, which has an antithetical "rosy air" suffused with sweetly holy emanations—"in wreathing orisons" and "vesper hymns," as if from "deep green convent valleys of the Manilla isles" (NN M-D 496). Such tender, evocative feelings are the context for Ahab's crisis that brings Pip into his cabin and keeps Starbuck (along with Pip) out of a boat and thus, so Ahab hopes, safe. Both "orisons" and "convent" have feminine overtones that join the second set of feminine images, occurring in "The Symphony," which is rich enough in them so as almost to be written as it were in a different key.

Here on the Line, we are told, Ahab had suffered the dire event with Moby Dick that cost him a leg and almost his very life. Balancing this trauma is Ahab's second, antithetical experience on the Line: his even greater sensing of death there, brought on by a dying whale and the setting sun. But Ishmael feels only sweetness, loveliness, plaintiveness. The same place is made to contrast two opposed responses, the one hellish and masculine and the other holy and feminine. Gradually, however, Ahab's thoughts undergo "'imminglings'" of a third feeling, and he is "'buoyed by breaths of once living things'" (NN M-D 497). But the great question is how the same place can inspire such opposed thoughts—how the latter can truly balance the former, how the once living things can have been as personally wrenching and destructive as Ahab's having had his leg ripped off? The two events have comparable magnitudes if Ahab's physical loss of limb is balanced by an earlier psychical loss—of his mother.

The great change in Ahab's present experience occurs the moment he witnesses the double death of sun (= son) and whale. The dying sun appears to inspire thoughts of himself as a kind of dying son. And if to ask how Ahab became acquainted with such "wonderousness" and "imminglings" that so soften his character is to ask where he was born, where better than in the place the passage suggests, a Spanish convent in a Manila valley, due north of the Line?[12] If Ahab had had a convent birth, the convent is the second Spanish religious place that Melville associates him with, the other being Elijah's recounting Ahab's "deadly skrimmage afore the altar in Santa, [Peru]" (NN M-D 92), the linking here of convent peacefulness and church violence displaying again Melville's habit of pairing contrasting opposites.

If we ask why Ishmael connects Ahab with memories of convent life, one explanation is that he believes he has known it: a hundred and fifty years ago it was a common solution for a dishonored woman to enter a convent for a concealed birth and to turn her child over to sisters who would arrange for adoption. Ahab inspires Ishmael to think of sisters at prayer and song: the missing voice is that of the mother. But she can be sensed mostly in very faint forms that, though they must leave us ever uncertain about her, yet are worthy of careful study because of something Richard Feynman once said about extending investigations into regions "we are not sure about." He tells us that "If the only laws that you find are those are those which you have just finished observing then you can never make any predictions. Yet the only utility of science is to go on and make guesses. So what we always do is to stick our necks out".[13] In literary criticism, we have been doing a similar thing and sticking our necks out for centuries because the utility of criticism is to go on and make intuitive guesses. If we don't, we will forever be confined to what we have just finished observing. I mean therefore to risk my neck concerning a matter I can never be sure about.

Ahab is "'buoyed by breath of once living things, exhaled as air, but water now.'" This may be the first reference to his mother and her vague death. A once living thing that is water now suggests a person who, having been buried at sea, has dissolved into water, thus leaving Ahab bereft and Ishmael without closure. Ahab's thought moves from his life source to his nurturing, to his isolation at sea: "'Born of earth, yet suckled by the sea; though hill and valley mothered me, ye billows are my foster brothers!'" (NN M-D 497) Moreover, green Manila, not barren Nantucket (NN M-D 565), is best described as having hills and valleys. And Manila brings us to Fedallah, a very curious whaleman.

A dark-skinned Ahab, 58 years old, needs a father who also is dark and about eighty years or older. On both scores Fedallah alone qualifies. By stressing Fedallah's age as beyond his ability to calculate (NN M-D 326), Stubb makes the dark Parsee the second oldest person aboard the ship after Fleece (NN M-D, 296) and old enough to be Ahab's father.

Ahab's mention of his "fishermen fathers" (NN M-D 165) connects Ahab and Fedallah because Fedallah, too, is a fisherman. He also has real importance because his name appears in a chapter title (Chapter 50). He is the one mature person aboard ship whom Ahab respects, turns to, values, and trusts, Pip being the mentally and immature, contrasting second. Yet Fedallah is the crewman who radiates evil qualities, not one of which he ever directs against Moby Dick or any shipmate. Toward whale and crew, Fedallah is completely indifferent. Why Melville should create him with vividly evil images when, for the pursuit of Moby Dick, simply making him a tough, old, cold-blooded whale hunter would serve, we are not told. His evil character must therefore have been earned by his treatment of a person or persons not involved in the present voyage. Who that might have been must wait while we address the more immediate question of Ahab's relationship to him.

Fedallah has important physical characteristics linking him to Ahab. Like Ahab, he is very "tall and swart"; and his black clothing and dark complexion give him an "ebonness" (NN M-D 217), which makes him similar in color to Ahab. Moreover, both complete a snake triad, Fedallah having a hiss (NN M-D 217) and a phallic tooth that seems "carved into a snake's head" (NN M-D 325), and Ahab having the look of an "anaconda of an old man". (NN M-D 178) If in the drama, as Henry James tells us, "[w]e are shut up wholly to cross relations, relations all within the action itself; no part of which is related to anything but some other part—save of course by the relation of the total to life,"[14] then in a novel/drama poetically treated we can expect great surprises because Ahab's father should exist among the characters (in the whale fishery, fathers and sons were easily found). And Fedallah is the chief and indeed only human candidate as Ahab's father, though doubled by fathering God.

Ahab is tied to Fedallah because Fedallah and his crew are on board due to Ahab's own "private measures" (NN M-D 230). These make a second set after Peleg's public hiring practices. Once aboard, Fedallah "soon evinced himself to be linked with Ahab's peculiar fortunes" by "some unaccountable tie" that gave him "some sort of half-hinted influence . . . it might have been even authority over him." Nothing matches blood for creating a tie and bestowing authority. One explanation for a very old, tall, swart crewman having such influence over an old, tall, bronze captain is that the crewman is the father of the captain.

The likely paternal relationships of Ahab and Fedallah and Ahab and Ishmael rank as two of the great surprises in the novel. And various hints connect the men as father and son. One set involves morphing shadows, which have Ahab so chancing "to stand that the Parsee occupied the shadow; while, if the Parsee's shadow was there at all it seemed only to blend with, and lengthen Ahab's" (NN M-D 328). Nothing, however, shows the united origin of Ahab and Fedallah so well as Ahab's defying God in "The Candles," where he puts "his foot upon the Parsee; and with fixed upward eye" addresses his heavenly adversary, saying, "'now I do glory in my genealogy. But thou art but my fiery father; my sweet mother I know not. O cruel! What hast thou done with her?'" (NN M-D 507–508). Symmetrically, above and below Ahab are his contrasting heavenly and earthly fathers; and the shrill irony of his question is that it should be (and can be) directed to Fedallah and himself, not to God.

Melville tells us that "a potent spell seemed secretly to join the twain," who stand "fixedly gazing upon each other; as if in the Parsee Ahab saw his forethrown shadow, in Ahab the Parsee his abandoned substance" ((NN M-D 507, 508). This image morphs Ahab with the Parsee's substance, whose substance could have been given, one would think, only with fathering conception. Mingled shadows, Fedallah's dominating Ahab's, suggest their sharing a common, or united, dark origin, and sharing it with another person, too, Fedallah having become so thin that seeing him made the men wonder "whether indeed he were a mere mortal substance, or else a tremulous shadow cast upon the deck by some unseen being's body" (NN M-D 537). With these words Melville may bring back onto the Pequod, in ghostly form, the spirit of someone who had once lived aboard the ship. And if Fedallah's evil sexual nature, underscored by his phallic tooth, was exercised upon some earlier person living aboard the vessel, his sister, say (a sister will neatly fit the novel's details, as we shall momentarily see), then incest committed with her could have produced a Fedallah-like Ahab. (This arrangement would give Ahab two dark, non-American, islander parents.) And incest, unrepented of, qualifies Fedallah as evil—and shows Melville already dealing with an important theme readdressed in *Pierre*.

Melville's hints—age, color, height, work—as to the identity of Ahab's father make maternal solutions necessary, too, since half a case—the paternal without the maternal half—would be systemically, awkwardly incomplete. Thus, a "tremulous shadow cast upon the deck" suggests a reference to a once-living person, clearly feminine, who is made from the merest of hints. She is now a shadow, a ghost, and symmetry requires a second one. Melville provides it when in "The Funeral" Ishmael refers to perhaps the most famous ghost of the eighteenth century, the Cock Lane ghost,[15] Fanny Lynes, whose having been a hoax makes her another contrasting opposite. Ishmael goes well out of his way to assure us that there "are other ghosts besides the Cock-Lane one, and [that] far deeper men than Doctor Johnson . . . believe in them" (NN M-D 309). This is a very surprising statement, since Ishmael's strong, challenging tone doubly affirms his belief in other ghosts and his certainty that men deeper than Johnson are believers in them, Ahab being the deepest man he knows. The statement clearly makes Ishmael a student of the subject and an intense believer, who, oddly, is made to think of two human ghosts upon seeing the body of a horribly violated, mutilated, stripped whale.

In any event, the wraith-like spirit for all its faintness is still able to make Fedallah seem overshadowed by her embodied spirit. And Melville makes subtly clear that what still attracts Fedallah is this person's "body," which has become a "tremulous shadow cast upon the deck" as if—so this supple, careful, poetic prose suggests—for further violation. Each word advances this idea, starting with the trembling that the feminine, watery shadow conveys.

Melville is careful to give Fedallah a connection with Manila: he heads a crew with the look of Manila's "aboriginal natives" (NN M-D 217), and he himself possesses "the ghostly aboriginality of earth's primal generations, which suggests that he too comes from the Philippines area. Fedallah's antiquity also links him to devils that "indulged in earthly amours" (NN M-D 231). Incest is the most devilish of them.

Fedallah's most notorious activity has been "'kidnapping people,'" according to Stubb. But in calling him the "'governor,'" Stubb also connects him to Ahab because the OED's first definition is "A steersman, pilot, captain of a vessel" (and Melville's usage postdates it by 340 years). On a second level the term can refer to Satan, and thus to Fedallah, since the fourth definition says, "spec. One who is in charge of a prison" (as a kidnapper would be). Melville is probably also aware of the slang meaning of the word as "father," which allows the term to refer to Fedallah as Ahab's father. Stubb suggests that Satan seems to have struck a deal (the "bond") with Fedallah, who will not be roasted in hell as long as he supplies Satan with proxies. Ahab would appear to double as roaster of Fedallah's victims by employing them, so as to escape being kidnapped himself (NN M-D 326–27). Stubb's typical humor doesn't obscure the serious point that Fedallah is guilty of great moral offenses. Kidnapping, incest and rape are such offenses, and if he forced them on an island girl—and who better than his sister?—she could have likely taken refuge in a Manila valley convent to give birth to Ahab, where he would have received the spiritual nourishing producing the memories that account for the vesper- and prayer-haunted seas that so move him.

Further suggested is the possibility that Fedallah much later kidnapped and hired her (as cook) and himself (as seaman) aboard the Pequod. She thus would be the second laboring female aboard ship, made necessary and symmetrically prepared for by Aunt Charity. As a sister to Bildad, her "beloved brother" (NN M-D 96), Aunt Charity requires a balancing element, powerfully filled if Fedallah has an unbeloved sister. No idea will be more contested than one introducing a character who is invisible. But the great strength of the idea comes from Melville's being a master toolmaker, having studied the triadic tools of Dante and Shakespeare, so as to be able to create all the triads that make this woman a logical necessity, and thus bring her into being. She is similar to gravity in that we never see her or it, but only the influences of each, in her case the doublings and triplings that show the pull and force she exerts, thereby clarifying Fedallah's and, Ahab's lustings, Ishmael's identity quest, and Queequeg's selfless giving. But the text presents her only as a logical conclusion that we can infer from Aunt Charity's labors aboard the Pequod and the evidence we have been carefully examining. Her existence isn't vouched for by a thread or two, but by a rich nexus of them, involving Fedallah, Ahab, Ishmael, Queequeg, and another that we shall learn more about in the chapter on Queequeg. These characters form a web showing the exquisite planning making so important a place for her in a triumph of art created by a master maker of powerful tools.

Thus, a convent infancy will explain parts of Ahab's wide religious knowledge and Ishmael's love of orisons and vesper hymns (NN M-D 496), which a congregation would have sung. In a convent, a pregnant girl could escape a predatory brother, who many years later returned to the isles, reunited himself with her, and forced her to leave with him. One of the most caustic strokes of fate imaginable made Ahab knowingly or unknowingly hire the two of them aboard their son's ship. Her having been a cook is suggested by Ishmael's aspiring to be "a Commodore, or a Captain, or a Cook," the capital letter emphasizing the latter term and showing the unusual respect Ishmael accords such work, while its very inclusion suggests that it has been part of his own employment history. (He even vouches for his cooking experience by a brief disquisition on broiled fowl, "judiciously buttered, and judgmentally salted and peppered" [NN M-D 5]). This matrix of matters is bound together by the nearly loveless family relationship of three persons, and it is their family closeness that gives so much power, strength, and emotional depth to the novel. It is one thing for a mere seaman to record a mere captain observing his dead boatman's "extended eyes turned full upon Ahab" when Fedallah's prophesy comes true (NN M-D 568), but quite another for a son to watch his father looking in horror upon a man who is the father of the one and the grandfather of the other. The latter instance is inexpressibly more powerful than the former one. And the novel is written with skills that allow the author to be credited with both views.

Aboard ship the mother would have been in the eye of a captain with the double problem of alcohol and lust, "his old spar," i.e., his penis, even when apparently gone,[16] "still pricking him at times" (NN M-D 471). Ahab's harpoon, which "burned . . . like a serpent's tongue," is a doubly phallic image that targets womanflesh and whaleflesh, Ahab's twin lusts. For the indescribable power and horror of this novel, Ahab would appear to have become the second rapist, of his own mother, in a drunken Pacific stupor that produced Ishmael (who ever after yearned for that body of water). This arrangement gives Ishmael, like Ahab, a non-American birth and, if true, illustrates the truth of Ishmael's remark that "not one in two of the many thousand men employed in the American whale fishery, are American born, though nearly all the officers are" (NN M-D 121), which he seems to know from his own history.

By charging God that "in the sacramental act [I was] burned by thee" (NN M-D 506), Ahab makes the burning his portion in the sacrament of penance, but attaches it to his former life as a Persian.[17] From Fedallah and his sister Ahab has acquired three bloodlines, giving him qualities Persian, Spanish, and aboriginal (making him very easily mistaken for a black in this country). Ahab of course insists that "my sweet mother, I know not" (NN M-D 508), and uses the present tense, which is an equivocation if Ahab had known her in the Biblical sense, say, twenty years ago when, trapped aboard a smallish ship with her two sexual assailants, she probably did double duty at a hot stove and in a cold bunk (or was cast down on a deck and dragged to one), where she was doubly assaulted, by brother or son, if not both. Possible support for this reading comes from Starbuck's seeing in Ahab's eyes "some lurid woe would shrivel me up, had I it" (NN M-D 169). "Lurid" woe is sensational and ghastly (OED1), which incest certainly is.

Our warrant for hypothesizing an earlier double hiring is Melville's visible, strong, symmetrical element of Ishmael's hiring both himself and Queequeg aboard ship. The doubled employments match seaman with harpooneer and harpooneer with cook, the latter two occupations having independent shipboard rank. If Melville's doublings mean anything at all—and he carries them so far as to say that as barreled oil in the hold, whales are again "sliding along beneath the surface as before" (NN M-D 427)—then the elegant symmetry of Fedallah hiring himself and his sister aboard the Pequod is what Melville's system exists to help us discern. Moreover, Melville's system appears to double every important element (only the slightest handful of which we have dealt with here), so that if nuns care for Ahab, another religious should have such cares, too—which we find upon learning of an unnamed, contrasting Arsacidean cannibal "priest's children" (NN M-D 454).

From such doublings we gain important insights into Ahab's religious ideas and his bitterness toward God. Ahab is a highly religious person, knowledgeable about two religions, as his familiarity with the Catholic hierarchy and papal traditions (NN M-D 166) and his Quaker speech show. He finally spurned all religions, out of anger at being God's plaything and cursed with monstrous burdens. Ironically, Ahab's burdens are lightened by thinking of his mother; for no sooner does Ahab see the Bachelor's olive-hued ladies than he looks "from the ship to the vial [of Nantucket soundings]" (NN M-D 495), and senses the hymn-filled air of orisons and vespers, in a pre-Joycean passage of association.

In any case, the Pacific spot may represent the place of Ishmael's conception. The soundings would appear to represent the Atlantic place, thousands of miles away, where the mother died and was buried at sea after giving birth to Ishmael and likely a twin, who would have died with her, since two births and two persons who die aboard ship are systemically required. Her sea burial had to have included another, that of a dead twin. And precisely here, we experience again the extraordinary power of Melville's symmetry, for twins were born, two persons died, two bodies were sea-buried, and Ishmael thereafter paused before coffin warehouses, fell in the rear of funerals, grieved for the graveless chapel-entablatured victims of the sea, ignored a prosperous port and better ships in order to sign aboard, for a 300th lay, a virtual madman's second-rate whaler, where his course and Ahab's collide and reunite them in Ahab's very boat in Pacific waters as Ishmael found a measure of peace because "the long supplication of my youth was answered" (NN M-D 482). Thus water, oceanic volumes of it, and not land, permit Ishmael the closeness with his mother that he yearns for. But such intuitive conclusions mean, as Feynman says, "[we] never are definitely right, [since] we can only be sure we are wrong."[18] Even so, Melville's symmetry is immaculate: Queequeg has been on an similar quest, has met Ishmael, and the pair have shared a love and found their peace. Even Ahab's triadicizing quest of hatred and death is much softened by his Pacific and Atlantic memories.

From guesses based on slight hints, from powerful symmetries, and from questioning Fedallah's objectless phallic evil, we can discern the direction and character of Melville's enlarged and unusually ambitious story. Slight as his hints often are, and ever so capable of allowing us to construe erroneously, they are joined by Melville's powerful symmetry, which potently embodies the ghostly actions on the past, resurrected and symmetrical. Melville's hints offer us glimpses of some of his subtlest, greatest, and most poetic work. Ahab and Ishmael's cherished mother is hardly more than the residue of soundings, shadows, and tracings in water. But without her, Melville's work would be missing an important symmetry and, even more important, the emotional center of the novel, which gives an unexpected depth to the whole. We can deny her, but only at the cost of missing the Pequod's better spirit and of damaging Melville's symmetrical account at one crucial point, to say nothing of all the other matters that she explains and accounts for, touching Ahab, Fedallah, Ishmael, and their identities. Her spirit shimmers in the reciprocal love of Ishmael and Queequeg and in Ahab's being humbled by imagined vespersong. To miss her is to miss the Pequod's Ghost and a haunting story. To accept her is not to see the "right" story, only a possible one.

The story is doubly haunting for another reason. If Ishmael has had a shipboard birth, the most economical way for this to have occurred is, as I have suggested, for him to be a twin,[19] giving Ishmael (and Ahab) a double loss, since one shipboard death requires another, which is most economically realized if Ishmael's birth has been followed by a birth of sufficient complication to cause the death of mother and child, making the event one of embittered joy. Ahab then would have one child and have lost another. Ishmael must beget very poignant, bittersweet feelings in Ahab, especially in their boat scene of possible accord. In the single episode comprising Chapters 116 and 117, Ahab speaks to the Parsee in Chapter 117, but first to an un-named person in Chapter 116, telling the latter person to "'Look! here'" and to "'see,'" as he directs his attention to the dying sperm whale turning toward the sun. If Ahab is speaking directly to Ishmael, is Ishmael too stubborn to acknowledge it? Melville splendidly captures the very human awkwardness of father and son, each wanting, needing the contact that he, so humanly, gives the gift of initiating to the other. Ahab is also (doubly) addressing Death itself, but his imperatives must be spoken to someone else, since Death, unlike a sleep-feigning Ishmael, need not be shown what it is doing. A few sentences of this address, however, have powerful implications if Ishmael, his possible dead twin, or both of them are understood as being addressed— and even if one of them is not (though the uncounted duplications in the novel make dual addressing here a virtual given). Has Ishmael stopped feigning sleep, or is Ahab fantasizing a reunion with him? We shall never know. But to report it, Ishmael must hear it. Urged to look at the dying whale as "'life [dying] sunwards full of faith'" (as the mother, symmetrically, was probably full of faith at her death); and to see that it is "'no sooner dead, than death whirls round the corpse, and it heads some other way'" (NN M-D 497), can Ishmael not be struck, as we are, that, for the symmetri-cal beauty of the passage, for the simple, the profound, the tragically brief, human, even tender moment of final, detached joy and peace, Ahab, morphing with a dying whale, turns sonwards, before death whirls round his corpse and heads it some other way? Melville endorses no reading of any passage in the novel, including of course this one; but by means of the symmetries and hints that make this reading possible he touches us very deeply.

And he sustains the moment. Never more human than in his attempts to destroy the least vestige of his shown or showing humanity, Ahab now addresses the whale, saying "'In vain . . . dost thou seek intercedings with yon all-quickening sun, that only calls forth life, but gives it not again.'" It is as if Ahab sees himself in the whale's final moments of seeking a union with the sun, only to bitterly deny that the sun /son really wants a union, as too taken up with setting / "sleeping"—with death, not life. But Ahab still has need for union, and he says again to Death, "'All thy unnamable imminglings float beneath me here; I am buoyed by breaths of once living things, exhaled as air, but water now'" (NN M-D 497). The buoyant water/Water sustains him. However bitterly he denies it, is he not also buoyed and quickened by Ishmael, mere feet away, and in this address is he not seeking intercedings with him? Ishmael might, of course, be denying Ahab. But for tenderness and unspeakable poignancy in a waning moment of barbarity—the horrible death of a great creature before the eyes of one if not two other creatures who are dying emotionally—the passage seems unmatchable.

8

Queequeg

Queequeg has a sister and a father (NN M-D 59, 55). No two facts about him lead to a fuller knowledge of his past than these two, and they also illustrate anew the enormous power of symmetry to extend the narrative into new, unsuspected places with almost unbelievable results. In a triadic structure, a sister means that Queequeg has another sibling somewhere in the world, and that the two children have an unnamed mother. Fate has predestined that Ishmael, Ahab, and Queequeg will finally be joined physically in Nantucket and on the postage-stamp deck of the Pequod. Is it possible there is a second dimension to this spatial joining, that of blood? Second dimensions are part of the unusual power of symmetry.

Ishmael assures us that his friend "and his ways were well worth unusual regarding" (NN M-D 27). Such regarding shows that Queequeg seems to enjoy inclusion in some very curious groups. For example, the triad of destinations shows that Ahab means to return to the Line and Ishmael means to return to the Pacific, which makes it likely that, symmetrically, Queequeg is a candidate as a third person who reaches an Atlantic destination, Nantucket, not entirely drifting there on the chance currents of life. (The events in the novel have long been regarded as chance matters; it is more rewarding to look at them as fate). The triad, in short, is one of intended destinations—Ahab for the Line, Moby Dick, and death; Ishmael for Nantucket and reunion; and Queequeg for Nantucket, family, and union.

Moreover, since Ahab masks his true intent in making his voyage and Ishmael masks his as an intent to see the world, can Queequeg asymmetrically really intend to learn from Christians? In short, isn't his reason for voyaging likely a mask for his true reasons? What prince with a genuine chance to inherit a throne deserts it for whaling?

Hasn't he likely seen "Christian" life aplenty even at home in Kokovoko? His ending up in Nantucket points us to the seer and whatever important matters he may have told Queequeg. It seems likely that this seer foretold Queequeg of his meeting with Ishmael and their serving aboard Ahab's Pequod. (Indeed, Queequeg likely was given an oral prediction of his future along with his two tattooed treatises, on cosmology and truth). Thus, three tall men—two harpooners and a seaman—are fated to collide when they converge upon the same deck. These three turn out to be the most religious men aboard the ship. They turn out to be tall, dark-skinned, and fixated on a white whale and on its Pacific grounds with their hymn- and prayer-scented winds. These three men inflict some of the bloodiest violence on the planet, but are drawn to convent vesper-haunted waters. Indeed, each one is devoted to water and is a meditator seeking his identity from water. These matters symmetrically suggest family resemblances and influences.

Of the doublings (and triplings) abundantly found in "Loomings" we soon note another: Ishmael the writer begins his account of Ishmael the whaleman (just as Melville certainly saw Dante-poet writing about Dante-pilgrim).[1] But the two Ishmaels, past and present, should be joined by a third person. Since we do not readily see one, we may identify that character with the help of an observation of Henry James, who calls attention to the importance of intensity as the dramatist's (and novelist's) all in all.[2] With this in mind, we can recognize that the three dozen water references in "Loomings" (not to mention its nearly four dozen water-implying terms), place more concentrated emphasis upon water in these opening five pages than some sea writers place upon it in lengthy works. Most important, Ishmael believes it holy and personifies it—"Water" and "Watery" (NN M-D 5, 486). Stressing the feminine "sweet mystery about the sea," he senses that "its gently awful stirrings seem to speak of some hidden soul beneath," and he likens those stirrings to "the fabled undulations of the Ephesian sod over the buried Evangelist St. John" (NN M-D 482), thus shrouding an unseen feminine soul in the sea with the mystical holiness of a sacred grave. In keeping with its well-known feminine nature, Ishmael endows it with great attractive powers, which draw untold numbers of men to her, most visibly Ishmael, Ahab, and Queequeg. Ishmael stresses the crucial importance of water to one's identity through Narcissus, who can see himself only in water, so crucial is the feminine element in his (and our) identity. Water provides "the image of the ungraspable phantom of life, and this is the key to it all" (NN M-D 5), that is, the very mother who bore Ishmael—because one phantom of life is an unseeable mother. Water is much more than an agent of conveyance; it is highly nuanced and may be the third character in "Loomings"—and elsewhere in the novel. And if "Water" gives identity, life, but also death, what identity (understood as female lineage) does it give Queequeg—and what fate? Powerfully felt in these passages is a swelling "huge, high harmony" of a poem "that sounds A little and a little, suddenly, By means of a separate sense," as Wallace Stevens says on a different occasion.

Melville gives us another key when he brilliantly connects Queequeg with Ishmael and Ahab, along with Fedallah and the unnamed mother (who seems to have dissolved into and become water), in a highly subtle manner through Aunt Charity. She is presented in "All Astir" bringing aboard a triad of whaling tools and ship supplies in two sets of items. Her loading labors strongly contrast the laziness of her much stronger brother Bildad, who carried "a long list of the articles needed" (NN M-D 96). Such taxing work sets up the powerful symmetry of two working women with religious interests and access to the Pequod through brothers who abuse their own sisters.

Abusively, Bildad's complacently accepting his sister's labor allows us to construct a triad in which another brother pocketed the cooking labors of his sister, whom he has also abused in a less conventional manner—sexually, for such is the parallel brought forth by Aunt Charity's associating herself with a long and phallic whaling lance, symbolizing tall Fedallah.

Aunt Charity's two sets of items symmetrically reveal the abuse and dysfunction involving Fedallah, Ahab, and Bildad. A jar of pickles, a bunch of quills, and a roll of flannel make up the first group. Next, this presumably pacific Quakeress brings aboard "a long oil-ladle, and a still longer whaling lance" (NN M-D 96).[3] Since the ladle and lance suggest occupation and phallic, stereotypical sexual functions representing tall Ahab and taller Fedallah (that is, dark-skinned, potent male adults), the much smaller sizes in the first set may represent children, gender, and certain potentials within them.

Thus, the glass container, brine (poetically reflecting an at-sea conception of Ishmael and his twin), and the contents of a jar of pickles may hint at a womb, amniotic fluid, and fetuses. These in turn point to the unnamed pregnant mother and her as yet unborn twins (and Queequeg as I shall show), who are the "priapic" vegetables, whose potential life together ended for the latter three with the twin births and the mother's death. The quills represent an uncircumcised male, for the potential prose and poetry that Ishmael means to write, who is a Stevensian poet-priest "of the invisible." The roll of flannel, the largest item in this set (just as Queequeg is physically larger than Ishmael and his twin), stresses the sense of warmth needed to put us in mind of Polynesian weather, Queequeg, and the arthritic condition (balancing Fleece's) that would likely await a South Sea islander aboard an ice-shrouded ship at Christmas. Through grouping, these phallic and gender symbols bind Queequeg to Ishmael and his lost twin, and these three children to the mother, to Ahab, and to Fedallah, the symmetrical group making up three related generations. Of equal importance, the physical color of Fedallah and his sister is passed on to the three living children, and provides the target of the racial abuse that Queequeg physically challenges and responds to when he and Ishmael are mocked aboard the Moss. Queequeg and Ishmael are black in the eyes of some Americans, who then and now have decided race by sight and (sometimes inaccurately) by skin color, not often by the work required in digging through more trustworthy records.

The triadic question this group raises is very important since, if the first element involves a defeated potential and the second a realized one, the flannel may represent either one. If Queequeg is alluded to by the flannel, his then needing protection against arthritis implies that he will live long enough to develop it. And since he doesn't contract arthritis aboard ship, the implication is that he survived to become arthritic after the sinking. This symmetry gives him a second illness to go with the fever he contracts while working among the barrels in the hold. We shall return to this matter shortly. Here we need only say that Melville's images function as poetry, uniting this group of people in an inseparable symbolic and relational matrix.

The three major males, working their way southward on an ice-covered ship, are also united by their belief in predestination, Ahab being a strong believer in it, Ishmael a genuine believer, and Queequeg an indirect one, through Yojo (NN M-D 68). That the three men should serve aboard the same ship seems fated. The moment we recognize them as a distinct group, we are struck by the power of the extraordinary drama Melville is plotting by bringing Ahab's son and brother onto Ahab's deck, together with their half-brother, Queequeg, and for a three-year voyage, no less! In all of American literature, what can compare with the psychological stresses that now will be produced? Consider merely the hiring of the two young men: Without even being told, Peleg knows Ishmael's name (NN M-D 78). Bildad may also know it, judging from his preposterous offer of a 777th lay to Ishmael, which arguably may represent his solution to getting rid of the looming problem that stands before him seeking placement within a hundred feet of Ahab for three years, in an attempt at personal solutions on a commercial ship. Bildad's greed of course wins out, and Ahab is left to face the ensuing problems as best he can.

By concentrating on Queequeg, I am suggesting that the three are brothers by the same mother, but different fathers. This is but one explanation as to why Ishmael "began to feel mysteriously drawn towards [Queequeg]" and why each took to the other "naturally and unbiddingly" (NN M-D 51). They seem to feel the mystery of kinship through shared familial responses and attitudes.

To begin with, Queequeg is a very strange kind of savage. His royal father fattens a few purchased slaves for use as ottomans, a practice which Queequeg, a selective abuser, also tries (NN M-D 100). Queequeg is a "prince" who labors as a harpooneer and accepts the common hardships of such a life. To qualify himself for it, he literally runs after a whaler, boards it, and seizes a ringbolt with a vow not to let go, "though hacked in pieces," in order to "see something more of Christendom than a specimen whaler or two" (NN M-D 56). This profound devotion to a strange religion has excited small interest as to its equally profound cause. He had "a wild desire to visit Christendom" and "was actuated by a profound desire to learn among the Christians, the arts whereby to make his people still happier than they were . . . and still better than they were " (NN M-D 56). Like Ishmael the teacher, Queequeg too, wants to serve people. Such aspirations in a "prince" might be explained if he had had favorable experiences with missionaries.

But Queequeg has had no such experiences that we know about. This leaves us to wonder who influenced him so favorably toward Christianity. The influence makes him intend to live among Christians and return to his own pagan people "as soon as he felt baptized again" (NN M-D 56), that is, presumably, as soon as he felt touched a second time, as he had been once before, by a sanctifying sense in someone he believed to have been purified through the rite—a woman, say, who had sought refuge in a convent. Queequeg has had a very unusual experience for a Polynesian "prince," and it has made a lasting impression on him.

The likeliest source of this feeling would have been a woman, since Queequeg somehow has been spiritually impressed by gentleness, service to others, and religious love. These traits are carefully heightened by his being repeatedly called a cannibal, a pagan, and a savage—which cannibalism entitles him to. His religious love is most visible perhaps in his favorable attitude toward a dominant culture that shows little respect for his "pagan" one. And his Christian interests are strong and active, as Ishmael discovers upon encountering Queequeg attending Father Mapple's chapel. A whalemen's chapel is not a pagan Polynesian's usual tourist stop. It is a place where one expects to find men who have fought whales asking protection for a pending voyage or giving thanks for a completed one. Father Mapple's walls display black-bordered (and lettered) tablets memorializing whalemen who never made it home. The one Christian woman, as I argued in the previous chapter, whose influence is powerfully presented in this novel, is the dark-skinned mother of Ahab and Ishmael. Moreover, Queequeg is a headhunter (and seller) and apparently a follower of Mohamed, and he observes Ramadan with a single-minded focus that is literally uninterruptible. Yet for all its single-mindedness, and thus its presumed evidence of Queequeg's devotion to this religion, it is overborne by an unusually devout Christian woman who inspired in him an interest in her faith.

The facts about Queequeg's family do not rule out his having had a Christian mother. His royal pagan father would appear to have been married, since we read of Queequeg's royal aunts on "the maternal side" (NN M-D 55). The definite article seems chosen to acknowledge that the king had a wife, who without being Queequeg's mother acted in a maternal capacity for him and thus would become the second step-mother in the novel after Ishmael's. Royal aunts imply a sister who had sufficient standing to marry the king. But Melville keeps her from view, thereby allowing us to connect the king with a liaison involving Queequeg's Christian mother, who gave birth to Queequeg.

The obvious question then becomes how such a woman got to Queequeg's island. Since whaling ships have made a couple of stops there, it is possible that his mother had been signed aboard a whaler, again through the agency of Fedallah, before the advent of the Pequod, and that that ship had visited Kokovoko, where Fedallah, an exploiter of the powerless, with a commodity at his mercy, sold her to the king.[5] And since the king buys people to sit on, he could also have bought one to lie upon. In any event, Fedallah appears thrice to have sold her for appetitive uses, twice to culinarily pleasure crews as cook and once to pleasure a king as bedmate. Such a history would explain why her Christian religion would be the most important solace in her life and the chief source of comfort that her faith could have to keep her spirit from being destroyed by her three exploiters—her rapist brother, their drunkenly rapist son, and a libidinous king who purchased rape. To endure such abuse would require just such a degree of faith that Melville is able to make us feel reflected by Ishmael and Queequeg, on whom it has been luminously imprinted. She is a great symmetrical achievement, coalescing through mere scraps, hints, and scents that recall hymns and convents and Manila valleys, and she is one of Melville's greatest confirmations that he will not court popularity and make reading easy for his readers. We must take him on his terms, not on ours. He was an impressionist, painting, as it were, not the figure, but the light of love and faith reflected onto others by the figure.[6]

If then Queequeg, Ishmael, and Ahab are half-brothers, their mother has had three labors, Ahab's, Ishmael's and his twin brother's (understood as a single birthing event), and Queequeg's, producing three children and a fetus that died in birth. Ishmael's love for his lost brother is intensely and psychologically treated where Melville has Ishmael speak of Queequeg as "my twin brother" (NN M-D 320) when they are almost umbilically connected at the waist by the monkey-rope. "Twin" is a needless adjective except to show another doubling (Queequeg as a brother replacing a twin brother in Ishmael's mind) along with Ishmael's strong need of the closest kind of family connections.

The text suggests one more bit of information about this extraordinary woman. She spent the longest time with Ahab and Fedallah (in convent and later at sea), the next longest time with Queequeg, and the shortest time with Ishmael, who has sought connection to and knowledge of her by signing aboard the Pequod and whose identity remains incomplete because of her absence from his life. He deserts merchantmen for a whaler because that specific ship will bring him to the Pacific grounds where he was conceived, and then to the Atlantic spot where he was born and where his mother and brother died. Needless to say, she has great influence and almost qualifies as a major character in this so-called womanless novel. And she owes her being to Melville's trust in us to do our share of the work and create her according to the symmetrical requirements of his system.[7] When we do our share, we encounter the accumulated horrors of what is usually called Ahab's monomania, but what we can now recognize as dysfunctional behavior, resulting in his and other families being sundered, rejoined, and estranged. Moreover, some crew members jettison important human feelings, as Stubb does in his impassive killing of whales, and submit themselves to a mad voyage under a captain whose dysfunctional hatred and rage they share by sometimes literally torturing unoffending mammals.[8] Ahab will pay any price to be avenged on Moby Dick, and the price he pays is something close to self-loathing and an almost total estrangement from his own flesh and blood, for "he seemed ready to sacrifice all mortal interests to that one passion" (NN M-D 211),[9] flesh and blood heading the list of our mortal interests.

Melville's treatment of such dysfunctionality, if not the earliest, will vie with the finest.[10] To help us recognize that Ishmael, Queequeg, and Ahab are half-brothers, Melville creates a highly important triad of evidence, while leaving us one difficult task to perform. At the Spouter-Inn, Ishmael shares a bed with Queequeg, which has had two other sets of occupants, the landlord and his wife, and later their two young boys. This triad shows the great importance of naming the group elements exactly. If we identify the bed's occupants as sleepers, we learn nothing. But when we examine the triad, we find that the first of the two elements is made up of Peter Coffin and his wife Sal, the second of their young sons Sam and little Johnny, and the third of Ishmael and Queequeg. Symmetry helps us determine the relationship of the latter pair on the basis of the related states of the known pairs, since a triad is comprised of three like elements, which makes family of Ishmael and Queequeg.

The two given elements of husband and wife and older son and younger son are family pairs, which suggest that the third element involves another family pair, who have the outward appearance of being unrelated so as to supply the triad with its important major difference. The most obvious qualifying pair (taking account of Queequeg's Polynesian blood) is that of an older half-brother to Ishmael, (which in turn makes him a younger half-brother to Ahab). The fit is exact, allowing us to confirm our important insight into the extraordinary relationship of the latter pair.[11] And the insight is doubled because Ahab's being father-brother to Ishmael through a common mother, and Ishmael's being half-brother to Queequeg through a common mother means that Ahab and Queequeg are half brothers through that same woman. Their relationship seems touched on when Ishmael describes Queequeg's "large, deep eyes, fiery black and bold, [where] there seemed tokens of a spirit that would dare a thousand devils" (NN M-D 50). Such a spirit puts us not only in mind of Ahab's defiant essence, but of Fedallah's powers and imputed devilish associations.

Queequeg can share qualities with both men if Fedallah's sister is his own mother, because my hypothesis has Ahab to be the son of Fedallah by his sister. More important, Queequeg alone among the harpooners has had an extraordinary experience with Moby Dick, whereas Tashtego and Daggoo have apparently merely seen Moby Dick from a distance. Because Queequeg feels the excitement of having counted the harpoons in his hide, he likely has been in a boat next to Ahab (NN M-D 162). Most important of all, he shares Ahab's strong taste for hunting Moby-Dick, which his excitement over seeing the implanted harpoons conveys. And such connections are important because if Fedallah and the nameless mother are brother and sister (of Philippine, Persian, aborigine blood), they will explain, as nothing else can, how Fedallah- and Ahab-like qualities appear in Queequeg. And since Ishmael reports on these qualities, he would presumably sense them as family traits, and hence would see and feel that Queequeg is crucial in his search for his own identity, and that the two of them are likely to be inseparably united.

A symmetrical system powerful enough to lead us to families and identities should also lead us to the giver of identities, names for the unnamed and the partially named. In Moby-Dick, four important characters are missing names, Ahab, Ishmael, Fedallah, and the unnamed mother. An elegant solution to this problem would be their all having the same surname, in a way that makes a perfect triad. In Chapter 108, a talking Ahab approaches the carpenter who is working on his new leg, but who is unable to identify the person Ahab addresses. Since Ishmael is the narrator, he may in fact be somewhere close by, though unseen by the carpenter. The carpenter, rebuked for thrusting a lantern into Ahab's face, explains, "'I thought, sir, that you spoke to carpenter.'" With the definite article omitted, Ahab believes the carpenter's noun is a proper noun, i.e., a surname: "'Carpenter, why that's—but no'" (NN M-D 471), and instantly catching himself, he changes the subject, though apparently he was going to say, "'why that's Ishmael.'" This mix-up allows us to see that Ishmael's last name would appear to be Carpenter. The surnames of Manila-raised Ahab, Fedallah, and the mother would then be Carpintero, the triad being completed by the common noun carpenter. Ishmael, born on Nantucket soundings, would be using the Anglicized form of the proper noun.

The same power that establishes surnames works equally well for first names. Ishmael's mother may be Esperanza, since Hope is a fitting name for her because of the group she would complete—Faith (fe d'allah = faith in God), and Charity being ful-filled by Esperanza. Fedallah and Esperanza are also obviously ironic.[12]

If Esperanza is an ironic name, part of its irony appears from a consideration of a condition that Queequeg, Ahab, and Ishmael each share in common and that derives straight from their unusual parenting: all three are illegitimate. Outside the Spouter-Inn, Ishmael seems to glance at Queequeg's and his own bastardy. There he beholds the iconic double try-pots sign identifying the place as catering to whalemen. Melville makes it serve to identify a second and third matter as well. "The horns of the cross-trees were sawed off," leaving "yes, two of them, one for Queequeg, and one for me" (NN M-D 66). These ominous reminders of gallows trees invite attachment to Queequeg as a murdering cannibal and headhunter and to Ishmael as a person bur-dened with the fear that his very birth somehow caused the death of his own twin and mother. Tied to this dark thought, however, is the lighter, humorous, and doubled significance of horns as symbols of cuckolding that brings on illegitimacy, though the humor is instantly muted because touched darkly with incest.

The final matter in a consideration of these three apparent half-brothers is whether they have any sense of their possible relationship with each other. Melville gives Ahab and Ishmael powerful reactions to each other, and Ishmael and Queequeg strong, enduring feelings toward each other. But the feelings of Ahab and Queequeg toward each other are much less obvious and therefore represent the major difference in this triad. Ahab's interest in Queequeg hinges largely on Queequeg's excitement over a harpooned Moby Dick (registered by Ahab's addressing Queequeg first, although he speaks last, instead of Tastego and Daggoo, who speak before him [NN M-D 162]) and on Ahab's comment on Queequeg's tattoos, "'Oh, devilish tantalization of the gods!'" His opportunity to give them this study would have been daily, at dinnertime, when Ahab joined Queequeg and the two other harpooners. The tantalizing matter for Ahab may have been that the tattoos, as a record of "a mystical treatise on the art of attaining truth" (NN M-D 480–81), are a subject that could have dealt with a woman who figured so deeply in each of their lives, though, of course, there are many other possible interpretations of this matter, as in every other one that I am dealing with. Still, there is a visible triad that helps us here: the tattooer understood the account he tattooed, Ishmael does not, but Ahab has "tantalizations"—that is, some skill at read-ing the old flesh-imprinted legend.

For Queequeg's part, his tattooing shows him having turned to "a departed prophet and seer of his island" (NN M-D 480), whose readings may have cost him royal favor, hence departure. Queequeg apparently had sought the man out for answers to personal questions, since one doesn't subject one's entire body to such pain for another man to use as an inscrutable written record of his interests.[13] The truth that Queequeg would have been interested in would be the same truth that drove him to travel 20,000 miles to end up in, of all places, Nantucket: namely, the truth about his identity and his mother.

What could a seer have told him but that she was dead and that knowledge of her would be attainable only through his two half-brothers? He could leave unsaid that the king could also tell Ishmael about her, if the son wanted to try that desperate avenue. But whether true or not, what is undeniable is that Queequeg's actions move him ever closer to Ahab and Ishmael, starting with his chaining himself to an American whaler, making his way to Sag Harbor, getting whaling experience to qualify him aboard the Pequod, then going on to New Bedford, only to proceed on and end his travels in Nantucket and on the very ship that Ahab commands and Ishmael seeks to serve aboard. Coincidence is all this is possible, except that it is so much more easily explained as indirect direction.

Queequeg's tattoos would appear to tell the truth about three half-brothers and a common mother, an extraordinary history that impels three men to meet up on one small deck in Nantucket harbor. What additionally is so striking about this convergence is that Ishmael's very wide intellectual knowledge of the profession of whaling and Queequeg's unordinary physical knowledge of hunting and killing whales joins them on the ship captained arguably by the best whale hunter alive. And the symmetrical convergence of these tall, dark-skinned men who are drawn to a specific area of the Pacific involves two young men in search of their identity and their past, just as it involves their other and older half-brother, who may fear what his identity and past entail.

II

At the end of the story, we are presented with two impossibilities, that Ishmael was the lone survivor, and that he expressed no sorrow about losing Queequeg, the man he loved most in this world. The absence of sorrow is explainable only if Melville made a huge blunder, or if Queequeg somehow survived and Ishmael has an inkling of it. That he did survive can be shown to accord with Melville's numeric system. Its symmetrical patterns require that if one person survives, a second does, too, along with a third. And equally important, this system makes us co-creators of the novel's conclusion. Other theories present the beautifully amusing spectacle of deconstructionists insisting that Melville's language is too slippery for stable meaning while displaying their lack of the skills needed to produce the story that the author challenges them to construct; and feminists who inveigh against Melville's female characters while they themselves are in the very act of failing to see one of the most perfectly felt characters in all of American literature. Melville trusts us, indeed wants us, to construct his story and his astonishing characters, and he has adopted a well-established triadic system, which is based on the one theory that is extraordinarily productive. That system endorses the only systemic construction by which we can do it. So, let us see what such construction produces.

To begin with, Melville gives us a triad of prophets, Elijah, Fedallah, and the tattooer. Elijah hints very broadly that Ahab and the Pequod are doomed, and Fedallah tells Ahab the ambiguous truth that "'Hemp only can kill you.'" Ahab interprets this to mean a land death from hanging (which Fedallah does not contradict), but without considering that his whaleboat line is made of hemp.

The heart of the prophecy assures Ahab that "'two hearses must verily be seen by thee on the sea; the first not made by mortal hands; and the visible wood of the last one must be grown in America'" (NN M-D 499). This last doubling leaves us to search for its third element. We may find it upon reading of Queequeg's coffin, which was made from "some heathenish, coffin-colored old lumber aboard, which . . . had been cut from the aboriginal groves of the Lackaday islands" (NN M-D 478). What Queequeg's seer and prophet said about his fate is unstated, but the subject surely was raised, since why else would Queequeg meet with such a person?[14] The triad, I believe, is completed if he told Queequeg that though his ship was doomed he would be saved by wood from a Pacific island. The elements of this triad show one forthright statement, a second broadly hinted one, and an ambiguous third one.

Ishmael himself provides a major inkling of evidence favoring the idea that Queequeg survived the sinking. In speaking of Queequeg's tattoos, Ishmael calls him a "riddle to unfold" whose mysteries were "destined in the end to moulder away with the living parchment whereon they were inscribed, and so be unsolved to the last" (NN M-D 481). There is a great difference between hieroglyphics that would molder into dust and those that would decompose in water. This suggests that Queequeg will die on land. And that Queequeg's tattoos likely became dust is suggested by a consideration of the triad of his lifesaving dives. They comprise one of his ways, along with his being the best swimmer and the best diver aboard ship, and they deserve the unusual regarding that Ishmael urges us to give such matters.

Aboard the Moss, Queequeg saved the life of one of his racial abusers, who fell overboard. Diving down and disappearing, Queequeg reappeared in a "few minutes more" (NN M-D 61), dragging his mocker to safety. Melville makes the abuser a lucky man to be swept into the sea with Queequeg aboard. His compassion for an abusive stranger is matched by his lung capacity, which rivals that of a Polynesian pearl diver: very few people can stay under water for a "few minutes." Queequeg's next dive, to save Tastego in the whale's head as it sank in the water, is but into a fifteen foot deep cavern, and therefore is of a shorter duration, which registers on the watching crew as "moment follow[ing] moment" (NN M-D 343). So far, we have two elements, the second because so much shorter than the first representing a major difference. Queequeg needs to make a third lifesaving dive, unless we want to believe that when the Pequod sinks, his love for Pip fails him and that Melville forgets the requirements of his symmetrical system. This third dive should be either shorter or longer than the other two, in order to show the customary proportional values of a triad.

When the ship sinks, Pip is in Ahab's cabin, terrified of drowning, and Queequeg is mounted on a mast far above him (NN M-D 566, 568). Pip's terror results from his near-drowning experience that has cost him his sanity and made him speak of himself to Queequeg as having already drowned. Taking Queequeg's hand in his coffin, Pip asked Queequeg to look for him in the Antilles, and "'if ye find him, then comfort him'" (NN M-D 479). As the ship slips beneath the water, Queequeg, mounted on his mast, must know as well as we do that Pip needs saving, and he must remember Pip's plea to be looked for and comforted. Thus, when Ishmael reports only on Tastego at his mast, we are left to wonder where Queequeg is. Melville's powerful system and Queequeg's own love for Pip suggest that, symmetrically, Queequeg has dived to save his friend, Queequeg being one of those rare persons who no sooner see the need for help than they respond to it, without regard for reward or their own safety.[15] To find and comfort Pip (and to fulfill Melville's triadic requirement), Queequeg must make this third dive.

Melville gives the reader the inestimable chance to complete the powerfully beautiful symmetry of Pip's taking Queequeg's hand in his coffin being balanced by Queequeg's taking Pip's hands on the sinking Pequod-coffin (tomb to all but three of the crew) after diving to find him. Because this dive would have been quite complicated, it would have been longer than the one he made from the Moss. Moreover, two of these three dives seem to involve the rescue of persons within a chamber, and all three must rescue people onto vessels: strong as Queequeg is, he could not swim the Pacific—at least not carrying Pip. So Queequeg must paddle out and meet another ship, board it with Pip, and gain safety somewhere. And to help us see this possibility, Melville has left us a key word on the occasion of Queequeg's paddling his canoe out to a whaler to take him to America. On that occasion Melville tells us, superfluously, except for its helpful emphasis, that Queequeg was "Alone in his canoe" (NN M-D 55), which means that the two vessels he paddles must contain a total of three occupants. And that occurs if Pip is with him on the final one.

The question is, what vessel is there to save the two of them? Moby Dick has turned the two extra whaleboats into chips, so they aren't available. But two extra boats require a third extra one. Thanks to symmetry and triads, we know that such a craft exists. When he was near death, Queequeg voiced a desire for two things, a coffin and "a canoe like those of Nantucket, all the more congenial to him, being a whaleman, that like a whale-boat these coffin canoes were without a keel".[16] We then immediately read that "when this strange circumstance was made known aft," which means made known to Ahab and most likely by Pip, "the carpenter was at once commanded to do Queequeg's bidding, whatever it might include" (NN M-D 478). Since the carpenter would have carried out this command to the letter, we can be as sure as Melville's system allows that the carpenter made Queequeg a coffin-canoe. We never see him making it, but then we didn't see him making two other items as well, the wheel for the tiller and Ahab's new wooden leg. So a boat exists, and it means that Queequeg has two things to retrieve on his dive—Pip and the boat. All then that is needed would be for Queequeg to carry Pip and follow the unlashed boat to the surface—the second object to surface, along with the life-buoy—on the far side of the craft where they could not see Ishmael, and Ishmael could not see them (thus completing the triad of three people who do not see each other, as one holds on to a life-buoy and the others to a boat). This much permits us to see yet more. Triadic structure shows us that a whole Pip who becomes broken must end as a partially restored Pip, thanks to Queequeg's love and ministering comfort.

Because, thanks to Melville's numeric system, this is possible and is indirectly forthcoming as Melville's and our own sequel, or second and finished novel, Ishmael need not mourn his great friend, since he could have had an inkling that Queequeg's survival was predestined: he reports on the beliefs in predestination of Ahab and Fedallah, and it is a belief he shares with them.

The sinking leaves Ishmael without his grandfather, father/brother, and, so he implies, half-brother, a triad in which two die and one lives. But the true triad is grandfather and father/brother, three relationships divided between two persons. And the water, the baptizing water, surely unites him, as it surely does Queequeg, with the soul of the Water, their mother, whereas the fate of Fedallah and Ahab is to be united, symmetrically, with the object of their hate, Moby Dick. Moreover, Queequeg and the devices made for him end up saving, as it were, two other lives at the end, Ishmael's and Pip's. And in Melville's conclusion we see yet once again another moment giving birth to inseparable opposites, this time, as with Ishmael's birth, the most powerful of all, death and life.

Melville has two endings, the first being the sinking of the Pequod and the second the meeting of Ishmael and the priest in Peru. Together they make up a triad when joined with the single opening of the novel in Nantucket. This triad, as we shall see, was copied by both Henry James and James Joyce, and it is this honor that truly elevates Melville's status as a great writer. Melville also places a triad of quests before us—Ishmael's, Queequeg's, and Ahab's. Ahab's quest after Moby Dick was a failure. Queequeg's quest to learn more about Christianity so as to help his people become better than they are is largely a success, thanks to his having lived with Ishmael. What he has learned has come from Ishmael through their mother, and it is such a lesson of love as would help Queequeg's people. But his quest is not a full success, since he never reads his tattooed history so as to know that Ahab is his half-brother and Fedallah his uncle. Worse yet, he loses Ishmael, though he saves Pip. Ishmael's quest, however, is a success, for he has lived with his half-brother, been in his father's boat, and at least seen Fedallah, his grandfather, though probably without being sure.

More important still, he ends up in Peru, with Spanish friends who offer the possibility that someone in their Spanish population is related to him through his partly Spanish mother.

Don Pedro and Don Sebastian draw out from Ishmael the Town-Ho story, become intensely interested in Steelkilt, and prompt Ishmael's offer of swearing on a Bible that the story is true. As Don Sebastian goes off to a nearby worthy priest for a holy book, Ishmael tells him to bring back the priest. The priest is wholly unnecessary in this matter, Ishmael's swearing being all that is needed. A holy book and a priest mean that a triad of holy things is in the making, the priest brought back being its second element. And in one or the other of them, there must be a third element, which we will examine in a moment, while we consider another uncompleted triad.

Fedallah and his sister represent two siblings calling for a completing third. And a Spanish priest will fit perfectly by joining Fedallah and Ishmael's mother to complete this group of a Parsee, a priest, and a highly devout woman. Moreover, Ishmael has more than a casual interest in this priest: he would not make his modest appearance without Ishmael's insisting on it. The sibling triad will be completed by either another Fedallah type or by a highly religious person, since the triad must be built on one or the other of these opposites. The priest neatly completes the triad's necessary minor difference (between himself and Ishmael's mother), the major one—the contrasting religious beliefs between Fedallah and his sister—being obvious. The minor difference shows the priest to be either more or less religious than his sister, the likelihood being that his faith has been strongly influenced and sustained by her stronger faith. Such a triad further suggests that their parents were a Catholic mother and a Muslim father. When Sebastian returns, Ishmael says, "'Now, venerable priest, [move] further into the light, and hold the Holy Book before me that I may touch it'" (NN M-D 259). Ishmael could easily swear in the shade, but then he wouldn't distinctly see the priest's face. This unnecessary request is explained if Ishmael knows that his mother had another brother, a very good one who balanced a very bad one, and wishes to see if family resemblances are visible between the priest, Fedallah, Ahab, Queequeg, and himself. Seen from the shadows, Ishmael's face would provide the priest with the shock of recognition that his own face coming forth into the light would have for Ishmael, who at that moment would realize his quest-fulfilling wish and know his identity. On the humble priest's face Ishmael would see the face of his mother, the priest's face being a brother's copy of his sister's face, thus completing an important triad and displaying the greater one of the three faces in the two reflections: Ishmael's in the water and his mother's in the priest's. These matters display one other important triad, the triad of delayed appearances. Ishmael must wait for Queequeg at the Spouter Inn, for Ahab on his quarterdeck, and for the priest at the Golden Inn. This is the end of Ishmael's quest for his mother. Begun unsuccessfully on land; continued then aboard a whaler, with partial success at Ahab's cabin; and now ended with a second voyage, bringing success in Peru. Ishmael's heartrending experience has left him penniless but successfully reunited with his brother, partially with his father, and spectrally with his mother.

The final word here should be that there is no final word. (We should, of course, note that Melville's conclusion shows that literature's beauty is without peer.) This study opens a door; it does not close one. The amount of work left to do on Moby-Dick is enormous, and no subject, especially the one I have addressed, has received its last word. I have only continued what Harrison Hayford began, who first opened the flood-gates of Melville's awaiting wonder-world. It is a wonder world, and to enter it we must use some of the same tools—symmetry, intuition, and prediction—that are used by our colleagues in mathematics and science. Sharing their tools will help to regain for literature its lost place next to them. That some writers have always used them shows the persistence of great thought over many centuries. But critics need to study writers much more than they need to read other academic critics. We have lost standing not only with our fellow scholars in abstract thought, but with too many of our own important writers, who practice it. And the practice leads straight to the true wonder world, where great numbers of astonishing rewards remain for discovery. The lesson of Queequeg and Ishmael is love, and the lesson of symmetry is fellowship in your group. And the lesson of a great work of art is exactly as James claimed: the great writer packs his coffer in "the one way that is mathematically right."[17] Melville's coffer thus contains three powerful stories: first, a whaling story, symbolizing, a second fugitive slave story,[18] and, third, a family story that grows out of Ishmael's personal quest, the whale story being one of death to whales and hunters, the fugitive slave story being one of chase, capture and death to the runaways, and the family story showing the reuniting of two brothers, Ishmael and Queequeg, with their father and grandfather and Ishmael's successfully "seeing" his mother's face. Our final triads show that Ishmael likely makes Peru the third place he settles in after the Pequod and the Spouter where he and his mother's brother are joined by the vision of his mother. These achievements were quickly recognized by Henry James and later by James Joyce (as we shall later see), so that in modern literature, Melville established himself as the great watershed dividing lesser structured work from fiendishly difficult efforts, which clearly look like attempts to surpass Melville's monumental work. Readers might take a moment to absorb the extraordinary magnitude of Melville's youthful achievement, one of the greatest ever achieved in literature.

9

The Black Ambassadors

Henry James was one of the best-read writers in American literature, with one glaring omission: he nowhere speaks of Melville. He does, however, refer to him, though the reference has apparently escaped attention. In a Paris talk with Maria Gostrey, Strether realizes that his mention of Madame de Vionnet has much surprised Miss Gostrey and says, "'You call it—your recognition—a shock?'" Then at the restaurant on the river when he sees Madame and Chad rowing toward him, he repeats the expression on sensing that she felt a shock on seeing him, a shock that he too felt on seeing them: "she had been the first at recognition, the first to feel, across the water—the shock."[1]

These two occasions produce three shocks, and display another of James's triadic figures, and they trace themselves to Melville's famous phrase on the shock of recognition, found in his essay on Hawthorne: "For genius, all over the world, stands hand in hand, and one shock of recognition runs the whole circle round" (Piazza Tales, NN, 249). That James should choose to place his two allusions to Melville in the novel he regarded as his best work brings to mind Melville's greatest novel which, as we have seen, has much evidence suggesting its main theme is a black one. If James's novel should also be about blacks, James may be honoring Melville, or even challenging him. In his Preface (NYE, I, xviii–xix), James criticizes the first person narrative without naming Melville, but in Hawthorne he appears to reach for the hand of a fellow genius.

James was a tantalizer and a challenger and, unlike the writers I earlier discuss, a writer who spoke repeatedly but not revealingly about his work, James wrote great Prefaces for most of his fiction. In their non-specific parts, they apply to any and all triadic structures, and he was the first writer in a thousand years to violate the code of silence concerning its structure, though without naming it.[2] Moreover James not only repeatedly tells us that whatever his things add up to, the addition in every case is ours, but hints at how to do the addition. This means that we can't get through the Preface to *The Ambassadors* without realizing that something racial awaits us in the story, though adding it up is our job, with important and highly useful hints from him. When, as artist, he saw his great theme and then identified the characters who would perform the actions exemplifying the theme, James says the work becomes sedentary and "involves as much ciphering, of sorts, as would merit the highest salary paid to a chief accountant" (NYE, I, x). This challenge places James' work in an objective tradition of writers who devise mathematical structures that make us aware of gaps needing filling. And he is the only writer to offer us a critical guide to his work. For their many pains, his Prefaces, the greatest feat of critical theory ever written, and obviously meant to bestow upon himself the triple crown of foremost writer of extended prose, foremost modern dramatist, and foremost critic ever, have been almost totally ignored, partly because F. R. Leavis declared them "unrepaying."[3] A fruitful way for us to break through James' shell of silence so as to know more about his allegiances may come from remembering not that he may have been a member of the LGBT group of his generation, but that, if so, he never came out and was horrified at the thought of being found out. Not ever coming out means a life continually lived under the pressure from the other to view yourself unfavorably, as the other does, thus making you live two distinct lives, which entitle you to a double biography, and, most important, that you likely hold solidarity with marginalized groups because you share in common with them a humiliating, furtive life forced upon you merely for being what you were born as. Our several million blacks of James' time knew, of course, such daily humiliation, and in their case it was often doubled by the males being legally counted as three-fifths of a man. Black women counted for nothing, not even as mothers, since many of their children were sold out from under them for cold cash, in cattle yards and auction pens where their mouths were offered for the inspection of any buyer. As a small boy, James knew a Kentucky mother and child, Aunt Silvia and Davy, who melted into the night in their run for freedom, hoping to escape the horrors of slave life.[4] This pair registered a deep memory in the mind of a boy who likely read the Liberator's reprinting of his father's work,[5] and grew up to encourage us to be one of those on whom nothing is lost, and holding himself to be a super-subtle observer, trying to understand all that he saw, while keeping us as ignorant as his secrecy, his almost daily unescorted walks, and his bonfires of papers, allowed.

James prods us to explain why in the Preface to a novel about a wayward son, we should find so many single word and phrasal allusions to slavery, such as "freedom," "constitutionally," "noose," "prejudice," "hung up just out of reach," "scent," "pursuit of the hidden slave with bloodhounds," "the basest of the servants of man," "capture," "chase with horn and hound," "hunt," "errand," "identity," and "passes," terms with a double bearing, but which, as here, extracted from their contexts read something like a slave chase. Many of them in context are void of a slavery bearing as James traces his process of discovering his main character, Lewis Lambert Strether, a man "burdened . . . with the oddity of a double consciousness" (NYE I, 5). Strether shares this oddity with many Afro-Americans who had a foot in each world, white and black, or were light enough to "pass" for white, and who viewed the world from two perspectives. The distinction of pointing out the condition and being the first to give it wide dissemination belongs to W. E. B. Du Bois, in *The Souls of Black Folk*, a copy of which William sent Henry, who called it "the only Southern book of any distinction that he had ever read."[6]

> [T]his American world . . . yields [the black] no true self-consciousness, but only lets him see himself through the revelation of the other [i.e., white] world. It is a peculiar sensation, this double consciousness, this sense of always looking at oneself through the eyes of others, of measuring one's soul by the tape of a world that looks on in amused contempt and pity. One ever feels his twoness,—an American, a Negro; two souls, two thoughts, two unreconciled strivings; two warring ideals in one dark body, whose dogged strength alone keeps it from being torn asunder.[7]

As a closeted gay person, James could identify with this double view of him and draw upon it to create Strether and other marginalized characters in his various fictions.

Du Bois and Strether share this doubled view of themselves. But it isn't the only thing they shared. Both had French names. Both were from Massachusetts. Each has brown skin. Both were editors. Both encountered women who took them for waiters. Each went to Europe. Both read and collected books. Each married and lost a son. Each was sensitive to the feelings and treatment of women and servants. Both men were extremely conscientious. Both were mulattoes. Both lived lives of psychological drama, played out as our great racial divide produced lynchings every week. More interesting still, at Harvard William James had been Du Bois's favorite teacher and the young man had often socialized at the James home. Apparently the two men had talked enough about Henry for Du Bois to get his English address and write to him before traveling to Europe (as Harvard's first black Ph.D.), where he hoped to meet him.[8] That event was frustrated because James would be away when Du Bois arrived, leaving us to recognize an unnoticed and important parallel: Strether's intended but failed Liverpool meeting with Waymarsh in the novel's opening paragraph appears indebted to Du Bois's failed European meeting with James. These matters show us that to the two persons James acknowledged as models for Strether, Howells and James himself, we must add W. E. B. Du Bois.

The Ambassadors' triadic structure is summarized in its title, there being exactly three persons involved in the same embassy, first Strether, then Sarah and Jim. And with such a structure, if we find Du Bois momentarily morphing, as it were, into Strether, we should find two more famous blacks doing the same for two other characters. Since Du Bois is clearly the one character with the most similarities to Strether, the central character of the novel, there should be two more characters with famous black antecedents, and I want to look at Waymarsh and Maria Gostrey for leads that will identify their models. Waymarsh is curiously described as looking like someone—unnamed—whom we should recognize in Strether's remembered image of Waymarsh:

He had a large handsome head and a large sallow seamed face—a striking significant physiognomic total, the upper range of which, the great political brow, the thick loose hair, the dark fuliginous eyes, recalled even to a generation whose standard had dreadfully deviated the impressive image, familiar by engravings and busts, of some great national worthy of the earlier part of the mid-century. He was of the personal type—and it was an element in the power and promise that in their early time Strether had found in him—of the American statesman, the statesman trained in "Congressional halls," of an elder day. The legend has been in later years that as the lower part of his face, which was weak, and slightly crooked, spoiled the likeness, this was the real reason for the growth of his beard, which might have seemed to spoil it for those not in the secret. (NYE, I, 25)

Frederick Douglass matches this description of eyes, hair, forehead, beard, weak jaw, and slightly crooked lower face as seen in engravings and busts of the time, and these features secure his place alongside Du Bois as the second element in our triad of paired blacks.

And finally, we sense doubleness when Maria Gostrey describes herself as a general guide—

> to 'Europe,' don't you know? I wait for people—I put them through. I pick them up—I set them down. I'm a sort of superior 'courier-maid.' I'm a companion at large. I take people, as I've told you, about. I never sought it—it has come to me. It has been my fate, and one's fate one accepts. It's a dreadful thing to have to say, in so wicked a world, but I verily believe that, as you see me, there's nothing I don't know. I know all the shops and the prices—but I know worse things still. I bear on my back the huge load of our national consciousness, or, in other words—for it comes to that—of our nation itself. Of what is our nation composed but of the men and women individually on my shoulders? I don't do it, you know, for any particular advantage. I don't do it, for instance—some people do, you know—for money." (NYE I, 18)

Joining Du Bois and Douglass is Harriet Tubman for James' astonishing opening of this novel, achieved by his using the three most radical American blacks of the time as partial models for his three most important characters—in plain view under the noses of critics who assured us that the author had nothing to do with blacks. Harriet Tubman, the Moses of her people, shouldered blacks, like Maria, for destinations outside the United States. Also, Tubman was very religious, as James quietly suggests with a single word, "verily." She helped penniless slaves, to escape from slavery, by dangerous trips, often out of the country, to Canada, on the Underground Railroad. And James appears to have had a special reason for honoring her with his abundant allusions in his greatest novel.

James' younger brother was Garth Wilkerson (Wilky) James, whom William called "'the best abolitionist you ever saw,'"[9] who, at 17, enlisted in the Civil War, transferred to the Massachusetts 54th (black) Regiment, was wounded in the assault on Fort Wagner, was hospitalized and just possibly ministered to by Harriet Tubman, who nursed the wounded of the 54th, before he was brought home on a stretcher by the father of a friend of Garth's, who, while vainly looking for his own son found Wilky instead. No Harriet Tubman anecdotes have come down to us, but James slips in enough little telling details about her so that it seems clear he is drawing upon a fund of knowledge he is not sharing with us. One such detail is Maria's confessing that "the most 'hopeless / of her country-folk were in general precisely those she liked best" (NYE I, 15). Another involves Harriet's well-known narcolepsy, in which she had premonitory visions, as is suggested by Miss Gostrey's phrase "it has come to me". These narcoleptic experiences have been traced to her having been struck in the head by a thrown object for blocking the pursuit of a man trying to apprehend an escaping black, causing her forehead to be permanently dented. Maria's head also is described as bearing dents: Maria, along with Strether, is "so finely brown and so sharply spare, each confessing so to dents of surface and aids to sight, to a disproportionate nose and a head delicately or grossly grizzled, they might have been brother and sister" (NYE I, 10). Their apparently African noses and grizzled heads need no comment as to their black heritage.

Maria and Strether share enough in common so that we do well to take them as brother and sister, and especially since James himself makes the suggestion. The novel gains a hundred-fold in significance if they really are. Moreover, Maria is at the moment shepherding no one to Europe, allowing her to devote herself to Strether, a very odd thing to offer to do without a blood tie to explain matters, except that they instantly hit it off. Furthermore, what James suggests remains sound when we consider that the only sure thing we can say is that Maria Gostrey is heading, at her own expense, toward Europe and Waymarsh, with his and her younger brother now in tow, and the question becomes why? And why does Maria know so much but still so little about Strether? But before we move on to answer that question, let us be clear that we have just seen James attach his three main characters to the three greatest black luminaries of the American 19th century while various James scholars have been busy promoting the view that James treated only whites, and those largely from the upper reaches of the dominant culture.

The question walks us straight up to the condition of black families before and shortly after the Civil War, which tells us that, except for Maria, James' fictional family had been slaves, that the family has a triad of children—two sons and a very young daughter. Maria's younger age tells us that she had been born after the father and two sons were sold off and following the Emancipation Proclamation, that she had stayed with the mother,[10] asked many questions about her siblings (there being nothing more natural than her having an active curiosity about two siblings she never met), that the mother couldn't possibly answer her questions (except to speak about their characters and personalities), and that the child vowed to search for them, which is one of the oldest stories we have about broken slave families. So, then, while on her way to see Waymarsh, Maria has the great good fortune of stumbling upon Strether who, unbeknownst to her, is a brother she's been searching for. And this is an explanation that will answer how she knows so much (and so little) about them. She simply intuits that she and Strether are quite alike. This isn't the only possible explanation, but it is a very helpful one, and it adds immeasurable power and pathos to James's story, even to this point, let alone to what lies ahead.

Power and pathos come into James's story about Maria because it sharply diverges from that of Harriet Tubman. As James gives us clues to this great difference, he dramatizes another aspect of the doubleness of being a black American. Maria appears to be a person trying to "pass" for white. Few things in the novel are more appealing than her affection for Strether and his friends, and few things more touching or sad than her various stratagems to avoid being seen too often in public with them. Passing made sense at the height of Jim Crow, when Chief Justice Roger Taney said that Negroes had no rights which a white man was bound to respect,[11] the effect of which was to make "passing" attractive to some blacks seeking respect, dignity, and opportunity. Maria's crossing the great color divide is suggested by her Paris apartment being her "final nest." Rich with her personal accumulations, it appeared dim, striking Strether, on a rare visit, as deficient in light, "almost dusky". It lacked the play of hard light to illuminate her features and her color. But Strether discerned within it "old ivory" (NYE I, 119), whose affinity testifies subtly to her interest in matters African.

Her stratagems for separation begin when Strether and Waymarsh plan to leave Chester for London by train. Also London-bound and going by train, Maria "made her own plan for an earlier one. (NYE I, 35). But her "confirmed fellowship" with them caused her to "to defer her journey and agree to accompany the gentlemen on their own, might a separate carriage mark her independence" (NYE I, 37). In effect, she turned their carriage on an English train into a kind of Jim Crow car.[12] Then, one night in London, Miss Gostrey let Strether know "that he wasn't to see her home. He was simply to put her, by herself, into a four-wheeler" (NYE I, 68). To his question, "'You won't take me with you?'" she replies, "'Not for the world'" When he declares he will then walk, she shows concern—"'In the rain?'" (NYE I, 74)—but not enough to invite him to ride. And in Paris, when Strether wants her to dine with him to meet little Bilham, Maria is all caution, asking, "'Are you giving dinners?'" which cleverly asks if they will be dining in private or in public. Strether misses the point here. Yet even on learning his dinners are in, she accepts if it will be "'Only once, you know,'" and with the provision, "'But I must be out of it—to the naked eye,'" suggesting she wants no false credit for extending hospitality to such a pair. When Strether proposes that she meet Chad, too, she assents, but nervously: "'I must see them each . . . Mr. Bilham naturally first. Only once—once for each; that will do. But face to face—for half an hour'" (NYE I, 121, 124). She relaxes and accepts, only to recoil and hedge, as if her white life were at stake when making trips back across the social divide.

Her caution is her constant companion. She is chary of inviting anyone for visits at her London and Paris places. Nor does she call on her new friends: rather, she meets them at a restaurant or a theater, at night. In Paris, she agrees to dine with Strether before going to the theater, but she fails to appear at dinner. "She hadn't dined with him, and it was characteristic of their relation that she made him embrace her refusal without in the least understanding it (NYE I, 129). Earlier, when she had dined with him in London, he had noticed how carefully she dressed to flatter her appearance; he was deeply aware of the red velvet band she wore round her throat, thereby adding value to "every other item—to that of her smile, and of the way she carried her head, to that of her complexion, of her lips, her teeth, her eyes, her hair". All these attractions were further enhanced by the "pink lights" at their table where "the lighted candles had rose-coloured shades". (NYE I, 51, 50) More than a hundred years ago, James apparently knew what lighting technicians know today, that if one wants to lighten the color of a black, use pink or red light.

But James' first and subtlest revelation about Miss Gostrey is made by means of gloves. When Strether first met her, she was "drawing on a pair of singularly fresh soft and elastic light gloves". A short time later, he saw her "stroking her gloves smoother" Later still, he noticed her looking at his hands, leading him "to wonder if a couple of sidelong glances from her meant he had best put on his gloves" (NYE I, 8, 10, 13). He, however, was interested in "smart neckties". But she issued a "prohibition of neckties and other items" and "permitted him at the most—the purchase of a pair of gloves" (NYE I, 41). A fair inference from these passages is that Miss Gostrey is sensitive to the contrast between pink nail and brown skin, between the color of the palm and that of the back of the hand, both giveaway features which she seems to want hidden by gloves. It isn't that black isn't beautiful to her, but that she knows how she will be treated if whites suspect she is black.

Much of the drama in the novel derives from the strategies its characters use to soften their treatment in a white world. By revealing these strategies, James is able to deal powerfully with some of literature's greatest themes, themes of identity, alienation, prejudice, shame, and allegiance, to deal with them inter-racially and internationally, and to do it all in deeply psychologically and dramatic ways. It is a psychological study of great dramatic intensity that allows us to watch Strether agonize about himself— "his want of money, of opportunity, of positive dignity" (NYE I, 87). The constant problem facing him is to gain dignity by accepting himself, his identity, his blackness. Simply yoking himself to Waymarsh helps only superficially because it doesn't bring him inner peace: an attachment to another is not an inner resolution about oneself. Strether has opportunities to pass, but when he covers his hands with gloves for Miss Gostrey's comfort, he is false to himself, and he knows it.

He quickly sees that his position is as false as Chad's is true. Chad accepts himself and knows how to live. Strether, however, is prepared only to encounter anew a mere boy.—unpolished and twenty-eight—whom he had known in America as "bold and wild" (NYE I, 149). Strether is stunned by a Chad who doesn't attest to Woolett, who is so different as to seem "a case of transformation unsurpassed" (NYE I, 137). Chad's idea of life is to live as he wishes and do as he wants, ideas that are alien to Woolett and Strether. Strether himself is doing what Chad's mother wants and is on her errand, the bills being paid by her and the errand helping Strether to become her husband (and Chad's stepfather) if Strether can but make the boy also do her bidding and return home to his place in the family business, a business in which Strether is happy not to be involved, feeling it tainted and wanting in dignity. He somehow doesn't quite see that his being an editor who suddenly one day is turned into "the mother's messenger" (NYE II, 290) to corral a wayward son shows that his editorial work is of less consequence than making her son heel—as the editor himself is doing. Strether feels like a "messenger at last reaching him after having run a mile through the dust" (NYE I, 97).

Expecting a boy, he finds instead a man. "He saw him in a flash as the young man marked out by women" (NYE I, 153), though Chad did his own selecting. Strether, in contrast, knows the unflattering experience of being the selected: "It wasn't even as if he had found Mrs. Newsome—so much more . . . had the mother performed the finding" (NYE I, 166) The upshot of her having done the finding is that he carries messages and runs errands. And the upshot of the delivered message is that Chad dug in and ignored it, showing Strether that what distinguishes the two of them is the pride, the self-respect, and the self-esteem of the young man: "Chad was—quite in fact insisted on being—as good as he thought" (NYE I, 171). Paris, Strether believed, and those who simply flowed with it—Paris made the difference.

Strether had expected a morally worse Chad, a Chad brutalized, immoral, pagan. it being the mother's idea that what held her child in the wicked city was a wicked woman, and Strether fully believed that it was a French woman—white, of course—who was keeping the boy from home. No other explanation of the young man's six-year absence had occurred to him, least of all that there could be anything wrong with Woolett and the United States. Nor did it occur to Strether that Mrs. Newsome could be less than an appealing figure to her son. He takes her for a total success, having money, power, and position. while failing to see that her messages and errands are attempts to make Chad into her image and break with his own kind. On first talking to Chad, he is making assumptions which he quickly finds the young man not to share. Nor is he aware of the kind of growth Chad has enjoyed away from Jim Crow America. Smelling about for a perfume, Strether easily misses the stench of inequality that drove Chad to Paris in the first place.

Chad has no more desire to return to the United States than has Maria Gostrey or little Bilham (who would "simply rather die" than go back) (NYE I, 178), or Miss Barrace, a point that somehow easily escapes readers of the novel. The ugliness of Jim Crow America, not the attractiveness of French equality and freedom seems to be the reason. Strether fails to hear his own patronizing tones as he comes wrapped in Woolett and delivering its solutions: He thinks he can even tell Chad things "that you won't know enough to ask me" (NYE I, 154). Strether admits, "I dare say we have imagined horrors. [about Chad's conduct]. But where's the harm if we haven't been wrong?" (NYE I, 156) (over lines like this, Richard Pryor's eyes sparkled like diamonds.) and hilariously follows that question with its twin: "there isn't any woman with you now?" When Chad sidesteps this, Strether is right there to point out, "You don't answer my question" (NYE I, 157–58). The beautiful little point here is that Strether treats Chad as an inferior, even while having felt in his attitude, "the hint of some self-respect, some sense of power" (NYE I, 156). Chad catches the ominous note in Strether's questions: "'You want to make a bonfire in fact' he laughed, 'and you pitch me on'" (NYE I, 151). This is likely an allusion to the infamous burning to death of a deckhand slave, one MacIntosh, on a St. Louis pier reported in many papers of the day and also written about by Charles Dickens, who told of whites "burn[ing] a slave alive at a slow fire in the city of St. Louis" and the judge, telling the jury impaneled to try the murderers, "that their most horrid deed was an act of public opinion, and, being so, must not be punished;" and he then "set the prisoners free, to walk the city, men of mark, and influence, and station, as they had been before,"[13] and he himself was reelected for his judiciousness.

Strether seems not to hear what Chad is laughing about, being in search of a pagan who has reverted to being a terrible African, and only wanting—unconsciously—to treat him as one. Amused, dismayed, Chad answers Strether's questions with an astute one of his own: "Don't you know how I like Paris itself?" which Strether can't believe he would prefer over Woolett, causing Chad to try again: "isn't that enough?" Strether, however, is still in pursuit of a femme fatale, which "made Chad, after a stare, throw himself back and try again. 'Do you think one's kept only by women?' . . . 'Is that,' the young man demanded, 'what they think at Woolett?'" On concluding, "'I must say then you show a low mind'" (NYE I, 158–59), James again shows us where Strether's efforts at returning Chad home really lead: "Chad had at any rate pulled his visitor up; he had even pulled up his admirable mother; he had absolutely, by a turn of the wrist and a jerk of the far-flung noose, pulled up, in a bunch Woolett browsing in its pride" (NYE I, 160). This triadic image of lynchings explains more than any other could Chad's wisdom in preferring France to the United States, and it is intensified by the "browsing" touch, which glances at innocent sheep, one of the oldest victim images in literature. The image is startlingly appropriate. Chad's people think he's involved with a white woman in Paris, an involvement that brought out the noose in the United States— brought it out, that is, when the involved male was black, and often as innocent as a lamb. James places the image in a well-known context, image and context making an ugly harmony because the conversation occurs late at night, "in the sleeping street" beneath a lamppost where Chad stood and "raised his face to the lamp" (NYE I, 156). A noose thrown over a lamppost, late at night, in a sleeping street, has a way, never forgotten, of raising its victim's face. To make a lovely Paris street bear witness to such distant realities occurring at that very moment in the United States, is an achievement that one would be able to praise more had Shakespeare not shown the way to an all-black minority cast by his own much earlier all-Jewish minority one, the earliest sustained example in literature of a work giving voice to the voiceless.[14]

Woolett sees Chad as coming home not to lynchings, but to perhaps the town's best business enterprise, with much upside potential growth in markets, monopoly, and sales. If Woolett is a black community, it would need, for its economic health, all the business vitality it can achieve. But if it is black, even more than economic health, it would need spirit, pride, and ideas. But having so little spirit and pride and so few ideas marks it, I think, as a black community, and one that is killing its soul with its product. In sketching Woolett as such a community and its product as denigrating, James has devoted some of his finest work in the novel. And just to be dead certain we see this, let me put it a bit more simply: when it is feared that Chad is being kept in Paris by a presumably white woman, James gives us images of a daytime burning alive and a night time lynching, and if we think these images are excessive we need to remember Emmett Till, murdered so viciously sixty years ago—an eye gouged out and shot in the head— that his casket should have been closed, but was kept open by his mother's order so that all could see the proof of white treatment of a young northern boy who was alleged to have whistled at a white woman.

Habituated as he was from his early career on to requiring the reader to meet him half way by doing "quite half the labour"[15] in creating the fictional piece, James recognized in his demands his own responsibilities, and he met them with a large array of arts and devices to sustain our interest, devices that reject any limitations as to what the author may or may not do. More than any contemporary writer (except Melville), he repeatedly demanded of his readers keen, close analysis, which he called "the Beautiful Gate itself of enjoyment"[16] If *The Ambassadors* is really about blacks, with a setting in Paris, James had no end of providing to do in order to represent the life and experience which blacks recognize as their imposed lot and portion in American life. The noose here comes to mind (as it did for Melville, in Ahab's death, the whale line flicking him up out of the boat by the neck). And if James was to make his reader do quite half the labor, an American setting at the height of Jim Crow would have made for little analysis on the reader's part. A Paris setting, however, shows James's awareness, confirmed by Conrad Kent Rivers' poetry, by James Baldwin's "Equal in Paris," and Josephine Baker's life, that Paris is the one western city where American blacks are accepted without social stigma, and this little point answers the question raised by James and taken up by F.R Leavis (unrepayingly), what does Paris symbolize for Strether? It symbolizes acceptance, dignity, and equality for blacks.

We should also ask, why fictional Woolett? That choice restricts our knowledge of Strether's New England home. The one clue as to its location is Strether's Boston accent. (NYE I, 207). Woolett thus seems to be either a suburb of Boston or a nearby community such as South Roxbury. Woolett contrasts strongly with some of the qualities Strether encounters in Paris, starting perhaps with the absence of violence and the things that replace it. Amid the talk, the high tide of argument, contention, and dispute, which he took in among the friends who gather in Chad's apartment, Strether was struck that "Nothing . . . well less resembles scenes of violence than even the liveliest of these occasions." Disagreement, in his experience, had been followed by blows. "Strether had never in his life heard so many opinions on so many subjects. There were opinions at Woolett, but only on three or four. The differences were there to match; if they were doubtless deep, though few, they were quiet,—they were, as might as might be said, almost as shy as if people had been ashamed of them. People showed little diffidence about such things, on the other hand, in the Boulevard Mallesherbes . . ." (NYE I, 173). In New England—New England proud of its town halls and open debate—what white community could have been characterized as having but three or four subjects for discussion, and deep difference, quiet differences, about which its people were ashamed? One proud Bostonian, Sidney Andrews, found such differences certainly, but found them only in the defeated South, of the reconstruction era. In "Three Months among the Reconstructionists," he says that such meager resources "will sadden the heart of any Northern man."[17] The North, Andrews believed, had no such affliction. As a great walker and a reader of Du Bois, James knew otherwise.

Together with its three or four opinions, Woolett had one business, a "big brave bouncing business' which "if it's only properly looked after, may well be on the way to become a monopoly" (NYE I, 59). Maria Gostrey wanted to know "what is the article produced? But Strether was reluctant to say: 'I'll tell you next time.' But when the next time came, he only said he'd tell her later on." Persisting, she learned "Only that as a small, trivial, rather ridiculous object of the commonest domestic use, it's just wanting in—what shall I say? Well, dignity, or the least approach to distinction" (NYE I, 60). If Woolett is ashamed of its opinions, Strether is ashamed of its product. E. M. Forster charges James with being too fastidious to name the item. He doesn't like that James left that for him to analyze. A bit irritated, Forster says that English novelists customarily do such work for their readers and straightforwardly name names: "but for James to indicate how their characters made their pile—it would not do." Forster's foolish conclusion is that "the author remains uninvolved"[18]. The fact is that Forster remains uninvolved. Only by arousing our curiosity and remaining silent himself can James hope to involve us, actively involve us, in doing our half of the work. His involvement is clear from his "effective provision" of clues in the passage—Strether's sense of shame, the alliteration, the product's wanting in dignity, its common domestic use, and its monopolistic possibilities. The item produced in a black community, which has become a big brave bouncing business, sounds—continuing the alliteration and balancing it with a dash of assonance—very much like a black bleach, of the sort the Johnson people in Chicago have been making for well over a hundred years. Blacks could very well get a monopoly in a skin bleach, since white businessmen have left black cosmetics pretty much alone. Moreover, a bleach provides no dignity and kills the soul of Woolett, for blacks have distinction as blacks, not as whites. Nothing better explains Chad's absolute refusal to return home to the family enterprise than its being a bleach, which his mother thinks would honor him, whereas six years in Paris have given him a taste of his full pride in being black. Strether seems to feel the mother's thinking is grotesque, and he curses the money produced by the Woolett product (NYE II, 317), for it reflects a depressing chapter of black American experience, when a race sought respect in the only way open to it, by obliterating its color. If a bleach ever brought respect, it more often brought humiliation, confusion, and a stronger sense of one's double identity.

When in the second paragraph of the novel James establishes Strether as having a double consciousness, he has created highly challenging problems for himself as an author—the psychological problem of showing Strether's blackness seeping back into his European experiences and the problem of the conflict that occurs when Parisian freedom collides with his Woolett repressions to bewilder him anew. All this registers on his sensitive perceptions, perceptions that amount almost to a double measure since they have been sharpened by his black experience. But as James wrote, "A psychological reason is, to my imagination, an object adorably pictorial; to catch the tint of its complexion—I feel as if that might inspire one to Titianesque efforts. There are few things more exciting to me, in short, than a psychological reason"[19] Much of the beauty of *The Ambassadors* involves the complexional tints produced when Strether's mind collides with the realities presented by Miss Gostrey's notions of what makes the man (at least as regards the hands); Waymarsh's frontal assaults on a jeweler's door; Chad's measuring the downward depth of Strether's mind; and Mrs. Newsome's magical conversion of Strether the editor into Strether the errand boy. Parisian freedom falls like rain on the parched soil of Strether's soul, that soul formed so capaciously, but burdened with humiliations, failures, missed opportunities—and Woolett. He has so little money that Waymarsh sends his telegram "reply paid" (NYE I, 3), little Bilham takes for granted he has known squalor, and Maria Gostrey sets him up in perhaps a second-rate hotel (NYE I, 98). Leon Edel thinks that Strether's experience reflects Darwinian determinism, especially when Strether "offers little Bilham the image of man as a creature molded and formed (The Master, 132)—and even 'conditioned' as we might say today—and therefore bereft of free will . . . . the individual assumes the form of the mold."[20] This is a sturdy observation, made sturdier if we add the more important point that the determinism flowed straight from Darwin's theory of the survival of the fittest. The pain of the passage comes from our realizing that many white Americans were, and are, making savagely sure that blacks were not fit to survive. Strether does the opposite in filling the plain molds of those trying hard to survive and tipping waiters and cabmen "too much" (NYE I, 179), apparently feeling fellowship with servants (NYE II, 252) and wanting to lighten their burden. White's treatment of him is sometimes brutally clear, as when on docking at Liverpool a group "had invited him to a tryst at the inn and had even invoked his aid for a 'look round' at the beauties of Liverpool"—in short, using him as a procurer, "but he had stolen away" (NYE I, 4), "tryst" probably defining the kind of beauties they had in mind. They might even have picked up his tab and thrown in a couple of ten-inch Havanas.

Waymarsh adds to Strether's burdens by expecting to be treated like a man and now and then giving Strether the job of seeing that it is done. Thus, his telegram makes him responsible for a room for his friend "only if not noisy." This is required of a man whose own room had a "dressing-glass . . . [that] struck him as blocking further, so strangely, the dimness of the window of his dull bedroom" (NYE I, 3, 9). Clearly, the room is dingily small. But the glass blocking further the window suggests its attachment to a chest or dresser, and together they would prevent a guest from appearing in the window and being seen from the street. All of these psychological matters show the simply endless, dense drama imparted to the novel and thereby explain why this novel was James's favorite: with each character and each episode the study he was engaged in provided a doubled content of strong, psychological matter exposing not only the individual double souls, but the American soul, the soul of the offending country. Ordinary white subjects could not come close to delivering content so deep, various, pervasive, and ironic. Even subjects that were free of any prejudicial taint and should have given Strether feelings of pride and accomplishment did just the opposite and distressed him. His job as editor of the Review is a case in point. It took the unpopular side, which would seem to be justice for minorities, and he admires Mrs. Newsome's courage in doing so. His editing it "seems to rescue a little, you see, from the wreck of hopes and ambitions, the refuse-heap of disappointments and failures, my one presentable little scrap of an identity" (NYE I, 65). The stunning image here clarifies the sort of inequality issues addressed in the Review, for one of the most familiar black figures in American life has been the junkman, forerunner to the sanitation workers Dr. King addressed in Memphis as he worked to gain them their earned wages and dignity—dignity so offensive to one frightened mind that he murdered Dr. King for his efforts. James had to have seen black junkmen in alleys separating scraps from trash or combing through refuse-heaps. The image, moreover, is so strong it makes us realize that Strether may have experienced such work, since the novel gives him only two jobs, that of editing and fetching Chad home. There is no reason why, in America, he couldn't have been a junk-man: he possesses its one great qualification, being black. A society which closes its avenues but opens its alleys to a race of people has made their identifying themselves as what they are almost intolerable. One of James's great subjects is this small scrap of Strether's identity, which painfully struggles to accept its blackness.

That struggle is made difficult by Strether's closeness to Waymarsh and Maria. Waymarsh confronts "problems" head on, and sometimes even on his own initiative, as at the jeweler's shop where Strether and Miss Gostrey almost cower across the street, unable to join their friend. The jeweler's store represents no problem whatever for Waymarsh but is one for his friends, who apparently equate it with its American counterpart, where they would not be welcomed. Of course, Waymarsh is helped to confront his by being an attorney, which gives him easier access to courts and a redress that Strether does not enjoy. Still, Waymarsh leaves a large wake, and Strether feels himself somehow expanding for being pulled along in it: "A place was too small for him after [their reunion] that had seemed large enough before" (NYE I, 23). Strether believes Waymarsh means the jeweler episode as striking a note of demonstration, and admits he and Miss Gostrey are left to show "almost a face of fear" as they stand "paralysed" (NYE I, 42–3). He credits his friend with being a "success of a kind that I haven't approached." by striking for freedom (NYE I, 44). From acts like that, Strether judges himself a failure. And Miss Gostrey casts a wider net, telling Strether "our realities are what has brought us together. We're beaten brothers in arms." (NYE, I, 45). Her reality at the moment is finding herself joined with Strether not in the fulfillment of the American dream, but in the frustration and denial of it. The black, she saw, was all too vulnerable to becoming a beaten brother and spoiling his perfection as a "good American," which she fears may be little Bilham's fate:

'Ah,' Miss Gostrey sighed, 'the name of the good American is as easily given as taken away! What is it, to begin with, to be one, and what's the extraordinary hurry? . . .

What I've seen so often spoiled,' she pursued, 'is the happy attitude itself, the state of faith and—what shall I call it?—the sense of beauty. . . . little Bilham has them to a charm. . . . The others have all wanted so dreadfully to do something, and they've gone and done it in too many cases indeed. It leaves them never the same afterwards; the charm's always somehow broken. Now he, I think, you know, really won't. He won't do the least dreadful little thing. . . . No—he's quite beautiful. He sees everything. He isn't a bit ashamed. He has every scrap of the courage of it that one could ask. Only think what he might do. One wants really—for fear of some accident—to keep him in view.' (NYE I, 131)

Her strategy for survival is not to stand out and to do nothing, so as to blend in, and her sense of helplessness against the mighty dominant group is perfectly expressed by her final remark about keeping her new friend "in view," probably while checking to be sure her gloves are on: suffering, personally and vicariously, comes with powerlessness. Her sense of his danger is exquisite; his not being ashamed exposes him to acting boldly, and acting boldly comes with believing in the ideals of his country—that he has been created equal and that in his own person he is beautiful and therefore able to develop as an American by exercising that faith and sense in public. But that would look like his being uppity, which too often invites being beaten back down, as happens to beaten brothers, especially when state and federal American courts freely gave and took away the name of the good American. Whites could be anything and be one; blacks could be everything and fail of being one. Such mockery I believe is what Maria is trying to see him spared. Since no black knew what being a good American was, well might she ask, "What is it, to begin with, to be one?"

Strether gives us an answer to this question at Chad's party where he promises little Bilham to help him financially. At the party, examples of courage are thick—Chad's in giving it for a sister who resents it, Madame de Vionnet's in seeming to acknowledge a black lineage by simply attending, even Sarah's by staying. All these may help to inspire Strether to pledge a different kind of allegiance, a prophetic allegiance being frequently copied today. Fond of little Bilham and of Mamie Pocock, realizing the couple are in love, and hating the Pocock's use of the girl as bait to lure Chad back to Woolett and the advertising of its sorry product, Strether wants to help the couple marry. When little Bilham points to his financial incapacity, Strether promises him his own money:

> "Well, I shan't live long; and I give you my word, now and here, that I'll leave you every penny of my own. I haven't many, unfortunately, but you shall have them all. And Miss Pocock, I think, has a few. I want, Strether went on, 'to have been at least to that extent constructive—even expiatory I've been sacrificing so to strange gods that I feel I want to put on record, somehow, my fidelity—fundamentally unchanged after all—to our own. I feel as if my hands were embrued with the blood of monstrous alien altar—of another faith altogether. There it is—it's done." (NYE II, 167–68)

This is a profound change of allegiance, and it is pledged at a time when Strether himself is losing everything. Failure to return Chad—insisting instead that he stay in

Paris—has cost Strether his standing with Mrs. Newsome and Sarah, and has straight-
way led to the latter replacing him and ending his mission. Actively setting himself
against the union of Chad and Mamie means he has further alienated Sarah by helping her sister-in-law to marry the penniless man of his choice instead of the rich one
of hers. Refusing to return Chad home to advertise the soulless product costs Strether
marriage with the mother, and thus security and status, of sorts, better than anything
he has yet known. In turn, these failures will cost him, as Maria Gostrey points out,
his editorship of the Review (NYE I, 65–6).

But against these failures, Strether gains one thing—his soul. That comes to him
when he stops temporizing and proclaims himself the black that he is by attending
Chad's black party. The exquisitely beautiful pledge of his fidelity to his own marks
that exact moment. When a social historian comes to date the time when the idea
of repudiation of mainstream American culture was first voiced, it should certainly
count as extraordinary that Henry James has earned a place in that study. Strether's
repudiation, James makes clear in the Preface, arose in part because Strether "has . . .
missed too much, though perhaps after all constitutionally qualified for a better part"
(NYE I, vi). And of the man who wrote as subtly as this last quotation shows, what else
can we believe of him than that being saturated with one's subject, as he advised, does
indeed lead to unusual achievements.

That saturation was partly fed by an ear sensitive to black speech, as we hear in a
triad of examples when Strether recalls rarely having seen Sarah "shy or dry," thought
Chad "unhurried, unflurried, unworried," and found himself wanting to sit down in
a Paris restaurant to something "fried and felicitous" (NYE II, 73, 65, 248). Such saturation (including James' likely knowledge of Douglass's having served as ambassador
to Haiti) gives to the novel its peculiar title, which contains just the perfect spice of
black extravagance witnessed by the adopted titles of King Oliver, Duke Ellington, and
Count Basie, and by the main character Lewis Lambert Strether, named after the hero
of Balzac's novel of that title. Much has been said as to why Strether was so named,
though one point has been missed. He bears the name of a white man, which from
the time of Daniel Webster Davis to Martin Luther King has been a characteristic way
for some black parents to name their children. It testified—it is now nearly dead—to
their sense of faith and beauty! These faiths have been reborn in Strether at the end of
the novel, when he prepares to return home to "A great difference"—but a difference

now within as well as without. Before leaving, he offers to name the Woolett product for Maria: "it would be a great commentary on everything," But she doesn't want to know—"She had done with the products of Woolett—for all the good she had got from them" (NYE II, 322). Apparently, she has used it, but not been turned white. Nor does she now want to be, there being no need for it in her final nest in Paris. .

Maria Gostrey has also been slowly transforming herself because she has now offered Strether a home with her, the woman who had to ride in a rail car separate from his, and who wanted to minimize their being seen together in public, that woman is now willing to share her inviting home with him. Is this change of heart the result of a person or an idea? In either case, the offer would be tempting, for Strether notices the table where he sits is "peculiarly polished" (NYE II, 319). Assuming that if what makes a table peculiarly polished is simply the fact of its being polished at all, then James seems to suggest that Maria has hitherto not been much of a housekeeper. In turn, this suggests either that she has hired a woman to do the work for her or has a visitor who obsesses about such matters. The woman who obsesses about such matters is usually a daughter's mother or mother-in-law who must break into action. A mother-in-law can be omitted since Maria has not married, which leaves us with a mother or a housekeeper. Here and there throughout the novel, Maria leaves Strether to write letters. Nothing exists to suggest her mother is dead. But we have clear evidence that Maria has guided two people to Europe, and in a triadic system that leaves us one short. It is much more likely that she's guided her own mother to Europe than that a housekeeper lives on the premises, so that her change of heart has been inspired by a person. Thus, when Strether gently turns down Maria's beautiful offer of living with her and leaves to return to the United States, he unwittingly loses the chance to be reunited with his own mother and thus loses the most precious person in the world to him, as James ends his realistic study of black life (which began with Strether missing Waymarsh), an ending reflecting how a slavery-shattered family looked almost a century and a quarter ago. However, James has probably doubled every event in the novel as Hugh Kenner claims for Joyce's *Ulysses*, and as Joyce likely learned from James, so that what I have described is but the first ending. Or rather, the first ending involves mother and daughter united and son separated. This means that the triad is incomplete, that we are presented with a gap, and that filling it requires that sometime in the future, Strether will return to Paris and find himself reunited with his mother and sister, as Ishmael was reunited with his uncle and the vision of his mother when he visits Maria's nest for a third time.[21] The final triad I shall deal with involves a matter well-known to many Jamesians, namely that various parts of the story are comical. In this final triad, the mere surface of the novel is the first element, the extended narrative the second element, and the comical sub-face found in the dialogue the third element. (I have left the extended narrative largely alone, except for the ending where, for the moment, Strether misses meeting Maria's—and his—mother.)

Forty years ago, as I was preparing for a next day's class, I suddenly experienced the words magically turning into comedy, and in my foolish elation shared my insight with my class. That class was made up of a dozen mostly young black students. The interpretation froze them into sitting through the hour with their eyes averted from mine, confused and troubled. I realized I had made a horrible mistake and that they could see nothing funny in dialogue so written that one side of it read in the ordinary manner while its underside, as it were, had to strike them as an early version of Sanford and Son. What the students' silence so eloquently testified to is that very little that happens to Strether is funny, despite James calling such treatment, in his Preface to *The American* (Blackmur, 31) working in two directions at once. That is exactly what he is doing. He is also doing more, but I did not see it then. He is gambling that his readers will see that he is demonstrating two opposed ways of telling the story, one respectful and the other not. James himself offers the strongest evidence in favor of his surface treatment in "The Art of Fiction" and his discussion of "Anthony Trollope". Speaking of Trollope's "suicidal" habit of assuring the reader that the story is make-believe, he says that "It is impossible to imagine what a novelist takes himself to be unless he regard himself as an historian and his narrative as a history. It is only as an historian that he has the smallest locus standi. As a narrator of fictitious events he is nowhere . . . he must relate events that are assumed to be real."[22] This shows us that James regards the historian narrator as a persona. He makes his case stronger in "The Art of Fiction" where in speaking of beauty and truth, he claims that "the deepest quality of a work of art will always be the quality of the mind of the producer. In proportion as that intelligence is fine will the novel, the picture, the statue partake of the substance of beauty and truth"[23] The historian-narrator is the persona dealing in truth and beauty, but the quality of mind displayed in mocking Strether and his friends does not belong to that narrator, but to a bigoted Jim Crow comedian. And how do we know they are separate personas? There has never been and never will be a Jim Crow view of blacks that honors the foremost American radical black voice (at the time), that of W.E.B. Du Bois, and his great radical predecessor Frederick Douglass, and their female counterpart who was hewn from the quarry of courage, Harriet Tubman. James's great gamble was in holding the mirror up to his time and all American times, and showing us, once more, the Du Boisean double view of blacks that this country has produced. The one is the view of the historian, the other the view of the bigot. And there is little question that James knew this and did this in producing his realistic masterpiece. He told the one true story you can tell about blacks in America, and he gambled that we would see that the degrading laugh comes from a second, and separate, persona, still very much alive, well, and active in this country.[24]

10

An Early Irish "Murphy Report"

Joyce became addicted to puzzles, and seems to have made his self-imposed exile from Ireland into a peculiarly difficult one by leaving its cause or causes unclear. But recent events in Ireland and Rome may offer us a fresh approach as to why he chose life on the continent to life in Dublin. The biographical fact that arguably has induced the profoundest sleep among Joyceans, his religious beliefs, may yet turn out to be the one experience that will shake them most awake, since it is one of the most important experiences of his life.

Richard Ellmann treats the matter with the attention it deserves by introducing us to the early chapter in Joyce's life when "After making his first communion, he received the honor of being chosen as altar boy" in the Irish Catholic Church.[1] That it proved to be an honor is, as we shall see, a trifle uncertain. But at the time, he "wrote a hymn to the Virgin Mary," studied in detail "The refinements of ritual [that] caught his imagination, and learned precisely the order of the priest's functions" (Ellmann, 30). In the Church, these are clear signs of a young boy headed toward a vocation. But this piety led to a highly different ending: Joyce refused to join the priesthood, refused to join in prayer at his mother's bedside as she lay dying, abandoned his country and Church, opposed his son and daughter being baptized in the Church, and opposed it for his grandson, these last three persons having no cat in his own alley-dustup with the Church, whatever its cause. This puzzling behavior endorses our considering whether the sexual abuse of Irish altar boys may have played a part in Joyce's dramatic about-face. For answer, Joyce gives us more puzzles—and perhaps some answers— the chief of them appearing in the introduction to and development of the most powerful—and overlooked—theme in *Ulysses*.

In the novel's very first sentence Joyce introduces the theme of sexual-predator priests in the person of flamboyant Buck Mulligan, a nearly naked faux priest in an untied, billowing gown, calling Stephen to him at the "altar," where he intones a morning "mass" and where Stephen would be cast as an "acolyte," though certainly a tardy one. Stephen's sullen anger at Buck helps us to dismiss the overtone of the spectacle as another of Buck's bad jokes, attempting to manipulate Stephen once more and regain standing with him. We easily miss Buck's initials B.M, which become triadic when joined with KMIA and KMRIA. In truth, Joyce's treatment of Buck is deceptive, since in the first line of the novel we don't know what role Buck will be made to play, though the first paragraph makes him a showy mocker of the Church. There is nothing at all to suggest that whatever Buck may be doing, Joyce may also be doing something else through the image of a faux priest followed by a tardy acolyte, and eighty-two pages later a real priest with a tardy altar boy, in a novel deeply indebted to the triadic structures of Shakespeare and Dante. Least of all do we suspect that Buck does double work by serving as the first element in a triad of morally errant priests: first elements are without fanfare. But for Joyce to ignore this perfectly set up theme of false priests would be impossibly sloppy work, throwing away his own careful foreshadowing of a real priest (whom Bloom likens to a toad), in a novel that Joyce obviously hoped and probably believed would successfully challenge, at least structurally, every other work of fiction for the laurel. Strong as this opening thumb in the reader's eye was, it offended only the Catholic Church and won no attention for the unseen priest problem. Hugh Kenner characterized *Ulysses*—and all Joyce—as trivia, and noted the corollary of "Joyce's policy of keeping all strong scenes offstage"[2] (which poses the great crux of how greatness can arise from detritus), and his observation remains intact to this day because it is true. Joyce delivers an eighteen-chapter tour of the minutiae and trivia of Dublin on a seemingly endless stretch of surface narrative that confirms our sense of the general dullness of the whole, until, through Bloom's eyes, we meet the acolyte who hangs back behind a priest, when he should precede him. Digging there produces the spark that transforms the character of the novel, and the utterly dull turns into unimaginable horror, and all by this exploding acetylene flame-point that accompanies Joyce's account of an altar boy. This is the start of a triadic analysis that will produce a more correct schemata of *Ulysses* than the work of either Ellmann, Kenner, or both together.

But well before the altar-boy account, the Church could have found another instance of Joyce's indelicate theme. An important sexual overtone appears at the Forty-Foot where a priest emerges with water rilling down and spurting *out* from his suited loins.[3] This partially completed triad of loin fluids is filled out by urine and semen. Appearing at this place, the cleric adds to the dramatic power of the theme because the Forty-Foot was a swimming spot favored by bathers nude and clad and at a time when the purity of priests was largely unimpeachable. And these matters seem to be the suggestions that Ellmann so brilliantly read as denoting "corruption".[4] Joyce, sotto voce, was merely reporting the truth that some Irish priests apparently were engaged in highly questionable sexual behavior. But no one dared to notice.

Ellmann dropped the matter here, where hard evidence for his case disappeared.[5] But thanks to Hugh Kenner's noticing that the doublings in the novel[6] are so frequent that almost "every scene in *Ulysses* is narrated at least twice" (Kenner, 76), pairing Buck's "mass" leads straight to Paddy Dignam's funeral "mass" and the candidates for Joyce's promised false priest and his altar boy. Being "real," they give Joyce the antithesis he needs for the triad he fulfills with them. Bloom calls Dignam's ceremony a "Requiem mass" (*U.* 6.602–3), but Don Gifford says "the funeral mass seems to have been omitted." He is correct, but he misses the crux, that Dignam though a member of the Church of Ireland, is being buried in the Catholic Church (probably to help an impoverished young Dignam be accepted at Clongowes) and that, like Ophelia, he is receiving "maim'd rites" because apostasy would have cost him good will and standing in the Church. Thus, when Bloom speaks of being "In the same boat" (*U.* 6.663), that is, with Kernan, he means, as Gifford notes, that like Kernan, Bloom also is non-practicing. With Dignam they complete the group of relatively minor offenders in this passage.

The powerful, poisonous offender in the passage appears as a true priest, in white, the color of purity, ironical as it shall be found to be:

A server [i.e., altar boy] bearing a brass bucket with something in it came through the door. The white smocked priest came after him, tidying his stole with one hand, balancing with the other a little book against his toad's belly.... The priest took a stick with a knob at the end of it [the aspergillum] out of the boy's bucket [the aspersorium] and shook it over the coffin. Then

he walked to the other end and shook it again. Then he came back and put it
back in the bucket. (*U.* 6.589–591; 614–616).

The specific process involved in this passage has drawn comment from one person,
Henry James, whom Joyce respected and apparently mentions (at *U.* 10.1216). James
speaks of himself as being "Addicted to seeing 'through,'—one thing through another,
accordingly, and still other things through *that*,"[7] though of course he is speaking generally and makes no claim even to be its originator. This triadic formula illustrates
Feynman's point about the imagination being straightjacketed, because the first thing
imagined must carry within it the features that will be found in the second thing imagined, and the second one must show the features that will be found in the third.

Starting then with the obvious in Joyce's imagined ritual, as we try to see "through"
the boy's brass bucket and the priest's brass sprinkler, which are clear phallic symbols,
the bucket and sprinkler neatly transform themselves into the second set—and here
things turn dark—that is, to the boy's anus (since we are told it is "the boy's bucket"),
and the sprinkler to the priest's member. Looking then "through" this second set, we
find the third set, color and shape, the brass color perfectly representing—and here
things turn much darker—fecalized anus and fecalized member, the "knob" on the
latter neatly representing the glans of the priest's member. (We notice, too, that just as
Buck is associated with bowels, so too is the real priest, and what is equally important,
Joyce appears to have gotten this association from Dante, who speaks bluntly about
"clerks and great men of letters, of great fame, all fouled with the same sin" i.e., sodomy. *Inf.* 15.106–8).[8] In addition, we have the brass bucket and sprinkler containing
water, the liquid representing the priest's sperm. Liquid is twice discharged from the
sprinkler's knob, and this fact supplies two elements of an incomplete triad which will
be completed by our mentally—and safely—supplying the third discharge as having
occurred before the boy and the priest come out the door for the ceremony. Joyce gives
his little scene the perfect details of the priest coming "after him"—in the double sense
of following and pursuing—while "tidying his stole," as would be done following a
sodomizing of the boy, requiring the slight adjustment needed to put all to rights after
such an act. After the ceremony, "the priest went off, followed by the server" (*U.* 6. 631).
Kernan notices that "The reverend gentleman read the service too quickly, don't you
[Bloom] think?" (*U.* 6.660), a fast reading shortening the time separating him from his

horrified victim. Breaking order by following the priest strongly suggests the boy delays being alone with a ravenous priest when they will be out of view.

More must come, of course, since a third element is needed to complete the triad that perfectly displays Dante's enormous power to influence Catholic writers of literature to the present day. And the triad does more: it shows Joyce at work on an Irish *Commedia*, balancing its massive load of trivia perfectly reflecting the daily stuff of ordinary life with a theme grave enough to accomplish that job, and reveals him to be a wholly complete artist on the level of theme as well as style.[9]

But before giving us this third element, Joyce's telling eye for irony has Bloom taken with the priest's petition, "Non intress in judicium cum servo tuo, Domine"—"Do not weigh the deeds of your servant, Lord"—which applies powerfully and triadically to the priest as well as to Dignam and the altar boy. Regarding the priest, his deeds offstage here are extremely black. And as if this irony were not enough, Joyce has Bloom kneel, saying, "My kneecap is hurting me. Ow" (*U.* 6.601, 613). This is a needless, trivial detail, but not as the first element of a triad that is mentally and protectively fulfilled by our seeing that two more kneecaps must hurt someone else who has knelt on the hard, stone floor. That person would likely have been the boy in a triad-fulfilling and third sexual act, this one of oral sex following his second sodomizing. Joyce achieves a maximum of intensity by setting this passage not in a priest's quarters as we so often have read about, but in a holy place, a church itself, where the sexual events butt squarely up against and bleed into a mass, however truncated, the tightness of the whole bursting with energies utterly belied by their casual, offhanded treatment. And all of this is adorned with no more excitement than accompanies the breathing of a sleeping child, and has been completely missed by readers, running or alert, the former of whom would likely find the passage boring and skip it entirely.

Joyce obviously has drawn support in exposing the dark side of the Church from Dante, whom Joyce acknowledged as "'my spiritual food'" (Ellmann, 218). In Canto XIX of *Inferno*, Dante stunned his readers by placing the simoniac popes, Boniface VIII, Nicholas III, and (unnamed) Clement V, deep in Hell in the crack of a rock—"le fissure de la pietra piatti" (Infer. XIX, 75)—clearly the Petrine rock on which Christ founded his Church, now in danger of being split in two and destroyed. Dante's handling is as direct (though he was not, as Joyce apparently is, the first to publish his news) and as confrontational as Joyce's is indirect and inoffensive. Diffident Bloom is the unsuspecting reporter, Joyce being much too wise to invoke comparisons with Dante on his own ground. But as quiet as the passage is, it too is thunderous and explosive, for in it Joyce (about seventy years before the revelations currently shaking Ireland, its clergy, and Rome) likely became the first person ever to treat the predatory act of pederasty by an Irish clergyman upon an altar boy in an Irish church on Irish soil, an act apparently repeated, following the ceremony and the return of the pair to the waiting room, because after the sprinkling the priest "put it [the aspergillum] back in the bucket." The horrifying image of the boy's backside as a "bucket" shows how he is valued by the priest; and the stunning point-for-point, inverse parallelism adds power to Joyce's contrasting treatment. Dante pictures battling popes, the highest members of the hierarchy, fighting each other for dominance, and destroying the Church by splitting and weakening the Petrine rock, the papacy. Joyce's symmetrically but inversely balanced scene shows the lower "members" of the clergy, the priests, destroying the Church as rams browsing in clover, the clover here, all sickeningly, being the little ones, the least powerful members, the children, preyed upon in acts equally suited to destroy them and the Church. Joyce subtly, unmistakably, signals the traumatizing effect of the act upon the altar boy by having him hanging back at the end of the ceremony. Joyce would have known that the altar boy preceded the priest: he fulfilled it many times in his own life, and, moreover, makes Stephen an altar boy, who "carried the boat of incense then at Clongowes" (*U.* 1.311). The power of the scene Bloom witnesses is increased by Joyce's restricting his treatment of the boy to his merest functions and nothing more: he exists for the priest's sexual use and is nothing in his own right. Joyce has protected the identity of this boy, if there was one, there being no apparent way to identify him.

But powerful as all of this is, the fuller measure of Joyce's power appears as Bloom stands behind Dignam's son Patrick, looking at his "furrowed neck" under the collar of his new white shirt (*U.* 6.576). Again, we can see one thing "through" another, the neck furrow morphing into the buttocks' furrow, and the latter furrow becoming the anal-ring furrow, the boy having in fact three rear furrows. The lower two could not be triadically summoned with that shuddering sort of economy that carries thought forward to the young Dignam doomed to the victimhood the boy's father suffered, nor of course from Bloom, but from the class of person identified by an exquisitely subtle synecdoche. It is introduced by the associated tactility of the boy's encircling white collar that points to a priest, and perhaps even to the very priest who stands watching the boy (assuming the senior Dignam's priest hasn't been rotated to another church, a policy issue Joyce apparently leaves unaddressed). In any case, this identification by literary device is important enough for Joyce to double it and drop a hint no less as to what we should be on the lookout for, though in typical Joycean fashion it appears three hundred pages later when Stephen speaks of "synechdoche. Part for the whole" (*U.* 15.4403).

But Joyce's full power is manifest when we consider Paddy Dignam a bit more carefully, and especially the question why he has left the Church to begin with. There is triadic evidence showing that he himself had been a victim like this altar boy. Bloom all innocently provides it in making a simple association when recalling Plumtree's potted meat, and continues, "Dignam's potted meat" (*U.* 8.744–45). Bloom is thinking of Dignam's potted, that is, coffined, flesh. But in a triadic system, a third element is required, and we have it, I believe, once we see that something had been inserted into Dignam's "meat," considered not just as a dispenser but, doubled, as a container. That introduces another anal intercourse image and gives us an excellent possibility as to why Dignam was driven finally from the Church that his wife still needs in order for their son to obtain an expensive education, where he seems marked to take his place in the long line of victims of some of the Irish clergy. Powerful as this is, it may pale a bit next to the likelihood that Dignam himself was sodomized by the man whose treatment finally caused him to leave the Church, and only by a twist of fate to be returned to it for burial by the very man who had been his victimizer. Put triadically, one altar boy and one priest give us two elements of a triad of actors in the sexual desecrations attending a mass. Without another priest to complete the group (Joyce shows, so far as I can determine, no other priest in the novel to be tainted with sins of pederasty), we need another altar boy. Joyce had to see that the body in the coffin would serve as no other possibly could. We cannot of course be certain of this. But it makes powerful sense because by fulfilling his own system, Joyce's identification produces a degree of irony wholly consistent with his powers, not mine.

As he was dying Dignam told his son Patrick "to be a good son to Ma. I couldn't hear the other things he said but I saw his tongue and his teeth trying to say it better" (*U.* 10, 1170–1172). Structure helps us resurrect these dying attempts as involving Mother and Fathers, the latter likely being divided into the one to respect and the one to fear and avoid. Love, and concern, for his son and his own impending death, could have forced Dignam to try to divulge a secret he meant to carry to his grave. The fluids from the aspergillum raining down on his coffin, just before its burial, suggest the sprinkler and its priest-agent could never bedew Dignam enough. This fate seems visually supported by the young Patrick Aloysius Dignam's looking into the window of Madame Doyle's shop, where in "the side mirrors two mourning Masters Dignam gaped silently" (*U.* 10.1132–33). They easily represent father and son at the same age. The support is made stronger because the young boy has been sent to Mangan's for pork steaks (*U.* 10.1154) that will probably become potted meat at home. Not one to miss an opportunity to intensify his structural parallel, Joyce has the boy "pawing" the meat he holds, just as the boy himself (by our "seeing through") and just as Paddy as a youngster were apparently also pawed. The pair of young Dignam's "pawings" complete the triad of "groped meats."

Power and shock are the constant effects attending Joyce's treatment of Paddy Dignam, possibly the worst alcoholic in the trio (completed by Kernan and Simon), who probably used alcohol to fight off his horrific memories, and whose funeral is accorded preeminence of place as the central event of the book, and the day that we celebrate to the present time: Bloomsday is also Dignamsday. Who fictional Dignam represents, we shall, I hope, never know. But what effect he had on Joyce seems clear enough.

Joyce was perhaps more deeply imbued with the Roman Catholic Church in general, and Thomistic theology in particular, than any other writer—Greene and Chesterton are but a distant second and third to him—so his refusal to have his children baptized in the Church can be truly called paranoid. This fear continued even twenty five years later, to 1932, and the intended baptizing of Giorgio's son Stephen, which had to be done secretly and the news kept from Joyce for many years. Joyce's exile has always exceeded its apparent cause—his writing costing him friends, publishers, and understanding in Ireland. Joyce's adamant opposition to Roman Catholic baptism was meant chiefly to protect his children, not at venting his personal anger or revenge. He seems entirely to have been acting for them, in a matter they could not address themselves, explanations to the women in their family probably being impossible. Joyce, moreover, was tolerant to a fault and made no moral decisions for others. But he was so protective a father that it is likely that pederasty in the Irish Catholic

Church provided a sufficient reason for him to leave Ireland the very moment the future mother of his children agreed to go with him. Given his fear of what the Church was doing to children, Joyce had to leave Ireland when Nora accepted him because children and baptism for them were virtually certain to follow.

Though Joyce's fear of priests could have come from personal experience, I doubt that it did, there being no apparent triad supporting Stephen's having been abused. Joyce's delicate nuancing separates Stephen from any function except that of a triadic occupant of the tower, and removes him then from the corruption which Buck emblemizes. Buck is clearly a faux priest, but Stephen becomes an acolyte only by virtue of being a figure fitting the personnel making up a mass: nothing else identifies him as belonging to its presentation. Whereas Buck carries his own bowl, razor and mirror, mimics the language of a mass, and adopts some of its gestures, Stephen does nothing. But the omphallus as predictive center of the universe accurately fulfills this function through Buck, the rilling priest, and the corruption they represent.

Joyce has Stephen himself remember an intensely frightening experience that occurred at Clongowes, from which we can deduce an extraordinary story. The event occurred as Stephen washed himself: "Water cold soft. When I put my face into it [the water] in the basin at Clongowes. Can't see! Who's behind me? Out quickly, quickly!" (U. 3.324–25). This matter clearly reflects his baptism because, structurally, it represents an inverse rite. The basin offers the symbol of an inverse font and the water the cleansing agent to remove the baptismal effects and all "dirt" that has come to cling to him at Clongowes. The person Stephen fears behind him—the second after (U. 3.502) obviously is intended to be an adult—a youngster would not strike such panic into Stephen—and therefore would likely not be a baptizing priest but a predator priest who uses the imprint of baptism as control over his charges so as sexually to abuse some of them.

Stephen appears to be in an accessible place, where he perhaps hears something, and fears a priest is intent on abusing him. Stephen is an altar boy, and the altar boy at Dignam's funeral who feared being in front of a priest who, apparently, behind him, posed a danger, helps us understand Stephen's panicky need to flee the room. Two more suggestions are apparent as well. The first is that the threat to Stephen is left unidentified and thus not personally felt as a repetition of something. This means that Stephen had learned of another boy who was being preyed upon by one of the Fathers.

The second involves Joyce's powerful water images showing Stephen in renunciatory acts, not swimming in the Forty-Foot, and later washing himself as if to undo his very baptism, which receives doubled intensity from our much later learning that Stephen has come to fear water so much that "his last bath . . . [took] place in the month of October of the preceding year"—that is, nine months ago (*U.* 17.238–39). We may suspect that the source of this aversion began in Clongowes, where water symbolized baptism and becoming imbued with the Father, and the act of washing represents the removal of that priestly power from his life. If Joyce experienced something like this at Clongowes, we may have an insight into his intense opposition to Giorgio's, Lucia's, and Stephen's being baptized in the Catholic Church.

Young Dignam displays a highly different and of course contrasting attitude toward the Catholic Church. Joyce helps us to see it in Patrick's carefully presented parental death, where the boy happily hopes that "Mr. Dignam, my father" is "in Purgatory now because he went to confession to Father Conroy on Saturday night" (*U.* 10.1172–74). The father's return to the fold is apparently meant to produce the good standing necessary for the boy to get his education. We clearly see the dramatic differences between the effect of Stephen's mother on her son and the death of Dignam on his son, Stephen leaving and Dignam relenting and returning to the Church, making Patrick proud of him. Patrick has a very conventional view of the Church, borne of his family's attitude, unlike Stephen, who fights, with a good degree of juvenile grandstanding that makes his bedside rupture all the more authentic as he struggles to free himself of the Dedalus pieties. And we see much more in the nuanced second collar image concerning the boy. What water and a basin show us about Stephen, the collar and its stud show us about Patrick. If water is the sign of the altered course of the soul, Patrick Dignam's collar is the sign of the altered course of one's vocation. "Master Dignam got his collar down and dawdled on (*U.* 10.1145).

His collar sprang up again and he tugged it down. The blooming stud was too small for the buttonhole of the shirt, blooming end to it" (*U.* 10.1156, 1165–67). By showing Patrick struggling to keep his collar on and in place and too irritated at the trouble it was causing, Joyce neatly underscores the boy's strong acceptance of and desire for the (Roman) collar and the life it symbolizes. Patrick's solution to the trouble is to propose a larger stud to replace the smaller, ineffective one. This proposal links priapic power with the religious life and appears to suggest that the second phase of his future clerical life, after being victimized as a child—represented by the small stud—will include his victimizing others as an adult—represented by the replacing, larger stud. Ugly as it is to see a sufferer on his way to becoming a victimizer himself, it is strictly accurate and the work of a master. We should also note that Joyce gives us a triad of three altar boys (the third unnamed) in an arrangement of one who appears to stay on and two who leave the Church—for the minor difference between the latter pair seems to be that Stephen's fierce intellectual opposition to the Church and fear of one type of its priests is balanced by the physical horror that would seem to drive the other one away. Young Dignam represents the major difference in that he is typical in thoroughly submitting to the Church and its life.[10]

This disturbing story continues, thanks to mathematics' powerful ability to bring forth an unseen, extended narrative which, in the case of *Ulysses*, would have outraged the Roman Catholic Church, though today it might struggle to produce a yawn among secular scholars who have small interest in the subject of Joyce and the Church. We have much more to learn about the past of Patrick's future priest-victimizer, and Bloom's observations and insistences point the way. He stresses the odd shape of the priest with a "toad's belly," which will "Burst sideways like a sheep in clover" (*U.* 6.591, 597–8). Lateral growth is found among the bizarre shapes produced by syphilis, which develops and morphs in peculiar ways in different persons. Also, according to a stage direction in "Circe," which we have no reason to doubt the accuracy of, Paddy Dignam, whose casket is apparently closed during his funeral, displayed, before he died, "Half of one ear, all the nose, and both thumbs,[as] ghouleaten" (*U.* 15.1208), and when dying had what appear to be tremors of the mouth and tongue as he tried to tell young Patrick something (*U.* 10.1171–72). Tremors of mouth and tongue characterize some patients with tertiary syphilis. This double set of symptoms, one in "real" life and the other in fantasy fiction, are of a piece, existing side by side in syphilitic symptomatology. Thus it is possible that Paddy had syphilis and that he got it as an altar boy from the priest. The question then becomes how the priest got infected and whom he infected.

First, as to how he became infected, the likely source for the priest's case would have been Bella Cohen's Nighttown establishment, venereal conditions and treatments being openly traded or acquired there. Bella's house attracted priests, as Zoe informs us. She speaks of an unnamed patron whom she recognized as a collarless priest (*U.* 15.2541–42), and because, as Kenner pointed out, so much is paired in the book, Joyce's system should provide for another earlier and undiscovered one. Moreover, when erroneously Zoe announces that Bloom has a chancre (*U.* 15.1304), we are assured of a couple of other infected persons, Joyce having created a structural universe of threes, as Ellmann pointed out (Ellmann, 1–2), and one of doubles, as Kenner said (Kenner, 76), in which we can trust. Obviously, Father Coffey is the prime candidate for that earlier priest. Father Conmee is the other mature cleric with the right probable age, providing the needed age fit, but he has the sanctimony of the old school and could not have found solace in Nighttown. Bella was the likely person to infect Coffey, though probably then a girl and employed in her mother's house that has now become her own. She is the likely one simply by her giving him the double pleasure he would enjoy from her erotic skill and his being able, anally, to humiliate a Jewess for her "share" in crucifying his "Lord." Triadic structure shows her bed partners (on 16 June) to be two in number (*U.* 15.3085), which requires a closing but earlier third to fill out this group. Her having a son, being educated at Oxford (*U.* 15.4297), means that she has at least one other child, one who, for the antithesis, will not be so favored. The least-favored person in "Circe" is the Blind Stripling, who appears in the second group of those comprising The Sins of the Past (*U.* 15.3045–46). If he is Bella's son he certainly would qualify as a Sin of her Past, and his steady bitterness, which may reflect the peculiar harshness of his fortune, would attest to the pure severity of his life as a blind piano tuner. With a whore for a possible mother, he probably came by his syphilis congenitally, and his father would likely be Father Coffey, if he had been Bella's priest-patron. The Stripling obviously has spent considerable time around pianos, where they served as well-known items of entertainment. (Bella has two of them, the second being a pianola that plays itself.) Coffey then has infected three victims, Paddy, the Blind Stripling, and, in the future, young Paddy. Bella, for her part, would appear also to have infected three, Coffey, her Oxford son, and one more, probably Zoe, who appears to be her final, and also favored, child, understanding her privileged position in the Cohen establishment as something of a mark of favor.

Zoe gives evidence pointing to a Jewish heritage. As the house greeter of three (Stephen, Lynch, and then Bloom), she acts the role of second, and substitute, hostess. We see this only because of structure, which clarifies relationships and shows us how carefully, thoughtfully Joyce has studied and weighed the dynamics of everything in his fictional account, giving us with Zoe whores Irish and Jewish under the management of two women who appear to be mother and daughter, along with a piano-tuner son and half-brother. Equally important, in identifying two houses Zoe promotes her house without any self-advertising: "You [Bloom] might go farther [down the street] and fare worse"(U. 15.128), and she even makes sure Bloom knows Bella is available in case she, not Zoe, is his choice. Moreover, Zoe knows personal things about Bella, such as her gambling luck, her bets, how she comes by her tips, and that her winnings go towards supporting her son at Oxford, where whoring and gambling provide his financial support. The tip on Throwaway has apparently made its way back to Bella, which will explain why "her luck's turned today" (U. 15.1283–90). Zoe shows familiarity with Bella and her culture and quotes Hebrew from the Song of Solomon, prompting Bloom to say he thought her a cut above the others (U. 15.1332–36), as a Jewess would likely seem to a Jewish observer.

The events in "Circe" steadily give way to Stephen's second crisis (after that at Clongowes), and he swings his ashplant with both hands at a chandelier and breaks one of its chimneys. This emphasis on violence (balancing Carr's) coming from a most unviolent person certainly involves Stephen's mother, but is highly nuanced and can better be understood when considered together with his Clongowes crisis. The great matters connecting them are the two panics he experiences, the cold water that Florry rushes out to get, the chimney Stephen breaks, the similarity of the two places, the religious themes active in each event, and the paternal ties so present and necessary in each.

Stephen's panic has been gathering all day long, starting with his rift with Buck who has chosen Haines over him, and causing him to move but not to return home, then his avoiding his father, his meeting Dilly in the last stages of "drowning," and his getting insufficiently drunk to block out these stresses, which open him to the hallucination he suffers. Stephen's second attack of panic occurs as he suddenly feels "Pas seul!" (the first attack came with his query, "Who's behind me?") Gifford paraphrases the French as meaning "Solo dance!" which is true, but only half the truth. The other half of its meaning is "Not alone!" More subtly, it suggests that this house of sexual gratification has become a place of sexual predation for him. His wanting no partner (the essence of brothel dancing) shows him gradually undergoing the change that ends with his attack on the chandelier. In his muddled mind, the cold water that will bring him around would represent a rebaptism because he associates sexual acts with baptismal power (water being the agent of baptism), and it will be administered by a whore who sees him as someone to have sex with. The double vision of the brothel, its workers, and clients is brilliantly rendered. Cold water will be unbearable, and Stephen's only protection is to break the chimney, which is a clear phallic symbol, and which identifies the clerical phallus as the object of his fear and the thing he is trying to destroy to keep it from harming him. Moreover, by reducing the light emitted by the chandelier Stephen may think he is not only separating himself from partners but making himself less visible. And finally, this matrix of responses, connections, and fears brilliantly shows that in his mind the whorehouse and the Church slip back and forth into each other, becoming each other, each being a place where sexual activities involve victims-young boys and young girls—powerless to avoid them, each place being the sexual hunting ground of Fathers and Brothers and fathers and brothers. It is this double, this structural pairing, that may be the great and needed function of "Circe," which, as Hugh Kenner pointed out, has no evident function on the "narrative level" (Kenner, 118). By pairing Church and whorehouse (brilliantly metaphysical), Joyce helps us to see they are like each other and thus suggests that if there is a difference between them, it is a difference in favor of the whorehouse. All sex there is consensual, and precious few of the participants would argue they are doing the Lord's work.

In his confused state, Icarus Stephen rises above his enemies, crying out, "*Pater! Free!*" followed by "Break my spirit will he?" (*U.* 15.3936–40). Joyce's use of the Latin form of Father is the doubling agent showing that Stephen has merged brothel and Church, Father and father, and escaped their twin attempt to crush his spirit into submission. The nuancing makes this work especially powerful. Feeding into its power is the broken figure of Dilly, who instead of seeking like Stephen a second and separate life seeks pathetically a second language, through a French grammar. That course will keep her in the house where Simon will continue, as Stephen apparently sees it, to crush her spirit, for Stephen believes that she is drowning and lost, which makes her like Ophelia (*U.* 10.875), and like a wife she shamelessly badgers Simon for money to feed her siblings at home. Joyce gives Stephen Gertrude's function of watching Ophelia drown (after hearing the girl sing about her tumbling to a king who calls her "Pretty Ophelia!" [*Hamlet*, 4.5.55])[11] and brutally doing nothing about it, just as Stephen appears to do nothing to help Dilly. Her own Church doesn't help her. Neither parent protects her. Through her confession, the Church would know about what some fathers were doing to daughters, and daughters would know to expect nothing from the Church. From inside the family, Stephen would have seen her plight, serving as Simon's second "wife." We see this conveyed through powerful symmetry when Simon, earlier, has ordered the girl to "Stand up straight for the love of the Lord Jesus," then "placed his hands on them [shoulders] and held them back" (*U.* 10.657–61). This act in a triadic system allows us to "see through" it to two other images of similar rounded protuberances, that is, where Simon pushes back her front side labia majora and her backside cheeks, for intercourse and sodomy. This set of father-spread and -violated female cheeks and lips is inversely and brilliantly paired with the Father-violated male buttock and anal furrows of young Dignam, their content being as ugly as their design is exquisite. And the design, of inverse male concavities and female convexities, displays the uppermost elements of each—male neck furrow, female shoulder protuberances—having no sexual function, but only analogical ones, Feynman's straitjacket upon our imagination that forms the unstated sexual specifics, the horrors of the whole being bearable only by virtue of the transforming beauty of the symmetries, nicely analogous to the neutralizing effect that Wordsworth notices rhyme achieving for murder and other violence in poetry. Needless to say, Joyce shows Simon to be in important respects quite fictional: Joyce's father apparently was not incestuously involved with a daughter. By working on the home as well as the Church, Joyce shows, as perhaps no one else, the pervasiveness of the sexual malady among us.

And the structure continues its work, revealing the plain, but powerfully rich, economical, double meaning in Simon's order "Stand up straight" as if addressed also to his unresponsive lank member and his petitioning the Lord Jesus for help. This is about as rank as it can be made. Joyce's six invisible sexual elements provide invisibility and strategic protection for every publisher since the time of Sylvia Beach. Without this double triad, which Joyce may have copied straight from Melville,[12] the novel is all trivia. With it, the novel has a deeply human content, and there is only one other novel I know of containing such a design, the great novel preceding Joyce's, Melville's *Moby-Dick.*[13] where the design and the sexual elements are as hidden and patterned as they are in *Ulysses.* Melville's hidden themes are as controversial as Joyce's, and both men saw that, clearly, you cannot have straightforward evidence and protection, too, and adopted patterned veiling, so that those who dismiss such work with foolish words like conjecture are in effect calling for suppression, though they may not know it. Joyce's construction assures him that nothing can directly be traced back to him or his printer. What it all comes to is the clear objective truth that Joyce's trivia with its intricate patterning is the only artifact he and his printer can be legally charged with.

Thanks to Dante's work, Joyce too is able to enjoy the appearance of unbridgeability while constructing a bridge that anyone can cross because symmetry shows how to do it. Thus, all the obscenities exist only in our minds, and ours and Joyce's seem forever separated, except through symmetrical additions. But unless his patterns lead us to deeper matters through an extended narrative, as I have tried to show, Joyce can be only the author of trivia that Oslo could regard as unworthy of a Nobel prize. This, too, is an objective truth. But fortunately there are the further objective truths, that he asked for mathematical analysis of his work, that he studied and loved Dante, and that he employed Dante's triadic structure, along with those of Shakespeare, Melville and James.

One astonishingly dazzling matter remains. The very structure of *Ulysses* is our greatest aid in understanding Joyce's accomplishment. That accomplishment is simply a second, and Irish, *Commedia*, which defines itself in the two halves of the novel. In the first half, Joyce's opens on a religious note with a faux priest refused submission by his designated acolyte. They serve as a paradigm for a real priest and his reluctant altar boy. They allow him to show, as we have seen, the second splitting of the Petrine rock, this one by the lower clergy in contrast to Dante's treatment of the papal offenders. In the second half of the novel, Joyce shifts over to a broad, brilliant parallel of Dante's account, and we see Stephen/Dante and his Circe/Inferno meeting with Bloom/Virgil, who is intent on uniting him with Molly/Beatrice, but first guides him through the brothel/hell and on to the dung heap of Eumaeus, Joyce's brilliant Purgatorio, which contains the clichéd purgings of Irish/English sins, in preparation for the honest uses of language by Molly/Beatrice on the Hill of Howth/Paradiso, and all this being squarely before our eyes, as Joyce focuses our attention on the element of minor difference, namely the Odyssean parallels—which like a second *Tale of a Tub* are meant to distract attacking whales—and which pale in comparison to the parallel that is truly dazzling—dazzling because it is so obvious—(once it is seen)—so well concealed—slipping beneath so many distinguished detectors—so very well presented, and so exquisitely funny. Stephen as Dante is modestly hilarious, but Bloom as Virgil is splendidly so, and Molly as Beatrice is pure comic genius—and the triadic values are perfect.

To suppress this would be to deface perhaps the second greatest structural accomplishment in literature—after *Finnegans Wake*. I prefer exactly what Joyce has produced, for his invisible elements remain forever invisible, protecting himself, his printer, and his readers, eluding the running reader and leaving me gaps to fill. Readers who believe otherwise are out of touch with one of Joyce's realities: In 1922 what chance of belief would Joyce have had by directly reporting on predator priests sodomizing altar boys and forcing oral sex upon them, and this followed by a second dose of similar sexual behavior involving Dilly and her father? And who was the printer that would have dared to publish such work? Joyce's only chance to say what he believed needed saying was through the use of a system of total, protective veiling. We either recognize the veiling of an intuitive, mathematical structure that our very greatest writers use, and adopt the welcoming response of our mathematician and physicist friends, or continue on displaying our great literary jewels as so many lusterless puerilities that shut us off from our academic neighbors who discuss their work and laugh at some of ours as the paste and glass that we quarterly recertify, one century at a time, as paste and glass.

Circean events show Stephen breaking the glass of a chandelier chimney that immediately becomes tied to his mother. She is described as *"noseless,"* perhaps reflecting that an intoxicated Stephen sees her as Simon's physical victim, too (*U.* 15.4159), the description suggesting she has lost it to syphilis, which would make it Simon's gift in Stephen's drunken mind, which, along with Paddy's ghouleaten nose and his wife's snubnose completes the triad of those displaying nose conditions. Small wonder Stephen shrieks at Simon the "corpsechewer!" (*U.* 15.4214), a term hitting off the eater of bodies who has fed on the body of Christ along with, triadically, his wife's nose and his daughter's hymen. Joyce's mother, we should note, never lost her nose and did not serve as the model for Stephen's mother, item for item. But the ending of Joyce's novel, like that of James's, was modeled on *Moby-Dick* and *The Ambassadors*. Joyce leaves us with a final triad: where does Stephen chose to live? The answer would appear to be with his two sisters, which means that Dilly doesn't drown

Such is a reading of the pure pattern that will continue to forestall the New York Post Office Authorities and the Customs Authorities of Folkestone from detaining and seizing any additional copies, a second time, on the basis of the various obscene matters I point out. My reading, however is not written in stone but in water. Joyce chose to write it in water, because that leaves no incriminating matters behind. *Ulysses* is a second Trojan horse and also a kind of second Tale of a second Tub. As horse, it launches attacks on the Catholic Church and on all writers competing with Joyce for top honors in their craft.[14] As Tub, it diverts attention from the Fathers and fathers and from their pride and their sins in Joyce's retelling of an old Greek and an Old Saxon story, added to by Saxo Grammaticus, Shakespeare, and now Joyce, in the Danish tale of *Hamlet* that Joyce so keenly studied. As Tub, it presents the appearance of being mere trivia. It is however, anything but trivia. But it was attacked as obscenity, and so successfully that the attacks succeeded in deflecting attention from the real obscenity it exposes concerning the Roman Catholic Church by identifying Joyce and *Ulysses* as the obscenity the world needed protection from. Even in Stephen's Green, his bust stands far removed from the springtime noon chatter of children's laughter, cries, and joy there by the pond, as if Dublin's children need shielding and separation from the "pollution" of *this* man, who was so preeminently their advocate, and whose bust needed separating as well from people who might have been inclined to attack it. One wonders if he and his family will ever be thought worthy of an apology. Oslo could award him the Nobel Prize posthumously, and Dublin could make February 2 a national holiday. That would leave the Church—no, highly unlikely. Still, just suppose. What if the Irish bishops, once a year, on Bloomsday, could devise a way to carry his bust over to the children and their parents at the pond and say a high mass in his and their honor, in perpetuity? Mightn't Irish eyes again be smiling?

Joyce perhaps expended more energy on *Ulysses* than Michaelangelo did on the Sistine ceiling or Ghiberti on his two sets of baptistery doors. When we ask what may possibly explain so great a thunderbolt, I suspect we need at least two answers. The first might be the huge burden of humiliations Joyce endured as the son of a ne'er-do-well Irish alcoholic in a colony of the literary colossus, imperial Great Britain, which regarded the Irish as little more than vermin, on whom education was wasted. The second seems supplied by Melville and James, from a second British colony, America, each writing novels of the highest unrecognized quality that only another genius of their order could fully appreciate and be challenged to surpass, as he had tried (in my view unsuccessfully) to surpass the great dramatist, Shakespeare, whom Joyce saw as the literary occupier of his country. Joyce's prodigious efforts structurally bested Shakespeare and everyone else, giving us the Beowulf poet and Joyce, the alpha and omega of "English" literary structuralism.

Afterword

Many readers at this point may feel overwhelmed or astonished and possibly having been unprepared for the interpretations placed before them. Such responses suggest that some readers expect writers to do their work for them and that they themselves have ignored many indicators which, to certain important writers, imply we have been on the wrong track. We have ignored the triadic emphases of the *Beowulf* poet, and Dante and Shakespeare and Melville and James and Joyce, in addition to the structural insights of Arthur Miller and the numerical findings of Harrison Hayford, Marvin Felheim, R. A. Foakes, and numerous Dante scholars. We have listened more to F. R. Leavis than to Henry James and ignored the latter's Prefaces. And we may have assumed that structural symmetries are mere ornament, may have looked superficially at the common habit of writers locating their stories a hundred years or so ago, and may have forgotten the pain felt by readers who have been made stories of. We have largely ignored science and mathematics as offering help to our studies, believing we are not powerfully connected to such disciplines, if at all. In short, we have been lazy and chosen the easy over the hard, until the present moment and our current interest in substituting our theories for those of the writers whose ideas about literature we seem sometimes willing to regard as amateurish. But none of this need be fatal. Triadic work will make more and greater discoveries than any I produce here. We need only start symmetrically filling in the gaps that confront us in our toughest texts.

Doing so does require that we intuit what will exactly fit the gap, and intuition will meet the reception physicists get from mathematicians, who have a mortal horror of not finding a thick floor of evidence underneath all moves forward. But for the writer, a move forward could mean arrest, a cell, and even death. None of the writers in this study could have supplied evidence for what they treat without losing readers or being punished. We have only to imagine Joyce alone exposing priests involved in sexually abusing children, or Shakespeare writing about Jews as ordinary people, or queens as poisoners, or a son plotting to overthrow the king, or Melville dealing with the savage treatment of pursued runaways, or James showing blacks being treated as human beings abroad but not at home, to understand the vulnerabilities the writers would have invited by disclosures. Literature's model therefore must be taken from writers like James and Miller and physicists like Feynman because they endorse intuitively filling gaps and because the moment the *writer* starts supplying evidence is the moment he becomes imperiled and responsible for his ideas, and literature will return to treating inoffensive puerilities. Assuming that I have read matters correctly, the most striking thing about them is how largely ineffective any of them have been in acting as a positive influence upon the problems they address. Other and earlier readers certainly saw what I have seen: each writer is proof of it. But, except for the mental sharpening that triadic structures produce, nothing has occurred to invalidate W. H. Auden's point that "poetry [or prose] makes nothing happen." Power in all of its usual forms—political, military, religious, editorial, or simply personal—remains too strong to challenge, and we are left with the same old conditions that get addressed according to the amount of speech that power is comfortable with. For we are talking about freedom of speech, and it requires vigorous and constant fighting to exert, let alone preserve. Every figurative device that literature employs offers an indirect way of saying what a writer may not risk saying straightforwardly. It isn't that prudence doth make cowards of us all, but that writers are often too sedentary, old, and digitally physical only, besides often having hemorrhoids, eye problems, and digestive disorders. They each told horrific truths about power, but not to it. To a people pleased to hear of their mighty exploits when they dared to share the roads of great leviathans, how welcome would the song have been that sang of raping along with pillaging and pointing out that those same warriors or their sons and grandsons returned to rape the offspring produced on earlier mighty exploits on the whale roads? To a theater invited to imagine Antonio spitting on Shylock and footing him like a stranger cur, would there really have been pleasure over learning that Antonio was his Christian brother who had bedded his wife and taken the high moral ground, or that Jessica had accepted his complaintless raising while she awaited her moment for cleaning him out and running off to help her indigent mother, made so in part by the moralist Antonio? Could a later Globe audience have found a ravenous Gertrude sexually consuming the infancy and boyhood of her son to be a proper study for their stage? Would they have been pleased with a structurally transformed Iago, victim son of a victimizing father? Would Melville's readers have favored *Moby-Dick*, knowing its structure reveals a powerful story of incest alongside a second story dealing with the hunting, maiming and butchering of harmless blacks, told by a dusky-skinned son on a quest seeking his dark-skinned Asian mother? Would James's readers have accepted *The Ambassadors* if they saw that it dealt with an almost entire black cast in various stages of rejecting Jim Crow America? And would Joyce's readers have likely thought that their church (but not Joyce) was guilty of horrific obscenities? believed their church was a far greater danger to their children than he was? or believed that he tried to protect them?

The Great Tradition noticed no themes of the gravity we find handled by the writers in *A Greater Tradition*. Putting aside a couple of the works I study, the others all deal with incest and dysfunctionality and the crushing truth that the ugliest kind of rotten-ness has been inflicted and practiced upon helpless, innocent children by the very per-sons who should have been their fiercest protectors. Almost every one of their pages deals with matters that are close to being unbelievable, including Gertrude's flicker of possible remorse over her battening on young Hamlet. That these things appear true seems due to our having largely succeeded in substituting illusions for the reality of our behavior. Writers like Ibsen, for example, believe that life is impossible without our deeply believing in illusions. But the illusion that we do not commit the grave matters that the writers of this study vouch for costs too much to believe, namely the perpetuation of our many abominations inflicted on helpless victims by other victims needing help.

These matters are among the many great themes that their writers introduce through the extended narrative they are at such pains to present. That extended nar-rative has an importance to them that academic critics have undervalued for a very long time, the value of their being able to tell an even greater story than appears on the surface of their work, a story that achieves for each writer the inestimable gift of his own extended life, because as long as we are denied the whole of the story, and know it, we will be motivated to continue returning to the work for the reading that will repay our efforts with its conclusion. An extended narrative has the added value of sifting out the dedicated from the mere running reader, for the latter gives up and turns elsewhere for easier fare. My readers may therefore be interested to know that in none of the ten chapters I present have I exhausted the extended narrative their works withhold, though I come closest to completing the story in my chapters on *Hamlet* and *The Merchant of Venice*. Henry James somewhere assures us of a truth that confronts the readers of each of my subjects, namely that the writer alone knows what his work contains. With the passing of what may be called the A. C. Bradley school of new criticism, the social forces ever at work filled that void with feminist, new historicist, deconstructionist, and other work, much of which seemed bent on expunging understandable English with jargon in all literary studies. This fork into the senseless has now produced the Ph.D. in literary theory, which is intent on replacing academic theory having ties to Aristotle and Plato with theory generated by Ph.D. students. I have attempted to restore my study to the old path, but now through mathematics, which I hope may prove useful to some who think it worthwhile to return to a broken but still useful line of study.

The enormous power of the triad brings forth the great subjects and themes in literature. In *Beowulf*, it identifies the theme of incest and its Christian redemption. In *The Merchant of Venice*, it identifies the huge Jewish side of the play that so many Jewish scholars have managed to miss. In *Hamlet*, it forces us to explain Horatio and succession, Osric and poisonings, and young Hamlet, Gertrude, incest and Yorick. In *Othello* it gives us a merely human Iago, not a monster. In *Moby-Dick*, it *adds* a character to the novel, extends the lives of two others, and makes us the gift of producing with Melville his triadically intended ending. In *The Ambassadors*, it shows that the novel deals not with whites but almost entirely with blacks, despite the certainty of Jamesians that it was the other way around. And in *Ulysses*, the triad assigns obscenity to its true creator, the Catholic Church, over fifty years before the Murphy Report. For a taste of what awaits the brave soul who applies the triadic method, say on *Richard the Third* and *Lear*, we need but imagine how Richard, Edmund, Goneril, and Regan might look under triadic transformation.

Notes

Chapter 1

1. Triadic pattern is intentional, it is unifying, and it is the insistent vehicle that brings us squarely before the great question, since so much of it is minor, even trivial, why are such matters being insisted upon? The answer seems to be, so that we will be forced to intuit that everything in the work is meant to display this pattern—in short, so that elements of the form will lead to elements of the essence, to use a distinction from Henry James' Preface to *The Portrait of A Lady*.

2. The symmetry used in literature differs from that found in physics and mathematics, the former variety being entirely linguistic and the latter numeric. Numeric symmetry is exquisitely precise, but linguistic symmetry is exquisitely wrought, so as not to give itself away. The writer is constantly pretending to be up to nothing at all, while devising an almost infinite number of disguises for his legerdemain. The played trick of pretending to be entirely natural is an exquisite game in itself.

Mario Livio speaks of Einstein's initial "grasp [of] the incredible power of symmetry, "'in *The Equation That Couldn't Be Solved* (New York, London, Toronto, Sydney, Simon and Shuster, 2005), 204. Einstein saw its power in cosmic matters. Critics deal with its incredible powers in the tiny universe of a text. In each case symmetry produces something out of nothing.

3. Prof. Michael McDaniel pointed out to me that Leonhard Euler, the Swiss mathematician, has proved that a given work can contain only a limited number of triadic inner structures. I have nor been able to verify whether any of the works I analyze can be shown to illustrate Euler's observation.

4. As I was finishing this study, I read William Goldbloom Bloch's *The Unimaginable Mathematics of Borges' Library of Babel*, Oxford: Oxford University Press, 2008, which may be the first fairly thorough study of mathematical influences on a work of literature. Bloch, however, apparently has no idea about the simpler application of mathematics to a literary work through the use of triads. Interested to see whether Borges adopted triads in his story, I began reading it, and soon found an epigraph, story, and footnotes concerning a librarian,

his father, and mother, in a physical structure of cells illuminated rather inadequately by two lights and the sunlight. These perfectly formed triads warrant someone examining the story in a rigorous way.

I should add that in *The Garden of Forking Paths*, Borges' character points out that the one way to get out of a maze is to continually turn left, which explains why Dante-Pilgrim and Virgil bear left in *Inferno*, the maze from which they successfully escape. The alert reader of Dante will recall that the pair make two right turns as well, giving the poet his triad of turns when we add the left one. Spoil-sports will point out the truth that we can't be sure Borges saw this, but the probability—and the fun—rests with thinking otherwise. As we shall later see, Joyce had his own fun, of a similar sort, with Hamlet.

The fun I speak of comes from observing the sly, deadpan face of the writer solving some crux that academics have noticed, unavailingly, for decades and are not close to solving simply because they spend a dozen or two sittings in reading twice or so a work that the poet or novelist has often spent many years in composing, the academic never seeing that without a "parity of labor" a successful solution is almost impossible. Years ago, W. H. Auden wrote a friend reminding him of their attendance at an MLA convention where the pair exchanged amused looks as academics explained literature which Auden thought they really knew little about. Usually, the amusement is concealed, as when Borges doesn't even mention Dante, or when Joyce speaks of nine persons dying in *Hamlet*, where academics believe the number merely eight. But in both cases, the writers get credit for solving a crux (from another writer who knows the truth) and doing it right under unsuspecting academic noses who may believe they don't miss the joke.

5. R. H. Hodgkin, *A History of the Anglo-Saxons* (Oxford: Clarendon Press, 1952), II, 521.

6. All quotations to the poem and a few critical articles are taken from *Beowulf: The Donaldson Translation*, ed. Joseph F. Tuso (New York and London: The W.W. Norton & Company), 1975.

7. John Grigsby, *Beowulf & Grendel* (London: Watkins Publishing, 2005), 146.

8. These terms do not embrace all triads. For example, Melville's "Call me Ishmael" is a perfect triad (proper noun, pronoun, and verb), which clearly show proportions, or should one say standing and preeminence? But it remains perfect only if we ignore the implied subject. Melville dodges the issue of the true subject in the sentence, You, which gives us four elements and two pronouns, one subject, one object. I think we are meant to ignore the implied pronoun and consider the sentence at face value. But fudging probably accompanies most categorization.

9. The pattern that John Leyerle ("The Interlace Structure of Beowulf," University of Toronto, Quarterly 37, 1–17, Oct. 1967) calls interlace work is what I call triadic. Feldheim was

the first to hint at the proportions of the elements of the structure, in Shakespeare Survey, 4 (1968), 102. I should also add that that Mario Livio's statement that "Symmetry imposes such rigid constraints" upon intuited symmetrical patterns "that the theory is being guided, almost inevitably, to the truth" (op. cit. 205) is also true for proportioned arrangement in literary triads, the proportioned arrangement being the relatively rigid constraint. The reader sees the constant battle the writer wages and wins against the slightest flaw in his choice of a word. Such unrelieved effort is truly heroic.

10. *The Holy Bible*, translated from the Latin Vulgate (Baltimore and New York: John Murphy Company), 1914.

11. Unprepared for, that is, unless he wrote somewhere close to and under the influence of the fine poetry being produced at Lindisfarne, which also fashioned excellent gold work. A third and even more important point remains. John Grigsby, *Beowulf and Grendel* (London: Watkins Publishing, 2005), shows the influence of Greek and Roman cereal gods, especially Nerthus, to the cultural fabric of the poem. No grain was more important to the matter than barley (see pp. 75–85, 171–96). On the doorstep of Lindisfarne stands Berwick-upon-Tweed. Berwick means barley farm.

12. The poet's device of slipping into the use of dramatic in place of narrative dialogue, I believe, did not escape Shakespeare's eye and invited him to view the material as easily adopted to dramatic ends, as we find him doing in Hamlet.

13. The supreme skill of this poet is seen when we realize that by putting his references to Cain, Flood, and Satanic crew in Denmark, he subtly has us transfer old Testament matters to a setting they did not occur in!

14. The vaguely described home of Grendel and his mother seems wholly a product of the poet's imagination. But he may have had help for its underwater setting because Lindisfarne and many other places share the highly interesting feature of daily being island and peninsula because receding tides produce a land approach that the rising tides remove. One look at these tidal changes, turning a peninsula into a horizontally distant island, could have given a poet his idea, mutatis mutandis, for the site of a vertically safe dwelling for his giants.

15. To these slight, possible clues as to the identity of Beowulf's natal home may be added the glories of symmetry apparent in the poem and visible in the greatest example of interlace work in the Lindisfarne Gospels, St Cuthbert's book, known to have been the product of the island monastery, which therefore could have provided an association for two of the most important Christian efforts to come forth at the time, one an artistic and the other a literary treasure. Both volumes also survived the 1731 fire in Sir Robert Cotton's library. The purely Lindisfarne associations are important because if they hold up, we know that Eadfrith, Bishop

of Lindisfarne from 698 to about 722, was the maker of the Gospels volume, bound by "Aethil-wald," and this information would bring us one step closer to identifying the author of the poem because Eadfirth and Aethilwald (Eadfirth's successor until 740) may likely have known the poet's identity. This speculation, of course, is close to palimpsest work. But then the eighth century itself exists as a palimpsest, and this gives speculation its needed margin for us to deal with material in a state of constant and advanced erasure. The reason for this seems apparent between transgressions of disobedience and murder.

16. Ruth Mellinkoff believes that "The Beowulf poet is obviously not interested in any vices associated with sex"—"Cain's monstrous progeny in Beowulf: part 1, Noachic tradition," Anglo-Saxon England 8 (1979), 155, n. 2.

17. From the similarities between the poem and Hamlet that I have noted, Shakespeare seems to have stored up various things for much later use in *Hamlet*, while in the interim adapting the triadic structure for use in *Romeo*, *The Taming*, etc., as well as in *The Merchant*, as we shall shortly see.

18. What is also very striking here is the near total absence of ego on the part of the Beowulf poet, Shakespeare, and Melville.

Chapter 2

1. Marvin Felheim, Shakespeare Studies, 4 (1968), 102.

2. My worked-in quotations are to *The Merchant of Venice* in The Complete Works of Shakespeare, ed. by George Lyman Kittredge, rev, by Irving Ribner (Waltham, Mass., Toronto: Ginn and Company, 1971).

3. "An Interview with Arthur Miller," Matthew C. Roudané, *Conversations with Arthur Miller*, Jackson and London: University Press of Mississippi., 1987, 368. 32. This exquisite gem, utterly neglected for twenty-five years, is perhaps the single most important insight into drama that we possess. Miller appears to have supplied the one point that about drama that Henry James refused to disclose.

4. I owe this point to Steven Blake, a student who played hockey, liked Shakespeare, and excelled at both.

5. Salo Wittmayer Baron, *Social and Religious History of the Jews*, New York: Columbia University Press, 9, 26. Baron points out that host countries watched their converso populations carefully because their members were notorious for socializing with their former communities, for backsliding, and returning to Judaism.

6. Shakespeare chooses this tensely packed speech to slip in the dazzling line, "if you poison us, do we not die?" (3.1.57), which besides looking squarely at Shylock looks as well

at a very much alive Queen and touches on Lopez's supposed poisoning of her, and does so with the words of Shylock who was often taken to have been modeled on Lopez. Anyone at the Globe catching the allusion might have sensed how skillful its writer was.

7. Harold Jenkins, "Much Ado About Nothing," SNL [Extra Issue], 1997, 5.

8. James Sharipro, SNL, 121–22.

9. James Sharipro, SNL, 199, 200.

10. Thinking of himself as a castrated ram suggests Antonio knows what offending organ Shylock has his eye on.

11. I owe this identification to Rabbi Michael Rascoe.

12. Portia is almost as wholly without relationships as are Horatio, Iago, and others like them, all cases showing that we must establish their relationships.

13. *The Theater Essays of Arthur Miller*, ed. by Robert A. Martin and Steven R. Centola (New York: Da Capo Press: 1996), 122–23.

14. Old Gobbo's dish is never given to Bassanio, as a careful reading of the text shows. Launcelot urges his father to give it, but no stage direction exists to show that it happens. The old man holds the dish at 2.2.124 and, still holding the dish, is sent back to Shylock by Bassanio, to whom presumably it will be given. Launcelot, we should note, anticipates the shrewd wisdom of Shakespeare's Fool, because in urging Old Gobbo to give the doves to Bassanio, he shows himself privy to Bassanio's need to reconcile with his father.

15. Portia's telling Morocco, "First, forward to the temple" (2.1.43) suggests she recognizes him as a Sephardic Jew, leaving the Duke and priests as the Christians. She may not recognize that though he, too, as a suitor, wants to win, winning for him, because he is gay, means, because of his promise to forswear marriage, losing her and all possibility of obtaining a wife, which he of course would welcome.

Chapter 3

I want to thank Sister Jean Milhaupt, O.P., Peter Straubel, and Leo W. Graff Jr., for their helpful criticism of my chapter, and especially Tessa Dayson for her electronic magicianship.

All Shakespeare citations are to G. Blakemore Evans, ed., *The Riverside Shakespeare* (Boston, Houghton Mifflin Company, 1974).

1. Niels Bohr, quoted by Victor Weiskopf, The Joy of Insight: Passions of a Physicist (New York: BasicBooks), 1991, 63.

2. Fredson Bowers, "Hamlet as Minister and Scourge," in *Twentieth Century Interpretations of Hamlet*, ed. David Bevington (Englewood Cliffs, N. J.: Prentice-Hall), 1968, 82–92. Bowers, Prosser, and Greg are merely eminent critics with differing views on the "Ghost." The "Ghost"

is so ignored that there are hardly individuals, let alone camps, that stand behind any identifiable banners.

3. Eleanor Prosser, *Hamlet and Revenge* (Stanford/London: Stanford University Press/ Oxford University Press), 1967.

4. W. W. Greg, "Hamlet's Hallucination" in Modern Language Review, 12, October, 1917), 395.

5. *Northrup Frye on Shakespeare*, ed. by Robert Sandler New Haven and London: Yale University Press, 1986, 86.

6. *Hamlet*, ed. T. J. B. Spencer (London: Penguin Books), 1980. "Introduction" by Anne Barton, 28–28, 34–35, 51.

7. John Dover Wilson, *What Happens in Hamlet* (Cambridge: At the University Press), 1970, 235.

8. Introduction to Hamlet in The Riverside Shakespeare, ed. G. Blakemore Evans (Boston: Houghton Miflin Company, 1974), 1137.

9. Wilson, 70.

10. Greg, 408.

11. Greg, loc. cit.

12. As Edmund informs us in Lear, 1.2.6, 10.

13. Barton, 34–35.

14. Mark Rose, *Shakespeare's Design* (Cambridge, Mass.: The Belknap Press of Harvard University Press),

15. *Witches, Devils, and Doctors in the Renaissance*: Johann Weyer, *De Praestigiis Daemonum*, ed. George Mora, M.D., et al. (Tempe, Arizona: Medieval & Renaissance Texts and Studies, 1998), 37, 39.

16. Weyer, 38

17. MND reminds us that some performers timed their productions for moonshine (3.1.53–54): the battlement appearance seems to be chosen to coincide with moonlessness.

18. Wilson, 66.

19. The First Player, traveling with his troupe, would be unemployed most likely because of the plague and would therefore be open to replacing at court some part of his lost income before returning to London, i.e., Copenhagen.

20. Franco Zeffirelli has the troupe enter Elsinore as it would an open, welcoming city, despite the probability that travelling companies, as S. P. Cerasano reminds us, likely "planned their routes taking into consideration where they thought that they would be welcomed, where the rewards were good, and where they would be provided for while in

residence."—"The Chamberlain's—King's Men" in *A Companion to Shakespeare*, edited by David Scott Kastan (Oxford: B. Blackwell, 1999), 338.

21. Stephen Greenblatt, *Hamlet in Purgatory* (Princeton and Oxford: Princeton University Press, 2010, 238–39.

22. Greg, 412.

23. Sir Israel Gollancz, *The Sources of Hamlet* with an Essay on the Legend (New York: Octagon Books Inc, 1967), 109

24. Rose, 63.

25. See Andrew Gurr, "Shakespeare's Playhouses," in David Scott Kastan, *A Companion to Shakespeare*, in Kastan, 371.

26. Alvin Kernan, *Shakespeare, the King's Playwright: Theater in the Stuart Court 1603–1613* (New Haven and London: Yale University Press, 1995), 43.

27. The incest theme implicitly confirms Gertrude's interest in young men—the King's younger brother and the King's young son.

28. Gollancz, 149

29. John Russell Brown, "The Setting for Hamlet" in Stratford-upon-Avon Studies 5, Hamlet, ed. by John Russell Brown and Bernard Harris (New York: St Martin's Press, 1964), 171, notes the rift in pointing out that Gertrude thrice ignores Claudius at 4.1.28, 38, and 44.

30. Hamlet's warning jibe to Polonius, "Let her not walk I' th' sun. Conception is a blessing, but as your daughter may conceive" (2.2.184–85) may refer to Claudius as "the [virile] sun breed[ing] maggots in a dead dog" (l.181) and the pregnancy that follows the walk. And Hamlet bluntly tells Ophelia "It would cost you a groaning [i.e. childbirth] to take off mine edge" (3.2.249).

31. Virgil K. Whitaker, *Shakespeare's Use of Learning: An Inquiry into the Growth of his Mind & Art* (San Marino, California: The Huntington Library, 1964), 344.

32. This attracting metal (3.2.110), referring of course to Ophelia's jewelry, which most likely was Claudius's gift to her, represents a tidy, double-barbed reminder to Gertrude that Ophelia can attract two men who incestuously interest Gertrude.

Chapter 4

I wish to thank Professor Leo W. Graff, Jr. and Brian Hull, M. D. for help in various aspects of this chapter. Credit for recognizing that Claudius's bloat might result from arsenic poisoning belongs to my former student Maureen Magras, whose insight and help I am happy to acknowledge.

1. Sir Israel Gollancz, *The Sources Hamlet* (New York: Octogon Books, Inc., 1967), [1].

2. Kemp Malone, *The Literary History of Hamlet: The Early Tradition* (New York: Haskell House, 1964), 2–5, 14–19.

3. Tacitus, Agricola, *Germany AND Dialogue on Orators*, trans., with an Introduction and Notes by Herbert W. Benario (Norman and London: University of Oklahoma Press, 1991), 83–84.

4. Malone, op. cit., 4–5; John Grigsby, *Beowulf & Grendel* (London: Watkins Publishing, 2005), 53, et. al

5. Arvin R. Eden and Jeff Opland, "Bartolommeo Eustachio's De Auditus Organis and the Unique Murder Plot in Shakespeare's Hamlet, New England Journal of Medicine, 307 (July, 1982), 259. Replying to Eden and Opland, Edward Shapiro says "that poison instilled into the ear was not new," as Marlowe's Edward the Second shows (1531).

6. Ibid, 260. This fictional accent is strengthened by A. D. Goddard who points out that "'Cursed hebona' is actually a harmless wildflower, Herb Bennet, also known as Blessed Herb and Avens in the vernacular in Shakespeare's day." Shakespeare Newsletter, 45:4 (Winter 1995), 85.

7. Stephen Greenblatt, in *Shakespearean Negotiations* (Berkeley, Los Angeles: University of California Press, 1988), 88–89, Greenblatt applies the point to the comedies. But it applies equally well to the tragedies, as Othello and Iago demonstrate.

8. *William Shakespeare: The Complete Works*, ed. Stanley Wells and Gary Taylor (Oxford: The Clarendon Press, 1992), 4.5.121, 125. All Shakespeare quotations are from this text.

9. Alfred Goodman Gilman, Louis S. Goodman, Theodore W. Rall, Ferid Murad, eds., *The Pharmacological Basic Therapeutics*, 7th ed., New York, MacMillan Publishing Co., 1985, 1617.

10. See the chapter, "The Persons Properly Called Poisoners" in Witches, Devils, and Doctors in the Renaissance: Johann Weyer, De Praestigilis Daemonium, General Editor, George Mora, M.D.: Associate Editor, Benjamin Kohl; Translation by John Shey; forward by John Weber, M.D.; Collaborators, Erik Midelfort, Helen Bacon (Tempe, Arizona: MRTS, 1998), 269–271. Curiously, Shakespeare worked in a theater the gold trim pigment of which was very likely arsenic trisulphide. See John Ronayne, "Totus Mundus Agit Histrionem: The Interior Decorative Scheme of the Bankside Globe in *Shakespeare's Globe Rebuilt*, ed. by J. R. Mulryne and Margaret Shewring (Cambridge in Association with Mulryne and Shewring, 1997, 142.

11. Gilman, et. al., 1615, 1617, 1616.

12. Charles Nicholl, in *The Chemical Theatre*, London, Boston, and Henley: Routledge & Kegan Paul, 1980, 15, reminds us of the debt owed by Elizabethans to Paracelsus, whose *De Natura Rerum*, 1573, "describes how to 'sublimate copper and reduce it by fixed arsenic to

a white substance, as white as Luna'". Elizabethan Paracelsians include John Hester, Francis Anthonie, Simon Forman, Thomas Moffett, James Forester, and others, who in their treatment of patients, probably did much to advance the reputation of the "inheritance powder." Ibid., 15. In *Shakespeare: The Evidence* (New York: St. Martin's Griffin, 1993), Ian Wilson argues that the death of the fifth Earl of Derby, at age thirty-five, in 1594, following vomiting and kidney failure, was due to "a single, highly lethal dose" of arscenic, "a favorite poison for the sixteenth century" 172–173. If true, this death would have interested Shakespeare, for the Earl of Derby was Ferdinando, Lord Strange, patron of an acting company in which Shakespeare himself may have entered the profession (103).

13. R. A. Foakes, "Hamlet: and the Court of Elsinore," *Shakespeare Survey*, no. 9 (1956): 36.

14. John Russell Brown, "The Setting for Hamlet" in Stratford-upon-Avon Studies 5, Hamlet, ed. by John Russell Brown and Bernard Harris (New York: St Martin's Press, 1964), 171.

15. Maurice Charney, *Shakespeare on Love and Lust* (New York: Columbia University Press, 2000, 201, also illuminates some of Claudius's curious reciprocal actions toward Gertrude.

16. Helge Kokeritz, ed., *Mr. William Shakespeare's Comedies, Histories, & Tragedies*, (New Haven / London: Yale University Press: Oxford University Press), 1955, 763.

17. Rebecca West, *The Court and the Castle* (New Haven: Yale University Press), 1957, 19–20.

18. "Some oddities of interpretation include the suggestion that . . . Hamlet sees Claudius as a possible seducer of Ophelia," Clifford Leech, "Studies in Hamlet, 1901–1955" in *Shakespeare Survey*, ed. Allardyce Nicoll, Cambridge University Press, 1956, IX, 4. In this fifty-four year old haystack, I have not been able to find the needle Leech alludes to.

19. The first gravedigger when asked if it is the law that Ophelia could possibly not have killed herself, cynically replies, "Ay, marry is't: crowner's quest law" (5.1.22). The coroner, he implies, has been squared. D. W. Robertson, Jr. ("Chaucer and the Economic and Social Consequences of the plague" in Social Unrest in the Late Middle Ages, ed. by Francis X. Newman [Binghamton, New York: MRTS, 1986, 53, 69, n. 24]) states that in medieval England, the time frame of Hamlet, "Extortion among coroners . . . became commonplace," and that "bribes became an invariable prelude to the performance of their duties. . . ."

20. West believes Gertrude is uncomprehending of Ophelia's plight, calling her a "stately defective" op. cit. 24. I think otherwise: the moment is charged with drama if Gertrude understands perfectly. It is also curious West sees so clearly that Ophelia is "a card that can be played to take several sorts of tricks," and that she is "sacrificed to family ambition" by her Pandarus-like father, but only for an "entanglement with [Hamlet]" loc. cit. Hamlet has no

ability to advance Polonius, who has managed to hang on as counselor in the court of the new king. Sacrificing Ophelia would have smoothed Polonius's passage to Claudius's side.

21. Leon Battista Alberti, Dinner Pieces, trans. by David Marsh (Binghamton, New York: MRTS, 1987), 140 has a character refer to the illuminating commonplace that "women's infidelity and lust can be harmful only when nasty rumors arise among the populace." If Gertrude works to squelch Ophelia's spreading of disquieting revelations about herself and Claudius, the irony is as obvious as is the Queen's interest in a permanent solution.

22. In "Merchant Culture in Fourteenth Century Venice: The Zibaldone da Canal," trans. with an introduction and notes by John E. Dotson (Binghamton, New York: MRTS, 1994), 105, n. 171, Dotson says that "'Perlle da pestar' were small seed pearls intended to be ground up and used as a medicine. Since pearls are alkaline, powdered pearl makes a pretty effective antacid. During the Middle Ages they had a great reputation as an antidote to poison." Claudius's hollowed out orient pearl, therefore, produced a large amount of antidote, which could possibly have been used to treat him. We should add that because ground pearl was not only a commodity but a cargo item, the practice and fear of poisoning was very widespread in Europe at this time, and this specific antidote would have been known to Shakespeare. Too often we forget that cargoes like this unloaded only a few hundred feet downriver from the Globe.

23. William. G. Wall, "The Importance of Being Osric: Death, Fate, and Foppery in Shakespeare's HAMLET," in The Shakespeare's Newsletter, XLII, W, 1992, 62.

24. Henry James, *Roderick Hudson*, Preface (New York: Charles Scribner's Sons,) 1907, xvi.

25. Barton's reconstruction of Garrick's fifth act neither includes Osric nor makes him necessary. Moreover, Garrick also has Claudius excitedly defend himself against Hamlet, which gives the king a physical strength that Shakespeare's text does not support. Ibid., 223.

26. I have used the Oxford text to illustrate, through the Additional Passages, the unmistakable importance of those passages to an understanding of the play in both the theater and the study. Dr. Wells' practice of relegating various lines to the status of Additional Passages (as with "rawer breath") does not produce an improved theater experience for us, nor would it have been helpful to the original Globe audiences. My generation doubts that anyone is capable of imposing tests on Shakespeare plays. But if a test should be imposed, my vote would be cast for drama, not Globe theater performance, which must always remain variable and unknown. It is drama that makes good theater, good acting, good reading, and good writing. Dr. Wells, moreover, endorses the current trendy emphasis on performance over text by carrying the argument to the extreme conclusion that "the text the author pens is not the play because *it can mean only through performance*" (Stanley Wells, *Shakespeare: A Life in Drama*, New York / London: Norton & Company, 1997, 2). My italics. I agree with Tom Stoppard who says

that playwrights say and do "whatever elevates the written word above all other contributions to the whole effect" ("Pragmatic Theater," NYRB, XLVI, September 23, 1999, 8.)

27. Gilman, et. al., op. cit., 1617.

28. Gilman, et. al., op. cit., 1616.

29. Perhaps to defend against Freudian reconstitutions of Hamlet's childhood, academic critics early on devised an unstated and unsponsored law, which no one steps forward to own and which is treated as so privileged as to be above and beyond criticism. It holds that offstage actions are unknowable—such as what happens to Osric when the play ends—and that references to such matters are improper. But what is truly improper is an arbitrary limitation on the exercise of the critical intelligence. We need to question all arbitrary critical laws that are held to be above questioning, especially because dogmatisms cleverly and constantly change their disguises.

30. Mark Rose, *Shakespeare's Design*. Cambridge, Mass.: The Belknap Press of Harvard University Press, 1972.

31. James Joyce, *Ulysses*, ed. Hans Walter Gabler with Wolfhard Steppe and Claus Melchior. New York: Vintage Books, 1986, 9, 132.

32. Don Giffard with Robert J. Seidman, *Ulysses Annotated*. 2nd ed., Berkeley, Los Angeles, London: University of California Press, 1988, 201.

33. My argument here is not that seating represents intelligence—anyone in the galleries could have failed to grasp the veiled character of Gertrude, just as some members of the pit could have succeeded in grasping it—but that the Globe actors in playing to the pit gave those spectators an excuse not to look in very deep. Over sixty years ago Caroline Spurgeon first pointed out the disease imagery in Hamlet. It has yet to be seriously examined as a diagnostic tool involving genuine medical matters.

Chapter 5

1. Rebecca West, *The Court and the Castle* (New Haven, Yale University Press, 1957), 21.

2. "Hamlet: the Prince or the Poem?" in *Selected Essays by C. S. Lewis*, ed. by Walter Hooper (Cambridge, England: At the University Press, 1969), 92.

3. Why this went unseen results largely from modern criticism's insane notion that Shakespeare is prohibited from dealing with pre- or post-curtain actions. He is able to deal with anything under the sun that his art can effectively devise. There is no limitation upon his artistic skills, but many upon the vision provided by modern criticism. And it is a pleasure to add that Shakespeare saw eye to eye with Michaelangelo on finishing what wasn't in view.

4. Avi Erlick, *Hamlet's Absent Father* (Princeton: Princeton University Press, 1977), 20.

5. *The Complete Works of Shakespeare*: Hamlet, ed. by Irving Ribner and George Lyman Kittredge (Ginn and Company: Waltham, Mass. / Toronto, 1971), 2.1.82–4. All further references to this work are to this edition and worked into my text.

6. Erlich, ibid, 157; West, op. cit, 17.

7. But his language here can be read as passive sexual compliance if she imposes it upon him.

8. Fredson Bowers, "'Hamlet' 'Sullied' or 'Solid' Flesh: a Bibliographical Case-History" (Shakespeare Survey, 1956). 9, 47. Though Wilson deserves some credit, Bowers deserves more.

9. Mark Rose, *Shakespeare's Design* (Cambridge, Mass.: Harvard University Press, 1972), 100.

10. Gertrude probably is not as insensitive as she appears. It's likely that her need to dominate Hamlet is doubled because Polonius is probably her brother. Only such closeness of relationship will explain the anomaly of his taking up part of her bedroom from which to spy on Hamlet. And his having abused her himself will then explain her enraged and intensified need to dominate Hamlet. The very name Polonius connects him and thus her with Poland, where he would have had the opportunity to peddle her to old Hamlet (fresh from smoting the Polacks) so as to indebt the king to him and be rewarded with the office of counselor.

11. R. H. Hodgkin, *A History of the Anglo-Saxons* (Oxford: Clarendon Press, 1952), II, 521.

12. This is one of the most beautiful actions in the play, and it is bestowed upon what appears to be a barely realized character, which should teach us how completely in possession of his story Shakespeare really is.

Chapter 6

1. Symmetry produces in a work of art much reader generated narrative that is done only with great difficulty during an ongoing performance, which is another reason I part company with those like Dr. Stanley Wells who want to limit our interpretations to those derived from performance.

2. Portions of this chapter were first presented in 1994 at a conference of the Shakespeare and Renaissance Association of West Virginia, which then published the paper.

3. Lodovico's name may be no accident. A well-know Sicilian inquisitor was named Ludovico a Paramo; he argued that "in banishing Adam and Eve from the Garden of Eden, God himself had set the pattern for secrecy and the absence of witnesses in trials of offenders against the faith."—Salo Wittmayer Baron. *A Social and Religious History of the Jews* 2nd ed. New York: Columbia University Press, 1962–83, XIII, 20. I wish to thank Professor the late Dr. Jose Soler, and also Ruth Olesan, for their help with portions of my Inquisition argument.

4. Irving Ribner, George Lyman Kittredge, *The Complete Works of Shakespeare* (Waltham, Massachusetts/Toronto: Ginn and Company, 1971). All citations from the play are taken from this text.

5. Juan de Llorente, *The History of the Inquisition in Spain*, trans. and abridged by Anon. (London: Geo B. Whittaker), 1827, 50–51. My other quotations from this volume are worked into my text.

6. The drawing appears in *Wanderings*: Chaim Potok's History of the Jews (New York: Alfred A. Knopf, 1978), 316–17, and may represent the famous auto-da-fe at Valladolid, 1536.

7. Among many parallels between Othello and Francisco Bussone de Camagnola, the most immediately striking include their precociously developed military talents, their both being Venetian outsiders, their great military prowess, their requests for residences befitting their dignities, their imperfect health, their hair-breadth 'scapes from a deadly breach, their both being mistrusted and watched, their having property confiscated, and their being recalled to Venice, where Carmagnola was tortured, tried, and beheaded on 5 May, 1432. These matters may be found in W. Carew Hazlitt, *The Venetian Republic* (London 1915, New York: AMS Press Inc., 1966), I, 858, 859, 870, 877, 883, 889, 899, 900–901, and 902, The most interesting similarity between the two comes from Carmagnola's frequent withdrawals from the field to the baths, under the guise of delicate health where he may have idled away time with his wife (Ibid. I. 870, 873, 876, 878, 881, 883, 884). Such possible dallying could have produced the idea that Othello is defensive about wanting Desdemona with him in Cyprus. Filippo Scholari, otherwise known as Pippo Spano, furnished Shakespeare with some hints for Cassio, such as needing a litter to transport him when ill (ibid. I, 815), and being quite militarily inept. Also, when Carmagnola's inaction produced meddling from Venice, and he denounced "self-sufficient civilians, who quitting their counting houses, came to teach war to the Child of War" (I, 878), we, of course, may hear an echo of Iago's complaint that the bookkeeper Cassio is only an "arithmetician" (1.1.19).

8. The ghettos of Venice had their own inns to confine Jewish visitors otherwise without room and board.

9. Thomas Caldicott Chubb, trans. *The Letters of Pietro Aretino* (New Haven: The Shoe String Press, Inc.)1967, 168, 325.

10. Brabantio's name—Brabant plus the Italian nominative io ending—tells us that he comes from the duchy, and that he seems to believe with Aretino that "Venice receives you, where others hunt you down"—Chubb, op. cit., 37.

11. Some readers will have realized that Othello is involved in the deaths of four persons, which breaks Shakespeare's triadic pattern. But then when we find that Desdemona is involved in four also—her own, her baby's, her mother's, and her father's, along with Iago who

is involved in hers and her child's, Emilia's, and his own, we see how neatly he repairs broken work. Iago's own is assured when he vows "From this time forth I never will speak word" (5.2.304), which fulfills one final triad, that of the three red-spotted cloths, the handkerchief, its copy, and the linen that will be used in his own waterboarding. This small area of the play is very exciting for the confluence of highly important matters that are found to join here, including the ground-breaking matter of the spotted cloths having a clear, metaphysical connection—"heterogeneous ideas linked by violence together"—allying Shakespeare with a poetic current that he obviously makes use of in this and later mature work. Triads, therefore, deserve close examination for more such discoveries, especially since their very structure involves proportions of most and least, which produce strong antitheses.

Chapter 7

1. Richard P. Blackmur, ed. *The Art of the Novel*: Critical Prefaces by Henry James. (New York and London: Charles Scribner's Sons, 1937), 122. We should note that ground, site, and foundation represent a triad]

2. Herman Melville, *Moby-Dick or The Whale*, ed. by Harrison Hayford, Hershel Parker, and G. Thomas Tanselle (Evanston and Chicago: Northwestern University Press and The Newberry Library, 1988), 152. All worked-in citations are to this edition.

3. According to the "Report of Commissioner of Fish and Fisheries" in Alexander Starbuck, *History of the American Whale Fishery* (Secaucus, New Jersey: Castle Books), 1989, 466–72.

4. In "Ishmael's Recovery: Injury, Illness, and Convalescence in Moby-Dick" Leviathan 8, March 2006, 22, James Emmett Ryan establishes Ishmael as, after Ahab, a second convalescent aboard ship. Ishmael's weak health makes his 300th lay all the more disgraceful, though of course one can argue that it may be more than an ill seaman deserves. And the ministrations to Ahab that I attribute to Ishmael are profoundly deepened by Ryan's argument of an Ishmael in poor health himself. Queequeg becomes the third convalescent aboard ship.

5. Fred V. Bernard. "The Question of Race in Moby-Dick." The Massachusetts Review XLIII (2002): 384–404.

6. Ian Stewart, *Why Beauty is Truth*, New York: Basic Books, 2007, 68, observes that "Elegance and simplicity are the touchstones of mathematics, and novel concepts, however strange they appear at first, tend to win out in the long run if they help to keep the subject elegant and simple" (his emphasis). The theory I am proposing not only keeps the subject elegant and simple, but positive. The obvious argument against my proposal is that it does not reflect Melville's intention. But it does, since the negative case assumes that Melville, out of youthful inexperience, neglected something so necessary as parents for Ishmael.

7. Joan Druett, *Hen Frigates: Wives of Merchant Captains under Sail* (New York: Simon and Schuster, 1998), 17, 51, 90.

8. Melville's prose is a vast triad made up of elements paired, tripled, and untouched or natural, which we find also in Joyce, who appears to have taken them from Melville.

9. Hershel Parker, *Herman Melville: A Biography* (Baltimore and London: The Johns Hopkins University Press, 2002), II, 10.

10. John Hope Franklin and Loren Schwenenger, *Runaway Slaves*. (New York and Oxford: Oxford University Press, 1999), 283. If Ishmael is a runaway, his color has made him to be mistaken for a black. The fear of capture that Ishmael exhibits from time to time may, however, only reflect his genuine dread of the consequences attendant on being picked up as one.

11. Ahab balances Perth as an alcoholic, the evidence of which is suggested by his acknowledging his thirsting "hollow" and his gritting his teeth when invited to drink aboard the Bachelor (NN M-D 165, 494).

12. Sister Jean Milhaupt, O.P. has pointed out to me that by my argument Ahab appears to be the offspring of a Philippine mother and an island aborigine and therefore cannot be a mulatto, and that Ishmael cannot be one either, since he appears to be an offspring of that offspring and the same Philippine mother. Strictly speaking, this is true. But both men lived out American lives in American ports and cities, where race existed in the eye of some white Americans who would have instantly sorted them with blacks, merely because of their color. In my MR article, I came at the racial subject from the evidence offered by color, social standing, customs, wages, and work opportunities. Coming at the same subject from the evidence of relationships, I now see that my earlier conclusion was inexact, since relationships suggest that the two men are a mix of Philippino and island aborigine who undergo, as Melville demonstrates in a dozen different ways, the same treatment that true mulattoes suffered: in short, Melville provides a doubled blood-group of mulattoes who suffer alike under our racial system. John Byrant claimed (without proof) that Ahab is white, and I argued that he is black. Both readings are gross distortions and wrong, according to my altered and nuanced reading of the evidence.

13. Richard Feynman, *The Character of Physical Law* (Cambridge, Mass. And London: The MIT Press, 1967), 76.

14. Blackmur, op. cit., 114.

15. *Boswell's Life of Johnson*, ed, Hill-Powell (Oxford: Oxford University Press, 1934) I, 406 and n. 3.

16. I am assuming that Moby Dick deprived Ahab of two appendages in their earlier encounter.

17. Having been a Persian makes Ahab reincarnated and shows Melville dealing with two of his lives. Also important is Ahab's hinted-at Persian connection with the Parsee. But

more important, Ahab seems to be denying the incestuous guilt we are examining because in reincarnation one acquires one's next life free of its previous physical peculiarities: he is suggesting his burning is from a previous life.

18. Feynman, 158.

19. One set of twins requires a second, and that set is evident when we read that Moby Dick "had actually been encountered in opposite latitudes at one and the same instant of time (NN M-D 182). The one possible way for such to have actually occurred is for Moby Dick to have a twin.

Chapter 8

1. Henry James's strictures on first-person narratives would include *Moby-Dick*, the brilliance of which James would be very hard pressed to match. For the strictures, see the Preface to *The Ambassadors, The Novels and Tales of Henry James* (New York: Charles Scribner's Sons, 1907), XXI, xviii–xix.

2. James opposes the first-person narrative because it makes it awkward to relate vital information about the protagonist. Melville avoids awkwardness by making things very difficult, that is, by tying smaller knots than James seems willing to use. His knots add greatly to our difficulty, but Melville gets as much said about his protagonist as James gets said, for example, about Strether. Joyce read both men, but borrowed, I believe, more from Melville, and produced *Ulysses* and *Finnegans Wake*, I believe, as books that would be unsurpassed for reader difficulty. In short, the difficulty of the latter two novels may be a direct response to *Moby-Dick*. Ibid, I, xvi.

3. The oil ladle symbol, while phallic, differs markedly from the lance symbol. The latter one vividly suggests deadly (i.e., climaxing) penetration into a bloody, flesh sheath, whereas the ladle image suggests the more benign dominant employment of transferring oil from try pot to barrel. Ahab's sexual assaults, therefore, seem connected more with alcoholic folly than with malevolence, more with predestination than with willed choice, though both are present.

4. Queequeg's abandoning Kokovoko for harpooneering suggests he is not in line to succeed his father, which in turn suggests his likely being illegitimate.

5. Fedallah seems then to sell her aboard the Pequod and thus to Ahab. As a person placed in Ahab's path, as it were, Ahab may feel led into temptation by a man who at least shares responsibility with Ahab for her fate.

6. This nameless woman is only a type and nothing more, a variation of patient Griselda, and certainly not a model for abused women. Though there is nothing nuanced about her, her presentation-less presentation represents art of a very high order.

7. Henry James allowed himself a boast about his indirect creation of Mrs. Newsome, Chad's mother, saying that Mrs. Newsome, in far off Woollett, "should yet be no less intensely than circuitously present through the whole thing, should be no less felt as to be reckoned with than the most direct exhibition, the finest portrayal at first hand, could make her." *The Novels and Tales of Henry James*, op. cit., XXI, xvi. Melville, I believe, deserves even more credit than James, since he not only broke the ground for James, but withheld naming the woman, indeed withheld vouching for her existence. James's super subtlety looks a bit clumsy in the comparison.

8. Whale-torn squid would probably not see their opponent as benign to themselves, which squares with Melville's vision of life above and below water as predatory.

9. Ishmael's "seemed" suggests he sees some hope of becoming one of Ahab's mortal interests.

10. Stubb is the ship's second officer showing dysfunctionality: he intentionally deserts Pip in the middle of the Pacific, so that Pip loses his mind; and he humiliates Fleece who must stand at attention, await a groin-blow, and preach to sharks. Whales, black males, and a colored woman make up the triad of inoffensives who suffer brutalizing in a novel that still may have ranking among the most violent of the century. We also need to recognize that while all the victims are black or colored, the victimizers are white or colored, but not black. This is a powerful expression of Melville's black racial theme.

11. The triad so identified still leaves ample room for other identifications, especially straight couple, straight children, and gay couple. However, a blood relationship between Ishmael and Queequeg does not exclude their being gay, though I find absolutely no evidence that they are.

12. These intuitions will be among the least readily accepted matters I present in this work, but they enjoy an important support. Ian Stewart points out that "Elegance and simplicity are the touchstones of mathematics. And novel concepts, however strange they appear at first, tend to win out in the long run if they help to keep the subject elegant and simple."—*Why Beauty is Truth*, 68. My namings keep matters elegant and simple.

13. There may be more than a hint in the mystery of Queequeg's hieroglyphics in that the seer was unwilling to make plain all the ugliness he saw, especially since it would involve the king, who had no compunction about killing, and eating, perceived opponents.

14. Most likely this shaman made his report to the king, which Queequeg would have learned about. The tattooing would likely represent a second and later meeting.

15. I owe this point, and help on many other matters, to Sara Leeland.

16. How Queequeg learned of these Nantucket canoes, we are not told. The three persons who could have told him are Ishmael, Ahab, or the seer.

17. Henry James, "Tennyson's Drama," in *Theory of Fiction: Henry James*, ed. by James E. Miller, Jr., (Lincoln and London: University of Nebraska Press, 1972), 98. Though James is speaking of the drama, the point applies equally well to triadicized novels. I should note that his criticisms of Tolstoi and Dostoyevsky as "loose, baggy monsters," is really an observation of their lacking the tight structure that comes from triads. Similarly, I believe his strictures against Jane Austen's novels address her unextended narratives.

18. F. V. Bernard, "The Question of Race in Moby-Dick," *Massachusetts Review* XLIII no. 3, (2002), 384–404.

Chapter 9

1. Henry James, *The Ambassadors* (New York: Charles Scribner's Sons, 1909), I, 226; II, 257. All subsequent citations, worked into my text, are taken from this edition.

2. Arthur Miller is the second to violate the silent code when he cuts to the heart of the matter and urges readers to fill the gaps that writers leave them. He obviously understands the asymmetric pattern writers leave for our fulfilling, but he does in two or three words what James devoted eighteen Prefaces to.

3. F. R. Leavis, *The Great Tradition* (New York: New York University Press, 1963), 126.

4. Henry James, *A Small Boy & Others* (New York: Charles Scribners Sons, 1941), 249–250.

5. Alfred Harbegger, *The Father: A Life of Henry James, Sr.* (New York: Farrar, Straus, and Giroux, 1994), 258.

6. Leon Edel, *The Master* (London: Rupert Hart-Davis, 1972), 284.

7. W. E. B. Du Bois, *The Souls of Black Folk: Essays and Sketches'* ed. Saunders Redding (Greenwich, Conn.: Fawcett Publications, 1961), 16–17.

8. Herbert Aptheker, ed., *The Correspondence of W.E.B. Du Bois* (Amherst: The University of Massachusetts Press, 1973), I, 134.

9. R. W. B. Lewis, *The Jameses: A Family Narrative* (New York: Farrar, Straus, and Giroux, 1991), 148.

10. James appears to use 1900 as his baseline date. Maria, then, being 35, would have been born in 1865 and free. Moreover, the triadic likelihood is that she was born of a different father, making the children half brothers and sister—three children distributed between two fathers.

11. Loren Miller, *The Petitioners: The Story of the Supreme Court of the United States and the Negro* (Cleveland and New York, Pantheon Press, 1967), 72. Taney's quotation stayed with James, who modified it slightly for use in a letter to William, Sept. 22, 1872.—*The Correspondence of William James*, ed. by Ignas Skrupskelis and Elizabeth M. Berkeley (Charlottesville and

London: University of Virginia Press, 1992), I, 170. It is worth noting that the racial aversion that white mainstream America showed to blacks and matters black extended also to scholarly attention given the subject, which helps to explain the otherwise surprising number of things slipping below editorial attention in most of the studies presented in these pages.

12. This arrangement suggests her strong fear of meeting someone, say from the ship, whose surprise on finding her with two blacks would give her game away in America where, on that person's return, the news would destroy her cover.

13. Charles Dicken's, *American Notes: A Journey* (New York: Fromm Publishing Corporation, 1985), 230.

14. In American literature, Melville was the first to do so for blacks, symbolized by the black monsters hunted to exhaustion by armed, white pursuers in *Moby-Dick*.

15. See James' review of George Eliot, "The Novels of George Eliot" The Atlantic Monthly, XVIII, 485: "When [the author] makes [the reader] well, that is, makes him interested, then the reader does quite half the labour." James goes on to say that such an authorial achievement may be a "secret," but James holds that it can be done. I take the secret to be his use of the mathematical triad.

16. R. P. Blackmur, *The Art of the Novel* (New York London: Charles Scribner's Sons), 227.

17. Sidney Andrews, "Three Months among the Reconstructionists," *Atlantic Monthly*, Feb. 1866.

18. E. M. Forster, *Aspects of the Novel* (New York: Harcourt, Brace & World, Inc: 1955), 218–19. If Forster had examined the novel in terms of James' symmetry, he could have identified the product that he believed James is so irresponsible about.

19. Roger Gard, ed. Henry James: *The Critical Muse: Selected Literary Criticism* (London: Penguin Books, 1987), 202.

20. *The Ambassadors*, Introduction, ed. Leon Edel (Boston: Houghton Miflin Company, 1960), viii. This Edelian text of the novel may be the most slovenly proofread edition of The Ambassadors ever to be printed.

21. This ending answers the question of what Strether was able to make of America upon returning to it from France—nothing, thus making France, not the United States, the country productive of restoring him to a single identity.

22. Gard, op. cit. 178. Already in 1884, the date of "The Art of Fiction," James apparently sees Du Bois's color line as the great fact of American life, great enough to cause him to recognize vast subjects in slight complexional tints.

23. Gard, op. cit., 205.

24. On the first page of his chapter on James, Leavis says "The Ambassadors seems to me to be not only not one of his [James's] great books, but to be a bad one ... it exhibits senility."

Readers interested in the question of why James charged most literary criticism with being infantile will probably recognize the tool of triadic symmetry and its astonishing power to double and triple the content of a work as the advantage James saw it having over all other structures. So far as I can see, Leavis is totally empty of any sense that *The Ambassadors* is three times as large as it seems to be, and without a hint that its characters are black and the novel itself a study of their treatment in America. Leavis has written a perfectly infantile chapter on James, while all the time believing that James was a pretentious fraud.

Chapter 10

1. Richard Ellmann, *James Joyce*, rev. ed. (Oxford, New York, Toronto, Melbourne: Oxford University Press, 1982), 30. Subsequent references to this volume are worked into my text.

2. Hugh Kenner, *Ulysses*, revised edition (Baltimore and London: The Johns Hopkins University Press, 1987), 90. Subsequent references to this volume are worked into my text. Kenner somehow managed to miss the obvious fact that a novel which is all trivia can only be trivia and anything but great,

3. Hans Walter Gabler, ed., *Ulysses* (New York: Vantage Books, 1986), 1.689–91. All references to this edition are worked into my text.

The London Sunday Times for 11/28/2009, 10, in its review of the Murphy report, "Church with a rotten core," says that Father Carney "may have colluded with two other priests, Fr. Francis McCarthy and Fr. Patrick Maguire, in finding victims in orphanages and at swimming pools." The Forty-Foot is a natural outdoor swimming pool.

4. Richard Ellmann, *Ulysses on the Liffey* (Oxford: Oxford University Press, 1972), 9. Subsequent quotations from this volume are worked into my text.

5. I believe that Ellmann understood what kind of corruption Joyce was hinting at, even though there is nothing in his surviving notes to establish the case.

6. Kenner notices (55) that the novel begins twice, without seeing that it ends once and thus completes the triad of openings and closings that Joyce surely saw in both Melville and James. Osric's death does not belong to that group but to the pair of flanking offstage deaths found in the play.

7. *The Art of the Novel: Critical Prefaces By Henry James*, ed. by R.P. Blackmur (New York: Charles Scribner's Sons, Ltd. London, 1937), 153–54. The double reference to James that Gifford notes at 10. 1216 sets up a need for a third Jamesian element, which may be supplied by "freshcheeked" Patrick and presumably dull-checked Dilly as they are subtly joined in Joyce's intricately designed triad of "cheeks."

8. *The Divine Comedy of Dante Alighieri*, ed. and trans. by Robert M. Durling (New York, Oxford: Oxford University Press, 1996), 1, 106–108. See also the note, 243.

9. Joyce's tour de force of styles in *Ulysses* seems meant to vie also with Shakespeare's in his various plays, there being as much difference between those of *Hamlet, Lear, Coriolanus,* and *Antony and Cleopatra*, as there is between diamonds, rubies, sapphires, and emeralds.

10. Joyce's triad in this instance is rather awkward because he is forced to substitute young Patrick for the unnamed altar boy to compose the elements of the triad's antithesis. That arrangement is awkward because it too visibly pairs unequals—Stephen from the here and now and Patrick from the vague and distant future. But pairing Stephen with the unnamed altar boy meant pairing two persons with excellent reasons to turn from the Church instead of one such person with another of a strong, opposite persuasion. Joyce liked the major and minor differences the latter pairing gave him over those of the former pair, and accepted the awkwardness

11. *The Riverside Shakespeare*, ed. by G. Blakemore Evans (Boston: Houghton Miflin Company, 1974), *Hamlet*, 4.5.55.

12. Melville's six symmetries are found on pp. 293, 329, 403, 419, 444, and 467 of Hayford's edition of *Moby-Dick*. They comprise symmetrical mouthfuls of whale blubber, the symmetrical head of the sperm whale, the symmetrical folded bulb on the prow of a French whaler, the whale's symmetrical tail, symmetrical dumplings, and a symmetrically applied constellation of stars painted on Stubb's oars. Analysis shows these items to divide into two groups of whale matter—head, tail and shark-bitten middle, and whaleship ornamental additions—bowsprit bulb, oar stars (fashioned by a carpenter), and dumplings (fashioned by a cook), the first group large, the second much smaller, except for the smallest of the large group and the largest of the small group, which seem to be similar in size. These six are the only matters in the entire novel that are described by the word symmetry and its derivatives. They will repay our most careful scrutiny.

13. Brigit Murphy at the Irish National Library, Kildare Street, told me that at the time Joyce borrowed its books, the library had a copy of *Moby-Dick* which Joyce could have read. As I recall, it was a reprint in a collection of reprinted novels and would have been available to Joyce at the time of his writing *Ulysses*.

14. Putting *La Divina Comedia* aside, I think Joyce might claim title to the greatest structural achievements in a single work, and Shakespeare to the greatest structural achievements in the totality of his works.

Bibliography

Agricola, Tacitus. *Germany and Dialogue on Orators.* Translated by Herbert Benario. Norman OK and London: University of Oklahoma Press. 1991.

Alberti, Leon Battista. *Dinner Pieces.* Translated by David Marsh. Binghamton NY: Medieval and Renaissance Texts and Studies. 1987.

Alighieri, Dante. *The Divine Comedy of Dante Alighieri.* Edited and Translated by Robert M. Durling. New York and London: Oxford University Press. 1996.

Andrews, Sidney. "Three Months Among the Reconstructionists." *Atlantic Monthly,* February 1866.

Aretino, Pietro. *The Letters of Pietro Aretino.* Translated by Thomas Caldicott Chubb. New Haven: The Shoestring Press Inc. 1967.

Baron, Salo Wittmayer. *A Social and Religious History of the Jews.* New York: Columbia University Press. 1962–1983.

Barton, Anne. Introduction to *Hamlet.* Edited by T. J. B. Spencer. London: Penguin Books. 1980.

Bernard, Fred V. "The Question of Race in Moby-Dick", *Massachusetts Review* XLIII. (2002).

Bloch, William Goldbloom. *The Unimaginable Mathematics of Borges' Library of Babel.* Oxford: Oxford University Press. 2008.

Bohr, Neils. Quoted in *The Joy of Insight: Passions of a Physicist.* Edited by Victor Weiskopf. New York: Basic Books. 1991.

Boswell, James. *Boswell's Life of Johnson.* Edited Hill-Powell. Oxford: Oxford University Press. 1934.

Brown, John Russell. "The Setting for Hamlet" *Stratford upon Avon Studies* no. 5. Edited by John Russell Brown and Bernard Harris. New York: St, Martin's Press. 1964.

Bowers, Fredson. "Hamlet as Minister and Scourge". In *Twentieth Century Interpretations of Hamlet.* Edited by David Bevington. Englewood Cliffs New Jersey: Prentice Hall. 1968. 82–92

Bowers, Fredson, "Hamlet's 'Sullied' and 'Solid' Flesh". *Shakespeare Survey*, Volume 9. Edited by Allardyce Nicoll, Cambridge: Cambridge University Press. 1956, 44–48

Bryant, John. "Moby Dick: Reading, Rewriting, and Editing." *Leviathan 9*, June (2007): 87–89.

Cersano, S. P., *A Companion to Shakespeare*. Edited by David Scott Kasten, Oxford: B. Blackwell. 1999.

Charney, Maurice. *Shakespeare on Love and Lust*, New York: Columbia University Press. 2000.

Contarini, Gasparo. *The Commonwealth and Government of Venice*, Translated by Sir Lewes Lewkenor. New York: Da Capo Press. 1969.

Dickens, Charles. *American Notes: A Journey*. New York: Fromm Publishing Corporation. 1985.

Donaldson, E. Talbot. *Beowulf: The Donaldson Translation*. Edited by Joseph Tuso, New York and London: W.W. Norton and Company. 1975.

Druett, Joan. *Wives of Merchant Captains Under Sail*. New York: Simon and Shuster. 1998.

Du Bois, W.E.B., *The Correspondence of W.E.B. Du Bois*. Edited by Herbert Aptheker. Amherst: The University of Massachusetts Press. 1973.

Du Bois, W.E.B., *The Souls of Black Folks: Essays and Sketches*. Edited by Saunders Redding. Greenwich Connecticut: Fawcett Publications. 1961.

Edel, Leon, *The Master*. London: Rupert Hart-Davis. 1972.

Eden, Alvin R. and Jeff Opland. "Bartolomeo Eustachios De Auditus Organis and The Unique Murder Plot in Shakespeare's Hamlet," *New England Journal of Medicine* no. 307 (July, 1992).

Ellman, Richard. *James Joyce*. Oxford, New York, Toronto and Melbourne: Oxford University Press. 1982.

Ellman, Richard. *Ulysses on the Liffey*. Oxford: Oxford University Press. 1972.

Erlick, Avi, *Hamlet's Absent Father*. Princeton: Princeton University Press. 1969.

Evans, G. Blackmore. *The Riverside Shakespeare*. Boston: Houghton Mifflin. 1974.

Felheim, Marvin. "The Merchant of Venice," *Shakespeare Studies Number 4*. Cambridge, Dubuque: Wm. C. Brown Company (1968). 94–108.

Feyman, Richard. *The Character of Physical Law*. Cambridge, England and London: The MIT Press. 1967.

Foakes, R. A. "Hamlet and the Court of Elsinore," *Shakespeare Survey*. Number 9. Edited by Allardyce Nicoll. Cambridge England and New York: Cambridge University Press. (1956). 35–43.

Forster, E. M. *Aspects of the Novel*. New York: Harcourt, Brace and World. 1955.

Franklin, John Hope and Loren Schwenenger. *Runaway Slaves*. New York and Oxford: Oxford University Press. 1999.

Frye, Northrup. *Northrup Frye on Shakespeare.* Edited by Robert Sandler. New Haven and London: Yale University Press. 1986.

Gifford, Don and Robert J. Seidman. *Ulysses Annotated.* Berkley, Los Angeles and London: University of California Press. 1988.

Goddard, A. D. *Shakespeare Newsletter* no. *45* Winter (1995).

Gollanez, Sir Israel. *The Sources of Hamlet.* New York: Octagon Books. 1967.

Greenblatt, Stephen. *Shakespearean Negotiations.* Berkley and Los Angeles: University of California Press. 1988.

Greenblatt, Stephen. *Hamlet in Purgatory.* Princeton and Oxford: Princeton University Press. 2010.

Greg, W. W. "Hamlet's Hallucination," *Modern Language Review*, no. 12 (October, 1917): 393–421.

Grigsby, John. *Beowulf and Grendel.* London: Watkins Publishing. 2005.

Gurr, Andrew, "Shakespeare's Playhouses." *A Companion to Shakespeare.* Edited by David Scott Kasten. Hoboken: Wiley-Blackwell Publishing. 1999.

Harbegger, Alfred. *The Father: A Life of Henry James Sr.* New York: Strauss and Giroux. 1994.

Hayford, Harrison. *Melville's Prisoners.* Evanston: Northwestern University Press. 2003.

Hazlitt, W. Carew. *The History of the Venetian Republic.* New York: AMS Press Inc. 1966.

Hodgkins, R. H. *A History of the Anglo-Saxons.* Oxford: The Clarendon Press. 1952.

James, Henry. *A Life in Letters.* Edited by Riley Horne. London and New York: Penguin Books Ltd. 2000.

James, Henry. *A Small Boy and Others.* New York: Charles Scribner's Sons. 1941.

James, Henry. *Roderick Hudson.* New York: Charles Scribner's Sons. 1905.

James, Henry. *The Ambassadors.* New York: Charles Scribner's Sons. 1909.

James, Henry. *The Ambassadors.* Edited by Leon Edel. Boston: Houghton Mifflin. 1960.

James, Henry. *The Art of the Novel.* Edited by Richard P. Blackmur. New York and London: Charles Scribner's Sons. 1937.

James, Henry. *Henry James: The Critical Muse Selected Literary Criticism.* Edited by Roger Gard. New York: Penguin Books. 1987.

James, Henry. *The Novels and Tales of Henry James.* New York: Charles Scribner's Sons. 1907.

James, Henry. "The Novels of George Eliot," *The Atlantic Monthly.* XVII.

James, Henry. *Theory of Fiction.* Edited by James E. Miller. Lincoln and London: University of Nebraska Press. 1971.

James, William. *The Correspondence of William James.* Edited by Ignas Skrupskelis and Elizabeth M. Berkley. Charlottesville and London: University of Virginia Press. 1992.

Jenkins, Harold. "Much Ado About Nothing." *Shakespeare Newsletter*, Extra Issue, (1997).

Joyce, James. *Ulysses.* Edited by Hans Walter Gabler. New York: Vantage Books. 1986.

Kastan, David Scott. *A Companion to Shakespeare.* Oxford: B. Blackwell. 1999.

Kenner, Hugh. *Ulysses.* Baltimore and London: Johns Hopkins University Press. 1987.

Kernan, Alvin. *Shakespeare: The King's Playwright.* New Haven and London: Yale University Press. 1995.

Kermode, Frank. "Introduction to Hamlet". *The Riverside Shakespeare.* Edited by G. Blakenore Evans. Boston: Houghton Mifflin. 1974.

Leavis, F. R. *The Great Tradition.* New York: New York University Press. 1963.

Leech, Clifford. "Studies in Hamlet 1901–1955." *Shakespeare Survey.* Edited by Alardyce Nicoll. Cambridge: Cambridge University Press. IX no. 4. 1–15.

Lewis, C. S. *The Prince or the Poem.* Edited by Walter Hooper. Cambridge England: University Press. 1964.

Lewis, R. W. B. *The Jameses: A Family Narrative.* New York: Farrar, Strauss and Giroux. 1991.

Leyerle, John. "The Interlace Structure of Beowulf." *University of Toronto Quarterly* 37, no. 1 (Oct. 1967): 1–17.

Livio, Mario. *The Equation That Couldn't be Solved.* New York, London and Sydney: Simon and Shuster. 2005.

Llorente, Juan de. *The History of the Inquisition in Spain.* Translated and Abridged by Anonymous. London: George B. Whittaker. 1827.

Malone, Kemp. *The Literary Tradition of Hamlet: The Early Tradition.* New York: Haskell House. 1964.

Mellinkoff, Ruth. "Cain's Monstrous Progeny in Beowulf: Part 1, Noarchic Tradition. *Anglo-Saxon England,* no. 8 (1979).

Melville, Herman. *Moby-Dick or The Whale.* Edited by Harrison Hayford, Hershel Parker and G. Thomas Tanselle. Evanston and Chicago: Northwestern University Press and The Newberry Library. 1988.

Melville, Herman. *The Piazza Tales.* Edited by Harrison Hayford, Alma A. MacDougall, G. Thomas Tanselle et. al. Evanston and Chicago: Northwestern University Press and The Newberry Library. 1987.

"Merchant Culture in Fourteenth Century Venice." Translated by John E. Dotson. *Medieval and Renaissance Texts and Studies.* Binghamton, New York: (1994).

Miller, Arthur. *The Theater Essays of Arthur Miller.* Edited by Robert A. Martin and Steven R. Centola. New York: De Capo Press. 1996.

Miller, Loren. *The Petitioners: The Story of the Supreme Court of the United States and the Negro.* Cleveland and New York: Pantheon Press. 1967.

Nicholl, Charles. *The Chemical Theatre.* London and Boston: Henly Routledge and Kegan Paul. 1980.

Parker, Hershel. *Herman Melville: A Biography.* Baltimore and London: The Johns Hopkins University Press. 2002.

Potok, Chaim. *Wanderings: Chaim Potok's History of the Jews.* New York: Alfred A. Knopf. 1978.

Prosser, Eleanor. *Hamlet and Revenge.* Stratford and London: Stratford University Press and Oxford University Press. 1967.

"Review of the Murphy Report." *The London Sunday Times.* November 28, 2009.

Robertson, D. W. Jr. "Chaucer and the Consequences of the Plague: Social Unrest in the Late Middle Ages." Edited by Francis X. Newman. *Medieval and Renaissance Texts and Studies.* Binghamton, New York. 1986.

Ronayne, John. *Totus Mundus Agit Histrionem: Shakespeare's Globe Rebuilt.* Edited by J. R. Mulryne and Margaret Shewring. Cambridge: Mulryne and Shewring. 1997.

Rose, Mark. *Shakespeare's Design.* Cambridge, Massachusetts: The Belnap Press of Harvard. 1972.

Roudané, Matthew. *Conversations with Arthur Miller.* Jackson and London: University Press of Mississippi. 1987.

Ryan, James Emmett. "Ishmael's Recovery: Injury, Illness and Recovery in Moby-Dick." *Leviathan 8.* March 2006. 17–34.

Shakespeare, William. *Mr. William Shakespeare's Comedies, Histories and Tragedies.* A Facsimile Edition. Prepared by Helge Kokeritz and Charles Tyler Prouty. New Haven and London: Yale University Press and Oxford University Press. 1954.

Shakespeare, William. *The Complete Works of Shakespeare.* Edited by George Lyman Kitterage. Revised by Irving Ribner. Waltham, Massachusetts and Toronto: Ginn and Company. 1971.

Shakespeare, William. *The Riverside Shakespeare.* Edited by G. Blakemore Evans. Boston: Houghton Mifflin Company. 1974.

Shakespeare, William. *The Complete Works.* Edited by Stanley Wells and Gary Taylor. Oxford: The Clarendon Press. 1992.

Shapiro, James. *Shakespeare Newsletter.* Extra Issue. 1997.

Starbuck, Alexander. *History of the American Whale Fisheries.* Secaucus, New Jersey: Castle Books. 1989.

Stewart, Ian. *Why Beauty is Truth*. New York: Basic Books. 2007.

Stoppard, Tom. "Pragmatic Theater." *New York Review of Books*. XLVI Sept. 23, 1999.

The Holy Bible. Translated from the Vulgate. Baltimore: John Murphy Company. 1914.

The Pharmalogical Basic Theraputics. 7th Edition. Edited by Alfred Goodman Gilman, Louis S. Goodman, Theodore W. Rall and Ferid Murad. New York: Macmillian Publishing Company. 1985.

Wall, William G. "The Importance of Being Osric: Death, Fate and Foppery in Shakespeare's Hamlet." *The Shakespeare Newsletter*. XLII. 1992. 62.

Wells, Stanley. *Shakespeare: A Life in Drama*. New York and London: Norton and Company. 1997.

West, Rebecca. *The Court and the Castle: Some Treatments of a Recurrent Theme*. New Haven: Yale University Press. 1955.

Weyer, Johann. *Witches, Devils and Doctors in the Renaissance*. Edited by George Mora MD, et al. Tempe, Arizona: Medieval and Renaissance Texts and Studies, no. 73. 1998.

Whitaker, Virgil K. *Shakespeare's Use of Learning: An Inquiry into the Growth of His Mind and Art*. San Marino California: The Huntington Library. 1964.

Wilson, Ian. *Shakespeare: The Evidence*. New York: St. Martin's Press. 1994.

Wilson, John Dover. *What Happens in Hamlet*. Cambridge: The University Press. 1970.

Index

A

Abel, 10, 12, 17, 24
  wife of emerging as Grendel's dam, 13, 15
Adam, 9, 14
Ahab, 134, 138
  ambivalence of concerning the hiring of
    Ishmael, 139
  attraction of the whaling ground where
    Moby-Dick nearly killed him, 143
  belief of in predestination, 158
  as "buoyed by the breath of once living
    things," 144–145
  change in after experiencing the double
    death of sun/son and whale, 144
  children of, 134–135
  concern of for the "pedlar," 139
  confession of as a sign of his humanity, 140
  cost to of his continual denial of Ishmael,
    140
  critics' approach to Ahab's softer side, 139
  death of, 184
  drinking problem of, 140, 149, 231n11, 232n3
  emotions of, 138
  explanations for the dark character of, 138
  Fedallah as the possible father of, 145–146,
    163
  former life of as a Persian, 150, 231–232n17
  as the greatest hunter, 131–132
  as half-brother to Queequeg and Ishmael, 161
  hints given by Melville as to the identity of
    Ahab's father, 147
  illegitimate birth of, 164
  killing of a whale by, 143
  and Lazarus, 140–141
  lust of, 148, 149
  masking of the true intent of the *Pequod*'s
    voyage by, 155–156
  mistaking of Starbuck for Ishmael, 139–140
  monomania of, 161
  mother of, 147–152, 231n12
  opposing thoughts of at the place where
    Moby-Dick took his leg, 143–144
  paternal relationships of, 146
  possible reason for the wide religious knowl-
    edge of, 149
  price paid by for revenge on Moby-Dick, 162
  protection of Pip by, 142
  as a rapist of his own mother, 149
  religious nature of, 150
  sexual assaults connected to his alcoholic
    folly, 232n3
  sharing of his quarters with Pip, 135
  signs of change in and reborn humanity of,
    142–143
  spell and shadows of Fedallah that dominate
    Ahab, 146–147
  united fate of with Fedallah, 169
  whale-watch of, 143

Alchemist, The (Johnson), 81

Ambassadors, The (H. James), 215, 235n20, 235–236n24

  astonishing opening of, 177

Ambassadors, The (H. James) (*continued*)

  beauty of, 187

  comic elements of, 193

  condition of black families before and after the Civil War in, 178–179

  description of Woolett as a black community in, 184

  image of the noose/lynching in, 183–184

  phrasal allusions to slavery in, 175

  racial theme of (as a novel of black in Paris), 174, 184–185

  reasons for much of the drama in, 181

  triadic structure of, 176

  See also *Ambassadors, The* (H. James), triads in

Ambassadors, The (H. James), triads in, 173, 216

  incomplete triad, 192–193

  triad of children, 178

  triad of the novel's surface, extended narrative, and comical elements, 193

American, The (H. James), Preface to, 193

Amleth, 55, 69

Andrews, Sidney, 185

angels, attempts to mate with human females, 9–10

Antonio, 27, 30, 32, 39, 46, 48, 50, 53, 214

  and the bond provision, 34

  as a Christian, 28, 35

  comedy inherent of in Antonio's chutzpah, 36

  complaints of Shylock concerning, 42

  desire of for revenge, 43–44

  lack of a wife, 43

  loss of both Leah and Jessica by, 36

  parading of his Christian and moral superiority over Shylock, 42–43

  playing of the religious card by, 30–31

  Portia's speech asking Shylock's mercy for Antonio, 47

  reason for Shylock's grudge against, 33

  reconciliation of with Shylock, 49

  request of that Shylock convert, 44

  as a self-righteous hypocrite, 35

  seduction of Shylock's wife considered just a trifle by, 43

  sexual swagger of, 33

  silence concerning where Antonio lives, 27–28

Aretino, Pietro, 118, 229n10

arsenic, 81, 90, 224–225n12

"Art of Fiction, The" (H. James), 193

Auden, W. H., 214

Aunt Charity, 148

  association of with the phallic symbol of a whaling lance, 157

  items of representing the abuse of Fedallah, Ahab, and Bildad, 15

  specific items she carries as representing a womb, 157–158

  symmetry of her two sets of items, 157

Austen, Jane, 23

auto-da-fe, 114, 117

B

Baker, Josephine, 185

Baldwin, James, 185

Barbary, 125, 126

Baron, Salo Wittmayer, 28, 52, 120, 123

Barton, Anne, 56

Basie, Count, 191

Bassanio, 38, 39–40, 42, 45, 46, 48, 50, 53

  relationship to Tubal, 51

  shock of upon hearing Shylock's reference to his father, 51

Beach, Sylvia, 209

Beatrice, 3, 5–6

Bellario, 40

Belleforest, 67, 79

Beowulf
Christian nature and strength of, 17
death of (as a Christian fighting Satan), 21–22, 23, 24
decapitation of Grendel's mother by, 15
fighting of Heorot's three opponents by, 7
half-brother to Wealhtheow, 13, 24
incestuous union of, 13–14, 15–16
offerings of the phallic cup to by Wealhtheow, 14, 16–17, 19

Beowulf
apparent Christianity of the queen in, 19–20
Cain as a prominent figure in, 8, 10, 11, 12, 17
Christian thrust of, 12, 14
the dragon as an agent of evil in, 20
Geatish woman in, 23, 24
infantile giants in and the charge of the poem as immature art, 7–8
influence of the New Testament on, 12, 22
the king's denial of pleasurable desire for the queen in, 19
lack of Christian images in, 8–9
monsters as symbols of strength in, 8
nuanced language of the characters in, 18
phallic images in, 13, 14, 15, 16–17, 19
possible recitation of to Christians, 9
redemptive acts of, 23
similarities of with *Hamlet*, 220n17
symmetry of, 219–220n15
See also *Beowulf*, triads in; phallic images, in *Beowulf*

Beowulf, triads in, 23–24, 25, 216
incomplete family triad, 24
the offering of the mead-cup by Wealhtheow and triadic necessity, 19
structure and proportion of the triads, 18–19
triad of the dragon's opponents, 21
triad of humans, Grendel, and the dragon, 8, 20–21
triad of incestuous unions, 11, 13, 14–15

Beowulf and Grendel (Grigsby), 9, 219n11

Beowulf poet, the, 1–2, 219n11
achievement of, 22
acuity of in presenting psychological tensions in various unions, 19–20
device of slipping used by, 219n12
disinterest of in sex, 220n16
as the first person to devise the triadic tool, 5
gamble of, 22–23
interest of in the Flood of the Old Testament, 8–9, 10–11
mingling by of English and Danish versions of *Beowulf*, 6–7
poetic subtlety of, 11–12
skill of, 2, 11, 219n13
structural greatness of, 23
use by of the sixth-century actions of Hrothgar in writing *Beowulf*, 10

Bernardo, 59, 74

Bianca, 129

Bildad, 157
greed of, 159

Bilham ("little Bilham"), 182, 187
fate of, 189
Strether's offer of financial help to, 190–191

blight, pre-Flood origins of, 2

Bloch, William Goldbloom, 217–218n4

Bloom, Leopold, 25, 199
chancre of, 206
observations of concerning Patrick Dignam's priest, 205
and Patrick Dignam, 200–201

Bloom, Molly, 25, 210

Bohr, Niels, 55

Bosch, Hieronymos, 87

Bowers, Fredson, 56, 97

Brabantio, 111, 118, 120, 125, 126
    charge of witchcraft against Iago, 113, 116
    desperate actions of due to state humiliations,
       119–120
    dramatic spectacle of as a demeaned Jewish
       senator, 120
    knowledge of Desdemona's love of fortune-
       telling, 116
    Othello's trust in, 121–122
    protection of himself and Desdemona by
       turning on Othello, 122–123
    treachery of regarding Desdemona, 126
    triad of those abused by, 126
Bradley, A. C., 216
Brown, John Russell, 83
Bryant, John, 143
buttons
    asymmetries involving, 3–4
    missing buttons analogy, 2–3

C

Cain, 24
    blood of, 22
    as a figure of malevolent evil, 14–15
    as incestuous companion of Grendel's dam, 15
    See also *Beowulf*, Cain as a prominent figure in
"Canon Yeoman's Tale" (Chaucer), 81
Carmagnola, 114, 229n7
Cassio, Michael, 112, 113, 126, 127
    and Desdemona, 115–116, 125–126
    desire of for both of Othello's positions,
       128–129
    failure of Roderigo to kill, 113
    manipulation as one of the skills of, 129
    treachery of, 129
Chaucer, Geoffrey, 23
    knowledge of chemicals, 81
Christianity, 9
    conversion of Jews to, 28

Christians, 9, 34, 118
    in Venice, 28
    villainy of toward Jews, 34
Cinthio, Giovanni, 113, 123
Claudius, 7, 58, 62, 68, 73, 75, 79, 90, 91
    amateurishness of, 83
    coronation of, 74
    as exemplar of Italianate villainy, 83
    incestuous union of with Gertrude, 12–13,
       97, 104–105
    initial warmth of toward Ophelia, 84
    as Ophelia's seducer, 85, 225n18
    physical weakness of, 80, 81
    poisoning of by Gertrude, 77, 78, 88
    questioning by of Hamlet regarding the
       argument of the Mousetrap, 128
    as a reflection of Cain, 12–13
    rift of with Gertrude, 83
    as wanting to be rid of his "plague" (Gertrude),
       83, 90
Cohen, Bella
    as the most likely person to have given syphi-
       lis to Father Coffey, 206
    Nighttown brothel of, 205–206
    Zoe's personal knowledge of, 207
Coleridge, Samuel Taylor, and the concept of
       "motiveless malignity," 111, 126
Commonwealth and Government of Venice,
       The (Contarini [trans. Lewkenor]),
       123–124
Contarini, Gasparo, 120, 123
cuckolding, 72, 74, 164
    humiliation of, 33
    inherent comedy of, 32, 33–34

D

Daggoo, 163, 164
Danes/Norwegians, contrasts between, 104
Dante, 3, 5, 18, 22, 24, 25, 131, 136, 148, 198, 213

influence of on Joyce concerning symmetry and structure, 210–211

influence on Joyce in exposing the dark side of Church, 199

placement of simoniac popes in hell by, 199–200

triadic structures of, 196, 210

use of terza rima by, 8

Darwin, Charles, 187

D'Avenant, William, 55

Davis, Daniel Webster, 191

De Cusa, Jacobus, 64, 65

de Llorente, Juan, 112, 114

De Praestigiis Daemonum (Weyer), 64

Dedalus, Stephen, 25, 90, 196

association of sexual acts with baptismal power by, 207–208

breaking of the chandelier chimney by and the ties to his mother, 207, 208, 211

experiences of as an altar boy, 203–204

frightening crisis and panic of at Clongowes, 203, 207

as Icarus Stephen, 208

meeting with Dilly, 207

rift with Buck, 207

second panic crisis of in the Nighttown brothel, 207–208

water images concerning, 204, 207–208

Denmark, 7

Desdemona, 113, 128, 129

advocacies of, 125–126

belief of in astrology, 117

Cassio taking the hand of, 115–116

chiromancy as her favorite form of fortune-telling, 116–117

as a Christian with Jewish blood, 122

consequences for being the wife of a disaffected Moor, 118

conversion of by coercion, 123

death of, 118, 119, 126

fear of but also attraction to magic, 117–118

greeting of to Lodovico that betrays her apprehension, 118

influence of the Inquisition on Othello's view of, 124

opponents/enemies of, 126–127

persons responsible for her death, 126

pregnancy of, 127

psychological chess played by, 117

reference of to Cassio's fortunes, 116

vulnerability of as a Jew, 119

with Othello in Cyprus, 114–115

"wretched fortune" of being called a whore, 116

determinism, Darwinian, 187

Deza, Diego, 120

Dickens, Charles, 23, 183

Dickinson, Emily, 2

Dido

Dido-Jessica's love is Aeneas-Shylock, 49

as Leah, 48–49

Dignam, Paddy, 197, 199

dying message of to his son, 201–202

funeral of, 203, 205

as a possible victim of syphilis contracted from a priest, 205–206

potted, coffined flesh of, 201

power and shock as the constant effects of Joyce's treatment of, 202

question of why he left the Church, 201

Dignam, Patrick Aloysius, 200–201

attitude of toward the Catholic Church, 204

collar of as a sign of the altered course of his vocation, 204–205

peering of into Madame Doyle's shop, 202

Dilly, 207, 211

similarities with Ophelia, 208

and Simon, 208–209

Divine Comedy, The (Dante), 22, 237n14
   insistent show of triads in, 29
Don Pedro, 170
Don Sebastian, 170
Donaldson, Talbot, 5, 23
doublings
   in *The Ambassadors*, 175–176, 177, 179, 192
   in *Beowulf*, 7
   Du Bois's double view of blacks, 194
   in *Hamlet*, 90–91
   in *Moby-Dick*, 135–136, 137, 144, 150, 152, 156
   in *Ulysses*, 197, 206, 208
Douglass, Frederick, 177, 191
Druett, Joan, 134
Dryden, John, 55
Du Bois, W. E. B., 175–176, 177, 185
   double view of blacks, 194
Duke, the (in *The Merchant of Venice*), 36, 46, 47, 221n15
Duke, the (in *Othello*), 118–120, 125, 127

E

Ecgtheow, 13
Eden, Avrim R., 79
Eden, garden of, 10
Edel, Leon, 187
Elijah, 144
Eliot, T. S., 23, 96, 109
   on *Hamlet*'s failure as a work of art, 93–94, 101, 103
   inadequacy of Eliot's argument concerning *Hamlet*, 106
Elizabeth I, plot against by Lopez, 26, 77, 79, 127
Ellington, Duke, 191
Ellmann, Richard, 195, 196, 197, 206, 236n5
Emilia, 118, 123, 126

"Equal in Paris" (Baldwin), 185
Erlick, Avi, 94, 95
Esperanza, 163–164
Eustachio, Bartholomew, 79
Eve, 9, 14

F

Father Coffey
   syphilis of, 206
   triad of Father Coffey's victims, 206
Father Conmee, 206
Father Mapple, 160
Fedallah, 143, 163, 164, 166, 232n5
   as Ahab's possible father, 145–146, 163
   connection of with Manilla, 147
   evil of (objectless phallic evil), 147, 151
   as the "governor," 148
   kidnapping of people by, 148
   physical color of, 158
   possible moral offenses of with his sister, 148–149
   selling of Queequeg's mother by, 160–161
   sexual nature of, 146–147
   united fate of with Ahab, 169
Felheim, Marvin, 25, 28, 52, 213
Feynman, Richard, 144, 151, 214
   on the imagination as straightjacketed, 198
Finnegan's Wake (Joyce), 232n2
   as the greatest structural accomplishment in literature, 211
First Player, 61, 63–64, 68, 70, 72, 81, 222n19
Fleece, 145, 158, 233n10
Flood, the, as recorded in the Old Testament, 8–9, 10–11
   images of and the role of in *Beowulf*, 20, 21
   need for, 14, 15
   See also Noah's ark
Florry, 207

Foakes, R. A., 71, 82

Forster, E. M., 235n18

Fortinbras, 20, 62, 64, 75
   connection with Hamlet, 74
   demands of, 74

Fowkes, R. J., 213

Franklin, John Hope, 139

Freawaru, 10

Freud, Sigmund, 94
   on Oedipus-Hamlet and Jocasta-Gertrude, 95

Frye, Northrop, 56

G

Garden of Forking Paths, The (Borges),
   217–218n4

"Garden of Worldly Delights, The" (Bosch), 87

Garrick, David, 55, 89, 226

Genesis, book of, 9–10

Gertrude, 16, 56, 63, 70, 91, 129, 214, 228n10
   active role of in the declining health of her
      husband, 87
   ardor of, 95
   as Claudius's "imperial jointress," 78, 83
   "compulsive ardure" of, 73
   extended verse passage of as a gem of fore-
      shadowing, 86
   guilt and soul sickness of, 86, 87–88
   Hamlet's reaction to her remarriage, 97
   imaged confession of, 73
   indifference and malevolence of, 73–74, 78
   jealousy of, 97–98
   knavery and craft of, 83–84
   knowledge of vegetation, 84
   lies of, 72–73
   likening of to Niobe, 79
   mocking ironies of, 86
   non-comprehension of Ophelia's plight,
      225–226n20
   passive role of in the death of Ophelia, 86–87
   poisoning of Claudius and Osric by, 77, 78
   Polonius as the brother of, 228n10
   possible sexual abuse of Hamlet as a child by,
      95–96, 100
   protection of Claudius by, 80
   Pryth and Ermutrud as incest-stained models
      of, 78
   reason for desiring revenge on Claudius, 84
   revenge on Claudius for the loss of her inces-
      tuous love, 85
   rift of with Claudius, 83
   self-revelations of, 226n21
   sexual hunger of for her son, 96, 223n27
   Wealhtheow as literary forbear of, 78

giants, 7–8, 10, 12

Gifford, Don, 90, 197, 207, 236n7

Globe Theater, audience of, 65, 67, 71–72, 89,
   214, 226–227n26, 227n33

God, 3, 8
   sacrifice of his son by, 12
   strategy of for expunging evil, 12
   victory of over Satan, 21–22

Gostrey, Maria, 173, 176, 182, 187, 191, 234n10
   ambivalence and caution of concerning
      Strether, 179–180
   caution as her constant companion, 180
   doubleness of, 177, 179
   family of, 178–179
   fear of for the fate of little Bilham, 189
   and the jewelry store episode, 188–189
   physical descriptions of, 178, 179
   questioning by of Strether concerning
      Woolett's business, 185–186
   revelation of through her gloves, 180–181
   as the sister of Strether, 179
   strategy of for survival, 189–190
   transformation of, 192

Gostrey, Maria (*continued*)
  unwillingness to return to the United States,
    182
Grammaticus, Saxo, 67, 69, 73, 78, 79, 212
Gratiano (in *The Merchant of Venice*), 3, 27, 31,
    37, 38, 46, 49
  as a Christian and great friend of Antonio, 28
  delivery of the Duke's invitation to dinner by,
    45–46
  and Nerissa, 39–40
  as the opposite of Shylock, 29
  reasons for Shylock's dislike of, 29–30
Gratiano (in *Othello*), 111, 112, 120
Greg, W. W., 56, 59
Grendel, 8, 9, 19
  "crucifixion" of Grendel's arm, 12
  death of, 24
  home of, 219n14
  portrayal of Grendel and his mother as
    monsters living underwater, 11
  severed limb of as a sexual trophy, 13, 15
Grendel's dam, 8, 15, 23
  Abel's wife as Grendel's dam, 13, 15
  blood of, 22
  death of, 20
  and Grendel's severed arm, 12, 18
Grigsby, John, 7, 9, 17, 19, 78, 219n11
Guildenstern, 80

H

Hamlet, 63, 68
  accusations of against Gertrude, 103–104
  attempted rejection of Gertrude by, 95
  berating of Gertrude by, 72
  as brought to the "Ghost" instead of the
    "Ghost" coming to him, 65
  closeness to Gertrude, 82
  confrontation with Gertrude after the
    Mousetrap, 99

coun,tercharges of against his mother, 99–100
death of, 60
divided thought concerning Gertrude, 82
duel with Laertes, 106
endorsement of Fortinbras's rights by, 74
failure of to answer Gertrude's question
    (". . . what act"), 101–102
foiling of plots by, 67
inquiries of to the sexton concerning Ophelia
    and Yorick, 107
knowledge of Polonius's spying on him, 70–71
legend of prior to Shakespeare's drama con-
    cerning, 78–79
loss of sexual performance and sexual bond-
    ing by, 105–106
madness of, 106–107
mocking attack on Osric by, 57, 95
mocking of Polonius by, 86
outwitting of his benetters by, 74–75
poisoning of, 77, 88
prayer of for the dissolution of his flesh,
    96–97
pressure on Hamlet to believe in the
    "Ghost," 67
"private time" given to Ophelia by, 97–98
questioning of the gravedigger by, 106–107
rage toward and hatred of his mother,
    100–102
reaction of to Gertrude's remarriage, 97
rejection of the earrings given to him by
    Ophelia, 105
response of to Horatio's inquiries concerning
    the "Ghost" as "business," 61–62
reviling of Ophelia as a common whore by, 85
and royal succession, 69
unexplained melancholy of, 105–106
use of picture images in confronting Ger-
    trude by, 101–103
warning jibe of to Polonius, 223n30

Hamlet (Shakespeare), 3, 7, 16, 22, 216, 227n29
   balanced elements of, 90
   double pairs of Italiante villains in, 90–91
   as dramatizing the political attempts of
      claimants to the Danish throne, 74
   failure of as a work of art, 93–94
   fencing match in, 106
   general rot of Denmark/Hamlet's court in,
      104–106
   Gertrude's extended verse passage in, 86
   illness of the old king in, 80–81
   importance of the Additional Passages to,
      226–227n26
   Italianate side of, 83
   psychological wounds carried by nearly
      everyone in, 108–109
   sexual energy imputed to the Danes in, 104
   Shakespeare's sleight of hand in, 64–65
   similarities of with *Beowulf*, 220n17
   symmetrical structure of, 64, 106–107
   tenderness and humor of the sexton in, 108
   tracing of the story back to *Beowulf*, 55
   triadic form in, 29
   See also *Hamlet* (Shakespeare), heart of the
      mystery of; *Hamlet* (Shakespeare), poison-
      ings in; *Hamlet* (Shakespeare), triads in;
      Hamlet's "Ghost"
Hamlet (Shakespeare), heart of the mystery of,
   93–94
   and the possible incestuous sexual abuse of
      Hamlet as a child by Gertrude, 95–96, 106
   and the sexual overtones of the episode in
      Ophelia's closet, 95
Hamlet (Shakespeare), poisonings in, 77
   drinking of poison by Gertrude, 87–88
   and Hamlet's "Ghost," 79
   the Mousetrap as an analogue for
      poisoning, 82
   orchard poisoning, 79

   a pearl as an antidote for, 87–88, 226n22
   poisoning of Claudius, 77, 78
   poisoning of Hamlet, 77, 88
   poisoning of Osric, 77
   prominence of, 79
   on the short lives of poisoners' agents, 89
   use of arsenic as a poison, 81, 224–225n12
   use of hebona as a poison, 79–80, 224n6
Hamlet (Shakespeare), triads in, 105–106, 216
   as offering proof of Gertrude's sexual hunger
      for her son, 96
   triad of Hamlet, Gertrude, and Ophelia,
      98–99
   triad of Hamlet's disgusts, 94
   triad of Hamlet's visits to various graves, 107
   triad of men that Gertrude physically
      struggles with, 95
   triad of periods in Hamlet's life, 94–95
   triad of pictures, 102–103
   triad of poisonings, 77
   triad of rejections, 95
   triad of the sexton's knowledge of three
      persons, 107
   triad of Yorick's royal laughers, 107–108
Hamlet's "Ghost," 55
   appearance of in a nightdress, 72
   appearance of in the Queen's chamber, 70
   appearances of to Horatio, 64, 75
   armor of, 67
   and the arras on the stage, 71–72
   as being purged of sins in purgatory, 65, 69
   as a challenge to Hamlet, 56
   as a Christian Ghost, 55
   claim of regarding the quick acting poison, 79
   duping function of, 55
   effect of on Danish succession, 63
   as fake or real, 56–57, 63, 71–73, 75
   as Hamlet's father (the dead King), 58–59, 68
   as Hamlet's private hallucination, 56

Hamlet (Shakespeare), triads in (*continued*)
Hamlet's suspicions concerning the
    "Ghost's" origin, 69–70
interrogation of, 64
majesty of, 66
as malevolent, 56
as mere spirit lacking armor, 56
ordering of Hamlet to kill Claudius by, 63
as a possible hoax originated by Horatio,
    67–68
testing of its authenticity, 68–69
Hardy, Thomas, 23
Hayford, Harrison, 136, 171, 213
Hazlitt, William, 51
hebona, 79–80, 224n6
Heorogar, 7
Heorot, 1–2, 10, 21
infernal enemies of, 2
magnificence of, 6
as a pagan temple of drunkenness, 15
Heoroweard, 7
Hodgkin, R. H., 6, 104
Homer, 24
Horatio, 40, 56, 62, 63, 75
acceptance of in both high and low
    worlds, 60
anomalies concerning, 58–59
appearance of in numerous coincidences,
    59–60
appearances of Hamlet's "Ghost" to, 64
benefit of from gender-partial criticism, 58
causing of the soldiers to breach military law
    by, 65–66
as a "chameleontic figure," 57, 75
conversion of to a believer in Hamlet's
    "Ghost," 64–65
courtly demeanor of, 57
illegitimacy of (as Claudius's son), 60–61, 72

possible hoax perpetrated by concerning
    Hamlet's "Ghost," 67–68
pressure by on Hamlet to kill Claudius, 60
treatment by critics of the character of,
    56–57
uncritical/objective view of, 57
Howells, William Dean, 176
Hrethric, 18
identification of as Roricus in Scandinavian
    legend, 19
Hrothgar, 7, 10, 14, 17, 18, 19
payment of for Heorot's delivery, 15–16
sons of (the royal children), 20
and the uninvited guest (Grendel), 19
Hrothulf, 18, 19
Hygelac, 10

I

Iago, 119, 120, 129
as belonging to the Jewish victims in *Othello*,
    124–125
bitterness toward his family, 126
family of, 125
grudge of against Brabantio, 125
handkerchief plot of, 127
inquisition of, 112–113
jealousy and hatred of Desdemona, 125
knowledge of Desdemona's deception with
    Brabantio, 126
reasons of for antagonizing Brabantio, 111
incest, 6, 78, 95
of Claudius and Gertrude, 12, 13, 97, 104–105
incestuous link of Wealhtheow and Beowulf,
    15–16
Freud's argument for the incestuous love of
    Hamlet for his mother, 94
of Polonius and Ophelia, 104, 105
possibility of in *Moby-Dick*, 147, 149–150

of the Queen in *Hamlet*, 77, 223n27

revenge of Gertrude on Claudius for the loss of her incestuous love, 85

triad of incestuous unions in *Beowulf*, 11, 13, 14–15, 216

triadic structure found within incestuous relationships, 94

Ingeld, 10

Inquisition, the, 118, 122

  conversos and Catholics interested in Lutheranism particularly singled out by, 124

  effect of on Othello, 124

  enumeration by of actions typical of "Judaizers," 123

  escape from, 113

  goal of, 112

  Lodovico as an officer of, 112

  onomancy of, 124

  rigorous interrogations of, 120–121

  and the settling of Iago's estate by, 112

  Shakespeare's audience's knowledge of, 127–128

  torture with a piece of cloth used by, 113–114

  treatment of its victims by, 124

  victims of, 113, 127–128

Ishmael, 131, 132, 139, 161, 231n10, 231n12, 233n9

  belief of in predestination, 158

  birth of, 137, 151, 157

  as black in the eyes of some Americans, 158

  as conceived and born in Ahab's quarters, 134

  connection by of Ahab with convent life, 144

  encounter with and effect of on Lazarus, 140, 141

  encounter of with the figure at his bedside, 136

  family resemblance of the priest and Ishmael, 170–171

first glimpse of his father, 135–136

grief of for his dead mother and himself, 135

as half-brother to Ahab and Queequeg, 161

illegitimate birth of, 164

on the importance of water to one's identity, 156–157

intense interest of in sailing from Nantucket instead of New Bedford, 133–134

lack of sorrow over losing Queequeg, 165–166

love of orisons and vesper hymns, 149

masking by of his true intent for voyaging on the *Pequod*, 155–156

mocking of by shipmates on the *Moss*, 158

mother of, 147–152

as the "pedlar," 139

in Peru, 169–170

psychological void of in his life, 135

and the race of his mother, 137

search of for his identity, 138, 148

as the second convalescent (after Ahab) aboard the *Pequod*, 230n4

sharing of a bed with Queequeg, 162

on the sweet feminine nature of the sea, 156

thwarted chimney climb of, 136

and the Town-Ho story, 170

J

James, Garth Wilkerson, 177–178

James, Henry, 4, 5, 22, 25, 51, 145, 169, 172, 198, 212, 213

  boast of concerning his indirect creation of Mrs. Newsome, 233n7

  on the choice of a character's motives by an author, 132

  as a closeted gay person, 175

  criticism of Tolstoi and Dostoyevsky by, 234n17

James, Henry (*continued*)
  demands of on his readers and the responsibilities due them, 184–185
  on George Eliot, 235n15
  knowledge of the humiliation suffered by blacks, 174
  lack of any mention of Melville except in an oblique reference, 173
  on literary criticism as infantile, 235–236n24
  possible honoring and challenging of Melville, 173
  Prefaces written by concerning his own fiction, 173–174
  on psychological reason, 187
  refusal of to praise Melville's achievements, 131
  and the repudiation of American culture, 191
  saturation of in his subjects leading to unusual achievements, 191
  sensitive ear of to black speech, 191
  strictures of on first-person narratives, 232nn1–2
James, William, 176
Jenkins, Harold, 33
Jerome, 10
Jessica, 30, 38, 48, 49, 214
  bastardy/questionable paternity of, 31, 32–33
  elopement of, 37
  fleeing of from Shylock's house, 36
  in Genoa, 33, 49, 51
  inheritance of Shylock's money, 42
  paternity of connected to the hatred between Shylock and Antonio, 35
  reuniting of with Jessica, 51
  Shylock's generosity toward, 36
  taunting of Shylock by Solanio concerning the complexion of Jessica, 31–32
  untroubled conscience of, 37
Jesus Christ, 23
  power of his transformative blood, 22
Jews, 44–45, 53, 111, 122
  as aliens, 33–34
  conversion of to Christianity, 28
  threat of to the sexual life of a nation, 34
Jim Crow America, 179, 182, 185, 193–194, 215
Joyce, Gorgio, 202, 204
Joyce, James, 4, 5, 22, 25, 131, 169, 198, 213
  addiction of to puzzles, 195
  as an altar boy, 195
  borrowing of from Melville, 232n2, 237n13
  energy expended by on the writing of *Ulysses*, 212
  and "English" literary structuralism, 212
  fear of priests perhaps stemming from personal experiences with, 203
  immersion of in the Roman Catholic Church, 202–203
  influence of Dante on in exposing the dark side of the Church, 199
  influence of Dante on concerning symmetry and structure, 210–211
  protective nature of as a father, 202–203
  tolerant nature of, 202
Joyce, Lucia, 204
Joyce, Stephen, 202, 204

K

Kenner, Hugh, 192, 206, 208, 236n6
  characterization of *Ulysses* as trivia, 196
Kermode, Frank, 57, 75
Kernan, Alvin, 73, 197, 202
King, Martin Luther, 188, 191

King Lear (Shakespeare), 216
Klaeber, Fredrick, 12
Kraki, Rolf, 5
    destruction of by Grendel, 6–7
Kyd, Thomas, 81

L

Laban, 35, 38
Laertes, 60, 62, 77, 79, 80, 90, 95
    duel with Hamlet, 106
    jumping of into Ophelia's grave and covering
        her, 104
Launcelot, 30, 31
    dispute of with Old Gobbo, 35
    intention of to flee Shylock's house, 36, 37
    irony involved in his age, 36
    Nerissa as a parallel to, 38
    offending of by Shylock, 48
    reuniting of with Shylock, 49
    Shylock as the father of, 35–36
    troubled conscience of, 37
    as the young master, 36
Lazarus, 140–141
    effect of on Ishmael, 141
    solace of found by in a black house/church,
        141–142
Leah, 30, 32–33, 45, 51
    fleeing of from Shylock's house, 36
    vulnerability of, 36
Leavis, F. R., 2, 174, 185, 213
    on *The Ambassadors*, 235-236n24
Lewis, C. S., 94
Lewkenor, Lewes, 123–124
literature
    distancing in, 10
    "English" literary structuralism, 212
    figurative devices of, 214

homogenous nature of prior to the introduc-
    tion of triadic structures, 4–5
masking devices of, 1, 2, 8, 77
readers' responses to, 213–216
See also mathematics/physics, and literature;
    narrative, extended
Livio, Mario, 217n2, 218–219n9
Lodovico, 111, 113
    and the act of "relajacion al brazo secular,"
        130
    Desdemona's greeting of, 118
    greeting of Othello by, 111–112
    as an officer of the Inquisition, 112
    response of to Desdemona's superstitions, 118
    significance of his name, 228n3
    turning of Iago over to Cassio by, 112
Lopez, Roderigo, 26, 77, 79
    execution of, 127
Lord Burghley, 77
Lorenzo, 27, 31, 38, 39, 49
    inheritance of Shylock's money by, 42, 44
Lucianus, 82
Lutheranism, Catholics interested in, 124

M

Madame de Vionnet, 190
Malone, Kemp, 78
Manrique, 114, 118
Marcellus, 59, 68, 74
    on the majesty of Hamlet's "Ghost," 66
Margery, 36
masking devices, 1, 2, 8, 77
mathematics/physics, and literature
    difference of symmetry in literature from
        that of mathematics or physics, 217n2
    elegance and simplicity as the touchstones of
        mathematics, 230n6, 233n12

mathematics/physics (*continued*)
  importance of the influence of mathematics
     and physics on, 213–214, 217–218n4
Melville, Herman, 4, 5, 22, 25, 184, 212, 213
  feminist criticism of his female characters, 166
  literary experiences of with Shakespeare and
     Dante, 131, 156
  on the shock of recognition, 173
  study by of the triadic tools of Dante and
     Shakespeare, 148
Merchant of Venice, The (Shakespeare), 3, 216
  the bond provision as a masterpiece of
     comedy in, 34
  change in the dramatic nature of from dark-
     ness to light, 47–48
  determining the Jewishness or Christianity
     of the characters in, 28–29
  family themes concerning conversos in, 111,
     120
  importance of the minor characters in, 37
  overall Jewish context of, 40
  question of whether it and its author are
     anti-Semitic, 26, 28–29, 30, 52
  sibling rivalry in, 30
  use of irony in, 35, 36
  See also *Merchant of Venice, The* (Shakespeare),
     triads in
Merchant of Venice, The (Shakespeare), triads in,
  216
  Inferno, Purgatorio, and Paradiso as similar to
     the gold, silver, and lead caskets, 25, 40, 42
  and the power of reconciliation and reunion
     reflected in triads, 46–47
  powerful triads of the concluding scene,
     48–49
  triad of Antonio, Bassanio, and friends, 51
  triad of children reunited with their fathers,
     49–50

triad of elders (the virtuous man, Antonio,
     Shylock), 40–41
triad of food portions, 46
triad of givers, 50
triad of Gratiano, Bassanio, and Antonio, 46
triad of Nerissa, Portia, and Shylock, 46, 51
triad of Shylock, Gratiano, and Antonio's
     houses, 28, 29, 52
triad of suffering fathers, 51–52
triad of two dining groups, 51
Milhaupt, Jean, 231n12
Miller, Arthur, 26–27, 31, 52, 53, 213, 220n3,
  234n2
  on the importance of relationships in a
     play, 40
  on the seriousness of the theater, 45
Milton, John, 12
Miss Barrace, 182
Moby-Dick (Melville), 3, 215, 232n19
  "The Cabin Table" chapter of, 134
  "The Carpet-Bag" chapter of, 140
  characters missing names in, 163
  "Cistern and Buckets" chapter of, 137
  "The Counterpane" chapter of, 135–136
  critical tools to use in the continuing study
     of, 171
  discussion/theme of Ahab's and Ishmael's
     mother in, 147–152
  doubling of a black delivery in "The Counter-
     pane," 137
  doublings and triplings of found in "The
     Loomings" chapter, 152, 156
  drama involved in having Ahab's son and
     brother on the *Pequod*, 158–159
  establishment of surnames and first names
     in, 163–164
  "The Funeral" chapter of, 147
  "The Glider" chapter of, 142

hidden themes in, 209
importance of the nature of water in, 156–157
"The Leg" chapter of, 140
"Loomings" chapter of, 134, 139
"Loomings" as an epigraph for the entire novel, 133
loose narrative form of, 143
masking of the true nature of reasons for the *Pequod*'s voyage, 155–156
numeric system of, 169
phallic images in, 133, 232n3
portrayal of blacks in, 235n12, 235n14
prophecy in, 166
the question of parentage as a major theme of, 131–132, 133, 162
repeated modifications of first-person limitations in, 138
six specific symmetries in, 237n12
symmetrical doubling and tripling in, 135–136, 150
symmetry of, 134, 142–143, 151, 161, 163, 169
symmetry of Queequeg and Pip in, 167–168
"The Symphony" chapter of (feminine overtones in), 143
treatment of dysfunctionality in, 162
two endings of, 169–170
See also *Moby-Dick* (Melville), triads in; phallic images, in *Moby-Dick*
Moby-Dick (Melville), triads in, 131, 168, 216
Ahab's triadicizing quest of hatred and death, 151
"Call me Ishmael" triad, 218n8
possibilities for the completion of the sibling triad, 170–171
triad of Ahab, Ishmael, and Queequeg, 158–159, 162, 164, 233n11
triad of ambassadors, 25
triad of delayed appearances, 171
triad of intended destinations, 155
triad of people who do not see each other, 169
triad of places Ishmael settles in, 171–172
triad of prophets (Elijah, Fedallah, the tattooer), 166
triad of Queequeg, Ishmael, and the lost twin, 158
triad of Queequeg's lifesaving dives, 167
triad of stories in, 171
triad of those who slept in the same Spouter Inn bed, 162
triad of three relationships divided between two persons, 169
triadic structure involving Queequeg, 155
Montano, 112
Moors, 111, 122
Morocco, 39, 221n15
Mousetrap, 68, 70, 81, 83, 87, 96, 98, 99
as an analogue for poisoning, 82
as exemplifying a doubled pair, 82
possible offensive matter in, 128
Mrs. Newsome, 182, 191
James's boast concerning the creation of, 233n7
Mulligan, Buck
association of with bowels, 198
as a faux priest, 203
rift with Stephen, 207
significance of the initials of (B. M.), 196

N

Nantucket, 133–134, 136, 155, 156, 165
narrative, extended, 215–216
in *The Ambassadors*, 193
in *Beowulf*, 4, 11
in *Hamlet*, 86
in *The Merchant of Venice*, 27, 52–53
in *Moby-Dick*, 142, 149

narrative (*continued*)
  in *Othello*, 111
  in *Ulysses*, 205, 210
Nerissa, 38, 44, 48, 53
  delivery by of the deed for Shylock's
      signing, 45
  and Gratiano, 40
  as a parallel to Launcelot, 38
Nerthus cult, and fertility practices, 9, 78
New Bedford, 133, 134, 165
New England, 185
New Testament, 12, 20
  influence of on *Beowulf*, 12
  salvific ideas in, 9
Newsome, Chad, 173
  acceptance of himself, 181
  failure of Strether to lure him back to
      Woolett, 181–183, 188, 190–191
  and Mamie Pocock, 190–191
  relationship with his mother, 181–182
  relationship with Strether, 181–182
  Strether's expectations of and assumptions
      concerning, 182
  Strether's treatment of as an inferior,
      183–184
Noah's ark, 11

O

Oedipus (Sophocles), 21
Old Gobbo, 30, 36
  dispute of with Launcelot, 35
  gift of doves by, 36, 37, 45, 46, 48, 221n14
  as representing love and the burying of
      grudges, 45
Old Testament, 8, 12, 20
Oliver, King, 191
Ophelia, 58, 60, 84, 91, 225n19
  death of by drowning, 74, 78, 83, 85, 86–87
  deplorable burial of, 78

funeral of, 105
hypothesis concerning the nature of her
    sin, 78
incest of with Polonius, 104, 105
jewelry of, 223n32
as the king's Valentine love, 84–85
"private time" given to Ophelia by Hamlet,
    97–98
rejection of Hamlet by, 95
Opland, Jeff, 79
Osric, 60, 91, 106
  classic symptoms of arsenic poisoning in, 90
  mocking attack on by Hamlet, 57, 95
  poisoning of, 77, 90
  as possibly Gertrude's agent in poisoning
      Claudius, 88–89
  terminal illness of, 89–90
  as a type (the cony, the gull) , 88
Othello
  baptism of, 114
  charge of witchcraft against, 113
  effect of the Inquisition on in regards to
      Desdemona, 124
  examination of concerning witchcraft
      charges against, 121–122
  famous reference of to fabulous men, 114
  flight of from Cyprus to Mauritania, 111,
      113, 115
  folly of, 116–117
  gambles taken by, 117
  and the Inquisition, 112–113
  involvement of in the death of four persons,
      229–230n11
  partial modeling of Othello on Carmagnola,
      114, 229n7
  reluctance of to name his royal ancestors,
      121
  in Spain, 114
  suspicion of heresy concerning, 114–115

suspicion as the predominant mood of, 123

trust of in Brabantio, 121–122

with Desdemona in Cyprus, 114–115

Othello (Shakespeare), 111

Contarini as a source for Shakespeare in the writing of, 120

conversos as a theme of Shakespeare's in, 120, 122–123, 124

dramatization of superstition in, 117–118, 123, 124

family themes in, 111, 125

how Iago fits the structure of powerful themes in, 124–125

on the Inquisition's treatment of its victims as a theme in, 124

medical and pharmaceutical images in, 126

occult properties of the handkerchief in, 113

tight-knit symmetry of, 127

See also *Othello* (Shakespeare), triads in

Othello (Shakespeare), triads in, 123, 129–130

triad of Desdemona's advocacies, 125–126

triad of Desdemona's superstitions, 117–118

triad of Othello, Desdemona, and Cassio in, 124

triad of persons whose deaths Iago is responsible for, 126

triad of those abused by Brabantio, 126

triad of those who kept Iago from advancement, 125

triad of women believers in the occult, 115

triadic need of Brabantio's for three children, 125

P

Paris, acceptance of American blacks in, 185

Parsee, the, 146, 152, 170, 231–232n17

as second oldest person aboard the *Pequod*, 145

Peleg, 132, 139

belief of in predestination, 158

Pequod

as a second parental vessel, 133

sinking of, 167–168, 169

Perth, 139, 231n11

phallic images

in *Beowulf*, 13, 14, 15, 16–17, 19

in *Moby-Dick*, 133, 157, 232n3

in *Ulysses*, 198, 208

Pip, 131, 138, 139, 143

Ahab's protection of, 142

sharing of quarters with Ahab, 135

Plumtree, 201

Pocock, Mamie, 190–191

Pocock, Sarah, 191

Polonius, 68, 77, 98, 99

alarm of, 71–72

association of with Jephthah, 84

funeral of, 105

Hamlet's warning to, 223n30

incest of with Ophelia, 104, 105

infection of with the pox, 105

spying of on Hamlet, 70–71

Player King, 81

Portia, 27, 30, 34, 53

alliance of with Bellario, 40

lack of paternal love in, 41

personality traits of, 38

as possibly a bastard, 41–42

rabbi father of, 40

recognition of Morocco as a Sephardic Jew by, 221n15

reunion and reconciliation of Shylock made possible by, 47

reuniting of with her father Shylock, 49

solution of to the strife between Shylock and Antonio, 44

as a soulmate of Jessica, 41

Portia (*continued*)
    speech of asking Shylock's mercy for
       Antonio, 47
    subtle musical help given to, 38–40
    treatment of Shylock as a human being by,
       47–48
Potok, Chaim, 114
Prosser, Eleanor, 56
Ptolemaic system, 82

Q

Queequeg, 132, 137, 232n4, 233n16
    actions of moving him closer to Ahab and
       Ishmael, 165
    anomalous birth images that accompany the
       rescue and delivery of, 134
    belief of in predestination, 158
    as black in the eyes of some Americans, 158
    Christian mother of, 160–162
    desire of when near death for a coffin and a
       canoe, 168
    as half-brother to Ahab and Ishmael, 161, 169
    as a headhunter, 160
    illegitimate birth of, 164
    influences on his interest in Christianity,
       159–160
    lifesaving dives of, 167–168
    love of for Pip, 167–168
    mocking of by shipmates on the *Moss*, 158
    as a Muslim, 160
    possible survival of, 165–167
    qualities shared by with Ishmael and Ahab,
       163
    retrieval of both Pip and the whaleboat by,
       168–169
    royalty of, 159
    and the seer, 156, 165, 233n14
    selflessness and giving of, 148

    sharing of a bed with Ishmael, 162
    sister and brother of, 155
    successful quest of for Christianity, 169
    tattooed treatises of (on cosmology and
       truth), 156, 233n13
    tattooing of, 164, 165, 166–167, 169, 233n14

R

Rascoe, Michael, 123
Revelation, book of, 21
Richard the Third (Shakespeare), 216
Rivers, Conrad Kent, 185
Roderigo, 119, 125, 126
    failure of to kill Cassio, 113
Roman Catholicism
    claim by of moral and intellectual superior-
      ity over other religions, 127–128
    priests of, 64
    See also Inquisition, the; *Ulysses*, overlooked
      theme of sexual-predatory priests in
Romeo and Juliet (Shakespeare), triadic form
    in, 29
Rose, Mark, 64
    on the balanced elements in *Hamlet*, 90
    on visual symmetries, 71
Rosencrantz, 80
royal courts, poets in, 2–3
    dismissal of poets from, 2
    nervousness of courts concerning working
      poets, 2
Runaway Slaves (Franklin and Schwenenger), 139
Ryan, James Emmett, 230n4

S

Sag Harbor, 165
Salerio, 27, 37
    taunting of Shylock by concerning the com-
      plexion of Jessica, 32–33

Satan
  Beowulf's death as a Christian fighting Satan, 21–22
  as the dragon in *Beowulf*, 21
  subjugation of by Mary in Revelation, 21
Scefing, Scyld, 5, 14
  sexuality of, 6
Schwenenger, Loren, 139
Scyldings, 5–6
Seidman, Robert J., 90
Shakespeare, William, 4, 5, 18, 22, 24, 25, 53, 131, 148, 212, 213, 227n3
  brothers of, 42
  creative architecture of, 52
  double genius of in appealing to both the pit and the gallery, 91
  duty of readers to devise answers to the great questions raised by, 41
  Hazlitt's and James's view of his plays as unactable, 51
  illustration of the type of comedy written by, 40–41
  influence of *Beowulf* and Danish traditions on in the writing of *Hamlet*, 104
  influences of concerning the use of discretion in drama, 123–124
  instinct of for the dramatic, 73
  Nerthus cultic influence on, 78–79
  triadic structures of, 196
  use of comedy as a means of reconciliation by, 45–46
  use of intense arrangements or persons and places in his work, 31
Shakespearean gaps, 27
Shapiro, James, 33
Shylock, 3, 53, 214
  carnality of, 32
  complaint of that Antonio disgraced him, 42
  countering of Antonio's campaign for revenge by, 44
  cuckolding of, 43
  cuckolding of as comedy, 32–33, 34
  emotional exhaustion of, 45
  generosity of toward Jessica, 36
  hatred of Antonio's Christianity by, 31
  "If you prick us, do we not bleed" line of, 32, 220–221n6
  irony of having to borrow money from Tubal, 50–51
  misidentification of as a victim of cuckolding, 34
  neighbors as the most vocal antagonists of, 31
  nursing of his anger toward Antonio for twenty years, 34
  reason for Shylock's grudge leading to revenge against Antonio, 33–34
  reasons for Shylock's dislike of Gratiano, 29–30
  reconciliation of with Antonio, 49
  relationships to his neighbors as a defining aspect of his character, 26–27
  reminder to Antonio of Laban's parti-coloured lambs, 35
  reunion and reconciliation of made possible by Portia's intervention, 47
  reuniting of with Jessica, 51
  reuniting of with Launcelot, 49
  reuniting of with Portia, 49
  taunting of by Salerio and Solanio concerning Shylock's daughter, 31–33
Simon, 202
  and Dilly, 208–209
  double meaning of his order to "Stand up straight," 209
Snaebjorn, 78

Solanio, 27
    anti-Semitism as an unlikely explanation for
        his attacks on Shylock, 37
    reasons for his intense anger toward Shylock,
        37
    taunting of Shylock by concerning the com-
        plexion of Jessica, 31–33
Sophocles, 21
Souls of Black Folks, The (Du Bois), 175
Spain, 114, 124–125
Spanish Armada, the, 127
Spear Danes, 6, 14
Spouter Inn, 140, 141, 162
Spurgeon, Caroline, 81
St Paul, 32
    on the fleshy nature of man, 34, 52
Starbuck, 138, 143
Stationers' Company, 128
Stevens, Wallace, 157
Stewart, Ian, 230n6, 233n12
stories, complete and incomplete nature of, 4–5
Strether, Lewis Lambert, 175, 193
    acceptance by of being black and gaining his
        soul as result of, 191
    ambivalence and caution of Maria toward,
        179–180
    attendance of at Chad's black party, 190, 191
    burdens of exacerbated by Waymarsh, 187–188
    closeness of to Waymarsh and Maria,
        188–189
    description of Waymarsh by, 176
    double view/consciousness of himself,
        175–176, 186–187
    as editor of the *Review*, 188, 191
    failure of to lure Chad back to Woolett,
        181–183, 188, 190–191
    identity of as one of James' great subjects, 188
    and the jewelry store episode, 188–189

    as Maria's brother, 179
    models for, 176
    offer of financial aid to little Bilham by,
        190–191
    questioning of by Maria concerning
        Woolett's business, 185–186
    reunion with his mother in Paris, 192–193
    struggle of concerning his self-identity, 181
    treatment of Chad as an inferior, 183–184
    and Waymarsh, 181, 192
Stubb, 138, 148, 233n10
    impassiveness of, 162
Sturlason, Snorri, 78
Sumatra, 140
symmetrical structures, modern, 23
    See also triadic literary structures,
        symmetrical
symmetry, 218–219n9, 228n1
    in *Beowulf*, 219–220n15
    difference of in literature from that of math-
        ematics or physics, 217n2
    Einstein's grasp of the power of, 217n2
    influence of Dante on Joyce concerning sym-
        metry, 210–211
    in *Moby-Dick*, 134, 142–143, 148, 151, 157,
        161, 163, 167–168, 169, 237n12
    in *Othello*, 127
    in *Ulysses*, 209, 210
    visual symmetry, 71

T

Tale of a Tub (Swift), 210, 212
Taney, Roger, 179
Tashtego, 134, 137, 163, 164
    saving of by Queequeg, 167
Tate, Nahum, 55
"Three Months among the Reconstructionists"
    (Andrews), 185

Throwaway, 207

Toledo, decrees of the assembly at, 112

Tolkien, J. R. R., 18

Torquemada, 120, 121

triadic literary structures, symmetrical, 2–5, 25–26, 106–107

   literature prior to the introduction of, 4–5

   triadic form in *Romeo and Juliet*, 29

   and the validation of editorial conjectures of damaged texts, 23

   writers' conundrums concerning, 4, 5

   and writers telling things "slant," 2

triads, 8, 213, 217n3, 218n8

   of Cain, Abel, and Wealtheow's sons, 24

   incomplete triads, 4

   power of, 216

   triadic pattern, 217n1, 218–219n9

   triadic structure found within incestuous relationships, 94

   unsolved triads, 4

   See also *Ambassadors, The* (H. James), triads in; *Beowulf*, triads in; *Divine Comedy, The* (Dante), insistent show of triads in; *Hamlet* (Shakespeare), triads in; *Merchant of Venice, The* (Shakespeare), triads in; *Moby-Dick* (Melville), triads in; *Othello* (Shakespeare), triads in; triadic literary structures, symmetrical; *Ulysses* (Joyce), triads in

Tubal, 49–50

   irony of loaning money to Shylock, 50–51

   relationship to Bassanio, 51

Tubman, Harriet, 177–178, 179

   narcolepsy of, 178

U

Ulysses (Joyce), 3, 192, 232n2, 237n9, 237n14

   alter-boy account in, 196

   attempts at the suppression of for obscenity, 209–210, 211–212

   "Circe" episode in, 205, 206

   endless surface narrative of, 196

   influence of Melville on, 209

   irony of the white-smocked priest in, 197–198

   invisible sexual elements in, 209, 211–212

   as a novel of two differing halves, 210

   Odyssean parallels in, 210

   overlooked theme of sexual-predatory priests in, 195–203, 205–206, 211, 212, 236n5

   pairing of the Church and the whorehouse in, 208

   parallel structure of with Dante's *Commedia*, 210–211

   powerful use of water images in, 204, 208

   as a second Tale of a second Tub, 212

   sexual male/female pairing in, 209

   sexual overtone occurrence at the Forty-Foot, 197, 236n3

   symmetry of, 209, 210

   as a tour of the minutiae and trivia of Dublin, 196

   two beginnings of, 236n6

   See also doublings, in Ulysses; phallic images, in *Ulysses*; Ulysses (Joyce), triads in

Ulysses (Joyce), triads in, 206, 216, 237n10

   "corpsechewer" triad in, 211

   double triad of invisible sexual elements in, 209

   triad of alcoholics in, 202

   triad of Buck's initials, 196

   triad of cheeks, 236n7

   triad of Father Coffey's victims, 206

   triad of loin fluids, 197–199

   triad of openings and closings, 236n6

   triad of Stephen, Bloom, and Molly, 25

V

Valdes, 121
vegetation cults, 78–79
venereal disease
    in Elizabethan England, 105
    symptoms of syphilis, 205
Venetian Senate, majesty of, 120
Venice, 123
    military threat to, 118–119
Virgil, 24
Vulgate, the, 10

W

Wall, William G., 88
Waymarsh, 181, 187
    closeness of to Strether, 188–189
    exacerbation of Strether's burdens by, 187–188
    Strether's remembered image of, 176
Wealhtheow, 13, 14, 18, 23, 24, 73
    incestuous link of with Beowulf, 15–16
    as literary forbear of Gertrude, 78
    offering of the mead-cup to Hrothgar,
        Beowulf, and possibly Hrothulf, 19
    trust of in Beowulf more than in Hrothgar, 20

    two offerings of the phallic cup by
        Wealhtheow to Beowulf, 14, 16–17
West, Rebecca, 85, 95
Whitaker, Virgil, 73
Wiglaf, 21
Wilson, John Dover, 56–57, 65, 88, 96
Woolett, 192
    biggest business of, 185–186
    as a black community in, 184
    Chad's refusal to return to, 181–183, 188,
        190–191
    need of for business and economic vitality,
        184

Y

Yojo, 158
Yorick, 106, 216
    triad of Yorick's royal laughers, 107–108

Z

Zeffirelli, Franco, 222–223n20
Zoe, 205, 206
    evidence for her Jewish heritage, 206–207
    familiarity with Bella, 207

CPSIA information can be obtained
at www.ICGtesting.com
Printed in the USA
FFHW011234151219
56538606-62393FF

9 781945 637582